Decoding AP Computer Science A

Moksh Jawa

Decoding AP Computer Science A

Moksh Jawa

Contents

Saurabh Khand

December 25th Evening

Start of my journey of changing my life

To those who are not as fortunate as me to receive an education. I truly hope that one day basic education is available to anyone who wants to learn.

To my amazing family.

To Washington High School for providing me an environment where I could strike the right balance between academics and pursuing my passions.

Preface

How This Book Came To Be:

This book did not come to life in a few days. This book is a product of my humble attempt to resolve a problem that gets worse by the year. The lack of computer science education, even in one of the most developed countries in the world, USA.

It all started in seventh grade, when my father introduced me to computer programming. He introduced me to a simple website and I was immediately fascinated by the idea of typing what seemed like an altered form of English to draw shapes or make objects move. With the fact that I could almost instantaneously see the results of what I was trying to do, my interest started to grow exponentially. At that time, even though, I hardly knew of the extensibility and power of computer science, I had already fallen for the subject. As I grew, my passion and love for the subject only continued to grow more and more. Long story short, I arrived at Washington High School as a nerdy freshman very excited to study AP Computer Science. However, I found, to my dismay, that the course wasn't offered. Luckily, that didn't stop me. That year, I self-studied AP Computer Science, jumping from one website to another, and, somehow, managed to receive a 5 on the exam that year. And that's when I thought to myself, "why can't all my other friends do the same thing as me?" as I hadn't done anything special. I asked around and discovered that not only was there no consolidated learning resource available, but also that most girls seem intimidated by the supposedly "boys-only" subject. To my surprise, it was, indeed, true. I couldn't find a resource that helped students learn APCS and do well in the exam as well. There were no APCS videos on Khan Academy. No reliable online course.

That's when my journey to do something so I could help out my fellow peers started. I wasn't even sure whether I would make an impact. The only thing I was sure about, at that point, was that I wanted to try something before giving up. So I started a Coding Club at Washington High School (WHS). Although the school didn't formally offer AP Computer Science course, that didn't mean it couldn't be taught informally, something I love about our education system. The goal of Coding Club was to spread APCS to students and make it easy for them to learn it. The meetings would be held as after school classes and quizzes, assignments, and worksheets would be handed out to students. The response to coding club was much better than expected. Creating content for AP Computer Science, helped me enhance my knowledge, strengthen my love for teaching computer science, and develop a newfound respect for all the hard work our teachers put in.

Despite the significant momentum the club gained, I wasn't sure if it was having the impact it could. There were 2 challenges. The first was that it was limited to students who were participating in the coding club. And second, it was virtually impossible for students to attend a 1-hour class every week and practice on their own before they came to the next one. Like they say, every lock has a key and every problem has a solution, this problem also present a wonderful solution. I did some research and realized there was no online course for APCS. By making one myself, students could study at their own pace and literally any student from across the world could use my course.

I set on the path of making the Khan Academy equivalent for AP Computer Science. My finished product was an online course called Decoding AP Computer Science A, which enabled high school students to successfully complete APCS. Today, there are over 2500 students enrolled and over 10,000 hours of computer science education has been delivered through this medium.

This encouraged me, but I didn't want to stop there. So, I started on yet another interesting, 9-month journey, that culminated in February 2016, to include yet another medium for spreading content. This book. I faced numerous challenges, along the way but this time a lot of people came to my rescue, and I am very thankful to everyone who supported me along the way. I hope that you find this book to be everything that you hoped for and more. :)

Goal/Vision:

This book has a simple goal: to provide anyone and everyone with an AP Computer Science education. I want this book to be accessible by any student or teacher, regardless of financial hardship. The next phase of my journey is to go raise funds from generous individuals, corporates or from the sale of this book and and ship this book free to anyone who needs it and cannot afford it. Computer science truly is a magical subject and it should be available to anyone who is interested in it. I hope that one day coding will be treated like a foreign language, a must-have, and that everyone can use it with a combination of knowledge and imagination to make an impact on the world.

Acknowledgements:

This book wouldn't have come to life if it hadn't been for the help of countless people.

I would like to thank my best friend, Taj Shaik, for being my supporter and helper. He helped me write the answer keys for practice tests and has supported me throughout the entire process. He's an amazing person (not to mention a Java expert!) and his support kept me running through the final paces of the book.

Thanks to Professor Ken Salisbury from Stanford and the team (Ellen, David, Nikhil, Sumit, Shirin, Hector, Shivali, Garrett, Sonny, Jaeyong, Mark, and Brian) I worked with at the Salisbury lab last summer. It was an incredible experience to work with this brilliant team and to see the power of computer science.

Thanks to Afra Fatima and Sri Lekha from NPU for helping with the development of practice questions.

Thank you to Raj Karamchedu for guiding me through the process of book publishing and helping me believe that I could write a book.

Thank you to my English teachers, Mrs. Jones and Mrs. Selinger, for reigniting my passion for writing.

Thank you to my high school's principal, Bob Moran, for giving me his time and attention, despite his busy schedule, to support my ventures to spread APCS education.

Thank you to Tempy didi [Radhika Sikand Bhatt] for guiding me in editing my book and helping me improve my writing.

Thank you to Andy Chen of Stanford University for mentoring me throughout this process and helping me explain difficult Java concepts.

Thank you to the nonprofit organization she++ for inspiring and encouraging high school students like myself to explore computer science and spread it to others.

Thank you to Createspace and Leanpub for being wonderful platforms for self-publishing and writing technical books.

Most importantly, a HUGE thank you to my family, my dad, mom, and little sister Vedika, for supporting me throughout this journey and continually providing encouragement.

Last but not least, thank you to my friends and everyone else for directly or indirectly helping with the development meant of this book.

This wouldn't have been possible if it wasn't for all of these wonderful people listed above.

Thank you.

Moksh Jawa

Fremont, CA

February 2016

Chapter 1 - Getting Set Up

1.1 Chapter Overview:

A journey of a thousand miles begins with a single step. This chapter is the first step to mastering AP Computer Science. To learning Java. To getting a 5 on the AP Computer Science test. We will be installing a few tools that will allow us to code in Java, making sure that this book is the right fit for you, and going over the AP Computer Science course syllabus and exam.

1.2 General Information:

Before diving right into the AP Computer Science curriculum, let's understand what AP Computer Science is all about and how you can perform well in it.

Paired with an Online Course

To enhance your learning experience, you can use this book with a free online course called Decoding AP Computer Science A as well. The course can be accessed at *http://www.apcs.tv*. This course is filled with video lectures and can help you get a better understanding of some of the more complicated concepts.

Is This Book Right for You?

Obviously, this book is a perfect fit for any high school student, who is keen to study AP Computer Science, as indicated by the title. If you are taking the class at your local high school, this book can help you study specific topics to achieve full comprehension or just give you a few more practice questions for your class or the AP Computer Science test. Similarly, if you don't have the luxury of taking AP Computer Science, this book covers every concept on the AP Computer Science exam as mandated by College Board.

Not in high school? Not a problem. This book also covers many introductory Java concepts while helping one prepare for AP Computer Science. Starting from the very basics, this book will help you get a quick jump into the computer science world. Although a lot of the text is focused specifically on the course, the concepts are universally applicable to computer science and can help anyone learn in a systematic manner.

As for prerequisites for using this book, it is recommended that you have a sufficient understanding of simple Algebra, as it is the underlying foundation of computer science. No coding experience required at all! As mentioned earlier, this book starts at the basics of computers and the Internet before diving into coding and assumes you, the reader, have absolutely zero knowledge about technology.

Overview of AP Computer Science

AP Computer Science is a college-level course for high school students that provides an introduction to the world of computer science. It aims to be the virtual equivalent of first computer science course you might take in college. Computer science is a vast subject comprising of a variety of programming languages that can be used for software development. This book will use a common programming language called Java. Don't worry if you don't understand what a programming language is yet. We will go over it in the next chapter. The primary objective of AP Computer Science is, according to College Board, "to understand core aspects of computer science which you can use to create solutions that are understandable and adaptable." For more in-depth information regarding APCS, visit College Board's website and review the course description.

Overview of the APCS Test

The AP Computer Science exam lasts three hours and is composed of two different sections, multiple choice and free response. Each section is equally weighted at 50%. The final result of the exam is a number ranging from 1 to 5 with 1 representing no recommendation, 2 possibly qualified, 3 qualified, 4 well qualified, and 5 extremely well qualified. "Qualified" means that you are capable of completing an introductory course on computer science at a university. This book will prepare you to get a 5.

The first section of the test is the multiple choice section. You will have 1 hour and 15 minutes to complete 40 multiple choice questions. Fortunately, and unlike other standardized tests, there is no penalty for getting a question wrong. Each question is worth one point and the scantron is scored by a machine

The second and last section of the test is the free response section. For this section, you have 1 hour and 45 minutes to complete 4 free response questions, usually consisting of multiple parts. You will often be given a situation and asked to write some code by hand to provide an efficient solution. Free response questions are scored by human readers who are usually high school and college computer science teachers from across the nation. Each of the 4 questions is worth 9 points and, unlike the multiple choice questions, partial credit may also be awarded.

Since the 2014 AP Computer Science test, there has been a notable change to the curriculum that AP Computer Science covers. The alteration is that the "GridWorld" case study is no longer included in the exam. It had previously accounted for a very significant 25% of the exam. This is important because the GridWorld case study may come up in other outdated study materials that you use and should be ignored.

As with any AP test, the AP Computer Science test is held in May of every year and the results are released around July. The exact date for the AP exam varies depending on the year. Overall, in order to get a "5" that would deem you as "extremely well qualified", you will have to approximately get above an 80% on the exam. Please note that the exact percentage varies from year to year depending on the curve set by the performance of other students taking the exam. The book aims to prepare you to score well on the AP test so that you can be confident that you will indeed get the desired "5." Visit College Board's website to read up more about the AP Computer Science test.

About Me

Because I will be guiding you throughout this entire process, I only thought it would be fair if I devote a paragraph to myself so that I'm not a mysterious voice behind some text. My name is Moksh Jawa and I am a 15-year-old rising junior at Washington High School. I self-studied and took the AP Computer Science exam in 9th grade and got a 5. I found it to be quite easy. However, it was not the same with my peers. I felt that preparation for this exam can be difficult for others due to the lack of good study materials. That truly inspired me to start helping spread computer science education and it's something I remain passionate about till this very day. Before authoring this book, I created a free online course called "Decoding AP Computer Science A" (pun intended) that got over 2500 students in the span of just a few months. Now, I've moved on to writing a book so that I can help spread computer science through yet another medium.

1.3 Downloading Requirements:

We will be installing two key components that are essential so that we can learn the Java programming language and start walking through AP Computer Science. These two requirements are the Java Development Kit (JDK) and Dr. Java. Both are free and available online.

Installing the Java Development Kit (JDK)

The Java Development Kit (JDK) is available as a free download on the website of a company called Oracle. It is needed so that we can compile and run our Java programs. As we get into computer science, we will go over the importance of the JDK and what computer programs are.

1. Firstly, search "Oracle Java SE Development Kit 8 Downloads" on any search engine and click the first link that should redirect you to a web page on the Oracle website. The web page should be labelled "Java SE Development Kit 8 Downloads" and it should look like Figure 1.1. If you are unable to locate the page, go to the following URL: *http://bit.ly/1NN2Sc7*
2. Then, select the Java SE Development Kit 8 download file that fits your operating system. A note to Window users, there are two options available – Windows x86 (32 bit) or x64 (64 bit). Pick the option that is appropriate for your version of windows.
3. For Windows users, a "Save As" dialogue box will appear. Save the file to disc. For Mac users, a .dmg file downloads.

4. Run the downloaded file. You may need to give the file administrator access or enter your user password.
5. Follow the installation wizard as directed.
6. After installation is complete, you can delete the installation file from Step 3 if you choose to.

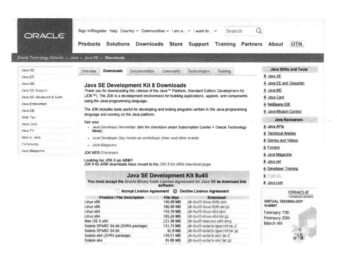

Figure 1.1

Installing Dr. Java

Dr. Java is a free programming environment for Java. Basically, you will be typing up all of your code in this computer program just like you type text in word processor like Microsoft Word. It was developed by Professor Corky Cartwright at Rick University and is a great Integrated Development Environment (IDE) for beginner programmers.

1. Navigate to the Dr. Java home page by visiting *http://www.drjava.org/*. You can make sure you are on the right web page by looking at Figure 1.2.
2. Select "Download Jar File". This file is the program itself – not an installation/set up program to install it. So to run DrJava, just double click the downloaded file. Alternatively, you can install the program locally. For Windows users, select "Download Windows App." For Mac users, select "Download Mac OS X App."

Figure 1.2

Other IDEs

This section is aimed primarily at students with some knowledge about computer science and an Integrated Development Environment (IDE). Dr. Java is a perfect example of an IDE because it's an "environment" in which you can write code and then test it. There are many other IDEs available for free online such as Eclipse and BlueJ. However, for this course, we will be using Dr. Java because it is more appropriate for beginners. If you have enough computer science experience to feel confident about using a different IDE, like Eclipse, feel free to follow along using an IDE of your choice. However, if you would like to play it safe, stick with Dr. Java.

1.4 Chapter Summary:

Congrats on making it through your first chapter! You are now ready to start learning more about computer science. You should now have the Java Development Kit (JDK) and Dr. Java so that you are prepared to write your first program. In addition, you should have a basic understanding of the expectations in the AP Computer Science course and exam. Get ready to get a 5 on the AP Computer Science test!

Chapter 2 - Introduction to Computers and the Internet

2.1 Chapter Overview:

In order to get a strong grasp of computer science, it is essential that you establish a strong fundamental base. Before you can start learning about computer science, you must understand how computer science came about, what a computer is made of, and the concepts, such as object-oriented programming, that rule the computer science world. In this chapter, we will be building a foundation so that the rest of the curriculum is easier to understand.

2.2 Computers and Computer Programs:

Before we dive into programming, let's take a look at some of the basic information about computing in today's world and how your computer works.

What is a Computer?

Whether you like it or not, you are completely surrounded by computers. A computer is an electronic device that can store, retrieve, and process data, or information. Practically everything around us, from a calculator to a smartphone, is a computer. Computers have advanced significantly over the last couple of decades and continue to dominate our daily routines. In fact, computers have become so advanced that there are supercomputers that can perform quadrillions of operations per second!

Software

But how do these computers know what to calculate? How do they know what to do? This is where computer programs come into play. A computer program is a set of instructions that tells the computer what to do. These various computer programs are often also referred to as software. Programming is the process of developing computer programs to make a computer do what you want it to do. Programmers create computer programs.

Programmers write these various instructions, or computer programs, using programming languages. Think of a programming language, or a computer language, as any other language like English, German, or Hindi. It's used to communicate with, in this case, computers. It has its own "grammar", or rules that need to be followed so that the communication can occur effectively. Java is an example of a programming language that can be used to tell a computer to do something. Java has its own syntax, or rules, that you have to follow so that the computer can understand what to do. The objective of AP Computer Science and this book, to a large extent, is to help you learn the Java programming language so that you can instruct computers. Similarly, in this book, we will start of by learning the fundamentals of Java (the abc's of English) and then slowly progress toward more complicated concepts (equivalent to structuring complex sentences).

Hardware

The keyboard, mouse, screen, and other physical devices are known as the hardware of the computer. Hardware and software are of equal importance and combine to form a computer. They compliment each other well and hardware stores and executes the software of a computer.

Components of a Computer

Almost every computer can be divided into various sections with different functions and roles. All of these components are essential to the efficiency of the computer.

1. *Input Unit*: Just as you may have guessed, this component of the computer is used to receive information from input devices such as keyboard, mouse, or a USB. It obtains this information and then makes it available to the other components of the computer so that they can interpret it and perform an action if needed. Your computer can also receive information from the Internet when you download music from iTunes or do anything of that sort.

2. *Output Unit*: This unit has the exact opposite function of the input unit: it takes information that the computer has processed and makes it available to output devices such as a screen or printer. The output unit is used whenever the computer displays anything or provides information to the user.

3. *Arithmetic and Logic Unit (ALU)*: This unit is essentially the "calculator" of the computer. It performs functions such as addition, subtraction, multiplication, division, and even comparing values. As indicated by the name, it performs basic computations involving arithmetic and logic.

4. *Central Processing Unit (CPU)*: The brain of the computer system is the central processing unit. It "runs the show" just as the nucleus does in a cell or a principal does a school. In modern computers, the arithmetic and logic unit is often contained with the CPU itself. The CPU of a computer dictates how the other units work in conjunction with each other. For example, the CPU can store information obtained through the memory unit (next) and then use the output unit to display the information from the memory unit on the computer screen. Multiple CPUs allow the computer to perform multiple operations at once and function faster. In essence, the Central Processing Unit is the boss of the computer and, hence, makes all the decisions and controls the actions of the other units as well.

5. *Memory Unit*: The memory unit serves as a temporary "warehouse" for information that the computer receives from other units, usually the input unit. However, the memory unit isn't just any ordinary storage unit. The information in the memory unit is volatile meaning that it is lost after the computer's power is turned off. The advantage to the memory unit is that all the information it stores will be available immediately for processing. It also stores information until it can be outputted using the output unit. The memory unit is often referred to as memory or primary memory.

6. *Secondary Storage Unit*: You be wondering if the memory unit only retains information until the computer's power is on, how a computer stores information that can be accessed even after the computer's power is turned off. This is where the secondary storage unit comes into play. The secondary storage unit is a long-term "warehouse" that stores information from other units. Because the information stored is preserved even when the computer is turned off, the information in the secondary storage unit is persistent. One drawback of storing information in this unit is that it takes longer to access the information then it would with the memory unit.

2.3 History of Computing:

A revolution in computing is was sparked by the development of the Internet and the World Wide Web and eventually led to the creation of the Java programming language. Let's look at how these innovations came about and what the inspiration was behind them.

History of the Internet and the World Wide Web

The Internet is a global system of interconnected computer networks that links several billion devices together. It was originally invented thanks to the USit Department of Defense which awarded contracts for network systems and used only to connect the computer systems of research organizations and universities. However, today, it's grown to be able to connect billions of computer devices together and available to practically anyone.

Many people confuse the Internet for the World Wide Web. Although they are closely related, they have different functions. The World Wide Web (commonly known as the Web) is an information system of webpages and media documents that can be viewed over the Internet. The addition of the World Wide Web helped significantly grow the popularity of the Internet and helped establish it as the primary communications mechanism.

The World Wide Web came to life thanks to British computer scientist Tim Berners-Lee of CERN, a renowned European nuclear research organization. Berners-Lee proposed this concept on March 12 1989 to improve CERN communication but later realized that it could be implemented on a global scale. After months of intense work and content generation, the Web finally become publicly accessible via the Internet on August 6 1991.

Today, the Internet and the World Wide Web combine to make the lives of billions of people significantly easier by making information available instantly and free-of-charge worldwide. The

Internet originally started off as a means of connecting research organizations so that researchers could be updated with latest advances and now it has revolutionized our lives and made sure that anyone can find out what's happening anywhere across the globe. Search engines, like Google, enable us to organize the vast information available and access it immediately.

History of Java

Java began as an internal project at Sun Microsystems in 1990 to develop an alternative to a programming language called C++. The motivation behind creating the Java programming language was for it to work with a lot of different devices, especially the newer and smarter devices that Sun believed would come to dominate our lives.

This internal project was led by James Gosling and resulted in a programming language called Oak because of the oak tree lying just outside of Sun Microsystem's offices. Later, Sun discovered that there was already a programming language by the name of Oak. When some Sun employees visited a coffee shop, they came up with Java and the name stuck.

Although development on the project was relatively smooth, the Java project ran into some hurdles along the way as well. As mentioned earlier, Sun's primary inspiration behind Java was to develop a programming language that would work seamlessly with newer and smarter devices, but, unfortunately, intelligent consumer-electronic devices were not growing as quickly as expected. By the summer of 1992, the team running the project had a fully-functional demo complete and Java was ready for the real world but Sun held back because it knew that the world wasn't ready for Java.

However, in 1993, the Web explodes in popularity and the Internet era, as we know it, begins. Sun engineers who have developed a project considered much ahead of its time realize the opportunity to allow others to use Java to create a more dynamic web experience filled with interactivity and animations. Java 1.0a became available for download in 1994 and was used by Sun engineers Patrick Naughton and Jonathan Payne to develop HotJava, the first-ever web browser that allowed moving objects and dynamic executable content. The first public release of Java came on May 23, 1995 as Java 1.02a and HotJava became available to the world. Java immediately became popular because it grew along with the Web that had reached a whopping 16 million users. By 1997 and in just a mere two years, Java had approximately 400,000 developers and was the #2 programming language in the world. Now, Sun Microsystems was able to start enabling Java for what it was originally created for: to develop smart appliances.

Today, Java is used for practically everything ranging from developing Android apps to improving web servers. Java has truly permeated throughout our lives and often we are unaware of its importance. The pagers that we receive as we wait in restaurants are developed using Java. In addition, Java is found in over 850 millions PCs worldwide.

2.4 Types of Programming Languages:

We know that programming languages are used by programmers to communicate instructions with computers. There are various types of programming languages that are determined based on whether they are directly understandable by the computer or require translation to be interpreted. Hundreds of programming languages exist today and they can be divided into 3 basic types:

1. Machine languages
2. Assembly languages
3. High-level languages

Machine Language

Machine language is a type of programming language that can be directly understood by the computer. It's essentially the computer's native tongue. Machine language is strings of numbers (usually 0s and 1s) that give the machine specific, and basic, instructions. Take a look at Figure 2.1 to see how machine language looks. As you can see, the code is just made up of 0's and 1's and is practically unreadable. Anyone would find this type of language very difficult to perceive and understand. Don't worry Java is a not like a machine language - it's much simpler comparatively. Another disadvantage of machine language is that it is machine dependent meaning that it is different for each type of computer.

Figure 2.1

```
000100110100000011110100
000101000101000001001011
010011100000011100110111
```

Assembly Language

Clearly, programming using machine language is too complicated and tedious for any programmer. Soon, a new type of programming language called assembly language came along that include English-like phrases that a human could understand for simple operations. You can see an example of assembly language in Figure 2.2. Compared to machine language, assembly language is a lot more understandable and simple since many of the phrases are recognizable. Note that the computer cannot understand assembly language directly; it only directly understands machine language. However, there are translator programs called assemblers that convert assembly language to machine language so that it can be interpreted by the computer. Therefore, programmers have an easier time giving instructions that a computer can understand.

Figure 2.2

```
start :
  mov ax, data
  mov ds, ax

  mov ax, first
  and ax, 00ffh
  shl ax, 08h
```

High-level Language

Although assembly language solved the problem of making code readable for programmers, it was still very tedious to use because it required a lot of work for even the simplest actions. As computer usage continued to increase, programmers needed a more efficient programming language that could enable programmers to give the computer more complicated instructions. High-level programming languages were developed as a solution and allowed programmers to accomplish tasks in as little as one line. As you can see in Figure 2.3, the programmer is able to add two different variables together to create a new one - something that would require multiple lines in assembly or machine language. Just like there are assemblers for assembly language, there are compilers that turn high-level language into machine language for the computer. Another advantage of high-level language over assembly language is that it is even closer to English and utilizes mathematical symbols like '+' as well. There are many high-level programming languages including Objective C, C++, and Java. In fact, Java is the most widely used high level language.

Figure 2.3

```
int a = 4;
int b = 5;
int c = a + b;
```

2.5 Object Oriented Programming (OOP):

In addition to being a high-level programming language, Java is also referred to as an object-oriented programming language. Essentially, a Java computer program is composed of pieces called objects and classes. This structure makes Java very appealing to developers because it promotes software reusability.

Java Class Libraries

Java is popular because it allows for code reusability, made possible by Java class libraries. Before we look at the class libraries, let's understand the components of a Java program that instruct the computer. A Java program is made up of pieces called classes which are composed of methods. Classes can essentially be considered the "building blocks" of any Java computer program. The methods perform tasks and return information.

Java class libraries are existing classes, or pieces, that any programmer can use while developing a computer program. Java class libraries are also known as Java APIs, or Application Programming Interfaces. As a programmer, there are two routes you can take while developing a computer program: you can either create every piece, or class, of the program yourself or you can utilize Java class libraries so that you don't have to create each class and can use some pre-existing ones.

There are two different aspects to learning Java. One is the actual Java programming language with which you create computer programs and the other is the Java class libraries, which are equally important because they make the life of a programmer significantly simpler. For example, let's say that you want a part of your Java computer program to include combining some text. In order to do that, you would have create a class in the program that would teach the computer how to combine text together. Alternatively, you could using a pre-existing class from the Java class libraries that would instruct the computer to combine the text rather than you having to do it yourself.

Important Tip

Objects ★

Next, let's understand what objects are. Objects are the essence of Java, but, first, let's look at them outside of Java - or, for that matter, outside of software. Everything around you is an object. For example, let's take a pencil. It's yellow. It's thin. It's hard. It writes and it erases. I have actually just listed some of the attributes and behaviors of an object with attributes being represented by adjectives and behaviors by verbs. The same goes for software objects, which make up computer programs. Every object, a software object or not, consists of attributes and behaviors.

Object-Class Relationship

The relationship between classes and objects is even more important than the objects and classes themselves. They complement each other and enable software reusability, a major factor in making Java a popular programming language.

The perfect analogy to describe the relationship between objects and classes is that classes are to objects as blueprints are to houses. Just as we build multiple houses with only one blueprint, we can create many objects using just a single class. In addition, objects have the abilities (or behaviors) to perform functions that are needed for Java computer programs. For example, a house can cool itself but the blueprint for the house cannot cool itself.

Object-Oriented Design

Object-oriented design, or OOD, models programs as real-world objects. It utilizes class relationships, or relationships in which objects in a class have the same attributes. For example, a class of fruits can contain many different fruits (objects) like bananas, apples, or oranges and they would all have the same attributes such as the ability to be eaten. It also takes advantage of inheritance relationship in which classes derive characteristics from other classes and then add on attributes of their own. Going back to the fruits class example, an object of the class orange could have inherited, or derived, the ability to be eaten from a class of fruits and then added on the characteristic of being orange. These two relationships define the structure of Java, an object-oriented programming language that applies object-oriented design, programs.

The process for object-oriented programming can be split into three unique steps. The first step is analyzing the objectives, or what the goal or purpose of a creating the program is. Next, create a design that follows object-oriented design and can help you determine how you can achieve the objectives. Lastly, implement the design and make the proposed program come to life. This last step involves typing up code and turning an abstract idea into a reality. Before you start writing code, it often useful to use pseudocode. Pseudocode is a method of expressing the logic of a program. It's like an outline of a speech. We will go over pseudocode in more detail in the coming chapters. Although this process seems very complicated and tedious, even the top-level programmers in the industry use it to make sure they are meeting the requirements for any given program adequately.

Unified Modeling Language (UML)

The Unified Modeling Language is a graphical language that displays object-oriented designs. You can see an example of UML in Figure 2.4. As you can probably tell, the purpose of UML is to enable programmers to map out the various use cases for a program and account for any possibility. In this particular example, you can see the entire logic of the program mapped out from start to finish. The Unified Modeling Language is used by even the most experienced programmers today because it helps them get their thoughts and plans visualized in an organized way.

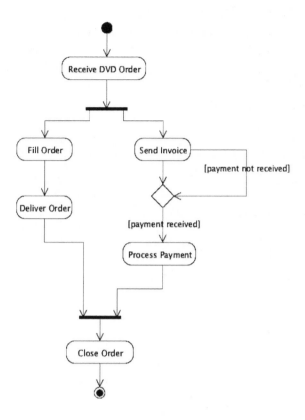

Figure 2.4

2.6 Developing a Java Program:

Now, we will take a look at the various steps involved in developing a Java program as well as where we type up our code. There's a lot that goes into creating a program and it's important to have a bird's eye view of the entire process before we dive into it.

Integrated Development Environment (IDE)

In Chapter 1, we downloaded Dr. Java a programming environment for Java. Dr. Java is also known as an Integrated Development Environment (IDE). An IDE is a software application that enables computer programmers to develop computer programs. It consists of a source code editor, a debugger, and a compiler. The source code editor is just similar to a text editor like Microsoft Word with the only difference being that it's focused on code rather than plain text. The debugger checks the code that typed up in the source code editor for any errors that would prevent the program from running. You can think of it as the component of Microsoft Word or any other text editor that places a red underline under mistakes in text except focused on errors in the code. We went over compilers earlier in the chapter, but, just to reiterate, they turn high-level language into machine language for the computer to understand. As you can probably tell, an IDE provides a comprehensive software development by allowing you to type up and compile the code.

Creating the Program

The first step in editing a Java program is using the source code editor. You type up the code for the Java program into the editor and then save the Java program file with .java extension.

Compiling the Program

Next, you compile the code and the IDE converts the code to machine language so that the computer can interpret it. This converted version of the Java program is saved as a .class file that can be executed and understood by the computer.

Executing the Program

This leads us to last step of the process in which we execute the program after creating and compiling it. Once you execute the program, it performs the task(s) that you have allocated for it. Execution is the last step of the process and is where you see the results of your creation and compilation of the program.

2.7 Chapter Summary:

In this chapter, we were able to gain a basic introduction to computers and the Internet. Along with touching upon the history of Java and the Internet, we also explored object-oriented programming, one of the most important concepts in computer science. Now that we have a fundamental base established, we can dive into actually creating our very own Java programs.

Chapter 3 - Introduction to Java

3.1 Chapter Overview:

Now that we have a basic understanding of the fundamental of computer science, we can finally dive into what AP Computer Science is all about: creating computer programs using Java. In my opinion, the best way to learn computer science is to immediately apply concepts that you learn and look at various programs and figure your way out through them. The objective of this chapter is for you to come out of it knowing the basics of Java and being able to create a simple Java program to display some text on the computer screen.

3.2 Hello World Program:

The Significance of the Hello World Program

The Hello World program is a classic program that is often used as an introduction to any programming language, including Java. The functionality of the Hello World program is very simple. All it does is print out the phrase "Hello World!" on the computer. First, we will look at the code that goes into telling the computer to display the phrase and, then, we will walk through it line by line. You can see the Hello World program and its output in Figure 3.1. This program demonstrates many basic fundamentals of Java and makes it excellent for beginners.

Figure 3.1 | HelloWorld.java

```
1   // HelloWorld.Java
2   /* Text-printing program.
3     This comment is shown as a traditional comment. */
4
5   public class HelloWorld
6   {
7     // main method begins execution of Java application
8     public static void main( String[] args )
9     {
10      System.out.println( "Hello World!" );
11    } // end main method
12  } // end HelloWorld Class
```

Output

```
> run HelloWorld
Hello World!
```

Getting the Hello World Program on Your Computer

First of all, open up Dr. Java on your computer. You should have it downloaded. If you do not, please refer back to Chapter 2. Create a New File (File > New) and save it as HelloWorld.java. Next, type up the code, or text, in Lines 1 - 12 exactly as you see it in Figure 2.1. Make sure that you do not ignore even a single character because they are all essential to the program. In addition, make sure you account for indents and spacing.

Once you have typed up the program, click the "Compile" button in the toolbar. You should see a message in the "Compiler Output" section towards the bottom of the screen that says "Compilation completed." If you see any error, or message other than that, you have made a mistake in copying the code for Hello World to your Dr. Java.

After successfully compiling the program without any errors, click the "Run" button in the toolbar. Once you click the "Run" button, notice that the bottom of the screen displays two lines: "> run HelloWorld" and "Hello World!" The first line indicates that the HelloWorld Java program is being run and the second line is the output of the program being run. Therefore, the program ran successfully and it printed out some text. Once you have the program typed up in Dr. Java and working, we can start looking at the code overall and line by line.

Patterns in the Code

There are couple of things that you may immediately notice once you have finished typing up the Hello World program. The first thing you may notice is that there is an array of colors. Each color has some connotation and as we look at more and more programs, you will start to understand what each color represents. Similarly, you may also note a lot of spacing such as indentations and blank lines. This spacing usually serves one of two different purposes. It either makes the code a little bit more spread out and readable so that it can be easily revised and interpreted by humans or it is mandatory so that the computer execute it. As we go through each line, you will realize where the spacing is needed and where it isn't.

Comments

Figure 3.2

```
1   // HelloWorld.Java
2   /* Text-printing program.
3      This comment is shown as a traditional comment. */
```

Line 1-3

The first three lines of the Hello World program start off with what looks like just plain English. These lines are known as comments. Comments are basically sidenotes that programmers place in their programs so that they can have a better idea of exactly what's going on. In this case, comments are used to display the name of the program and its functionality. The amazing thing about comments are that they do not affect the program at all whatsoever so you can change any of the text within them or remove them completely and the functionality of the program will not be affected. Although comments do not seem very useful, they come in handy once you start developing larger and more advanced Java programs where it's difficult to keep track of the functionality of all of the code. It's good to build a practice of using comments. There are two widely used comments in Java and both are on display in these three lines: end-of-line comments and traditional comments.

An end-of-line comment is a comment that begins with //. As you can see on Line 1, the comment begins with // so therefore it is a end-of-line comment. An end-of-line comment can only span across one line and it can begin anywhere on the line including the middle (see Line 11 or 12).

A traditional comment differs from an end-of-line comment because it can span multiple lines which makes it useful for a particularly long comment. It starts with /* and ends with */.

Both types of comments serve the same purpose and differ in length and declaration. It's also important to note that // or /* */ need to be used to indicate a comment is being used otherwise that computer will try to interpret the text and that will cause an error.

Blank Spaces and Lines

Line 4

This line is not particularly important to the program as it's just simply a blank line. Extra spaces and blank lines are use to make computer programs more easier to read and they are, just like comments, ignored by the computer and do not affect the functionality of the program.

Declaring a Class

Figure 3.3

```
5   public class HelloWorld
6   {
```

Line 5-6

Line 5 is where we finally dive into the actual program - this is where the computer starts interpreting whatever is typed. This line is considered to be a class declaration because you, the programmer, are informing the computer about a class. We went over classes briefly in Chapter 2 and it's important to remember that they are the basic building blocks of every Java program and each program has one class.

Let's examine Line 5 word by word. First, let's look at "class", the second word in the line. "Class" is a keyword that lets the computer know that we will be declaring a class. Recall that a class is the basic building block of a Java program. Next, "public", the first word, is also another keyword but it has a different purpose. It's a little bit advanced so we'll go over it a little bit later in the book. Don't worry if these concepts seem confusing. We're just starting to look at them and you'll start to grasp them before you know. The last word in the line is "HelloWorld." It simply represents the name of the class. You may notice that the file name is HelloWorld.java and the class name is HelloWorld. This is not a coincidence. The file name and class name must match for a Java program to function. There are also some guidelines that you should follow while naming a class. The name of a class is considered to be an identifier, meaning that it can consist of letters, numbers, underscores, and dollar signs and cannot have any spaces or begin with a digit. In addition, class names and word within them are usually capitalized (HelloWorld). Some valid class names are Moksh_Is_Awesome$1000 or $Jawa. On the other hand, 1000$Moksh_Is_Awesome (starts with a digit) or Jawa12 $50 (contains a space) are some invalid identifiers.

Next, in Line 6, all we see is a simple left brace, {. This signifies the beginning of the body of the class. A left brace is always used after a class declaration and can represent the start of the body of practically anything. Similarly, a corresponding right brace, }, marks the end of the body. It's also important to note that everything inside of the body, Lines 7-11, is indented. This is an example of one of the most important spacing guidelines in Java: all the text within a body is indented.

Declaring a Method

Figure 3.4

```
7   // main method begins execution of Java application
8   public static void main( String[] args )
9   {
```

Line 7-9

Line 7 is a review of what we just learned. It is an end-of-line comment as indicated by the green text color and the two slashes that begin the line. Recall that this line has no impact on the functionality of the Hello World program and it's simply there to let us know what's happening in the program - the purpose of the main method in this case.

Line 8 is where the fun of the Java program begins. Just like we declared a class in Line 5, we are declaring a method in Line 8. Remember that a method is a component of a class that performs tasks and returns information. Line 8 is the basic starting point for any Java program. Every class usually contains multiple methods including only one main method. A main method is a requirement or else the Java program will not function. When a Java program is run, the main method is executed and it either performs the tasks itself or instructs other methods to return information.

Let's take a look at Line 8 word by word. The first word you see is `public`, which, if you recall from the class declaration, is a keyword that we will be addressing later in the book. The same goes for `static`. The `void` keyword signifies that the method does not return information and we will be understanding its importance to methods a little bit later. Then comes the most important word in the entire line: `main`. Just like `HelloWorld` in the class declaration determined the name of the class, `main` does the same for the method name, which is also an identifier. Logically, the computer identifies the method with the name `main` as the main method. Lastly, (`String[] args`) is a required component of a main method declaration and we will go over why it's there when discuss methods more in depth.

Finally, on Line 9, we have yet another left brace and, as you probably guessed, represents the start of the body of the method. It was used in the exactly same way with the class declaration. Likewise, a right brace will follow later in the program to signify the end of the method body and the text inside body is indented.

Outputting Text in Java

Figure 3.5

```
9     {
10        System.out.println( "Hello World!" );
11    } // end main method
```

Line 10

Line 10 is the most important line of this entire program; it makes the HelloWorld program print out "Hello World!" Notice that it is indented as it is contained within the body of the method. This line contains many traces of concepts we have briefly touched but are yet to completely understand so don't worry if you feel a bit lost.

The first part of this line is `System.out`. `System.out` represents an object known as the standard output object. This object allows any Java program to display text. The System.out object has a method called `println()` that prints a line of text. The "Hello World!" in between the parentheses represents what the method will print out. In this case, it is "Hello World!" but it can be replaced by anything (as long as it has quotation marks around it) and that will be printed out. For example, if Line 10 was changed to `System.out.println("Moksh is the best!");`, then the program would print out "Moksh is the best!" The phrase contained inside of the parentheses is known as an argument of a method and, soon, you will learn more about arguments and how important they are to Java programming. Lastly, there's a semicolon (;) after the closing parenthesis. It represents the end of a statement. Although it does not seem very significant, removing the semicolon will prevent the program from compiling due to an error. A semicolon, like indentation or braces, is another requirement of programming in Java.

Right Braces to End Classes and Methods

Figure 3.6

```
11     } // end main method
12  } // end HelloWorld Class
```

Line 11-12

For the last two lines of your first Java program, we finally see the much-awaited right brace, }. Remember that right braces complement the left braces by ending the bodies of a class or method. In addition, after the right brace closes the body, the following code no longer has to be indented like the text within the body. Following the right braces you can see two end-of-line comments which, just to reiterate, do not impact the program and simply let us know when the bodies of the HelloWorld class and main method are ending.

3.3 Importing Packages:

One of the primary advantages of Java is that it promotes software reusability thanks to the Java Class Libraries. There are thousands of classes available for programmers to use and, in this section, we will be exploring how these classes are organized and how programmers like you can use them in your Java program.

Packages

A package is a group of related classes. Remember that a class is like a blueprint and is the fundamental building block of Java programs. We also went over Java Class Libraries, or Java APIs, which are existing classes that any programmer can use while developing a computer program. The Java Class Libraries are filled with an enormous amount of classes and this is where packages come into play. Packages are used to organize, or group, the various classes based on their similarities. An example of a package is the java.lang package which contains a lot of classes that are commonly used by Java programmers and essential to the majority of Java programs. Similarly, there are many other packages that Java programmers would like to use in their programs. However, an essential question comes up: how does a Java programmer use an external package in his or her Java program?

Import Statement

The answer to that question is to import the package using the import statement. Quite simply, the import statements allows you to import, or utilize, a package or a class that you require for your Java program.

Figure 3.7

```
1   import packageName.*;
2   import packageName.className;
3   import packageName.subpackageName.*;
```

We can see a couple examples of import statements in Figure 3.7. Using the import statement on Line 1, we can easily import an entire package. It's that simple. Import is the keyword that enables the importing to happen. packageName would logically be replaced with whatever the name of the package is (for example: java.lang). The asterisk, *, at following the package name tells the computer to import of all of the classes within the package. Lastly, there is a semicolon (;) at the end because this is a statement and Java requires that you put a semicolon at the end of statements.

There are also situations where you don't want to import all of the classes within a package and just need to use one. In that case. the import statement on Line 2 comes in very handy. The import statement is very similar to the one on Line 1 with the only difference coming from replacing the asterisk that enabled all classes to be imported with a name of a class within the package so only that class is imported.

Finally, there are some packages that are so big that they have to be split into subpackages first. An import statement for such a situation can be seen on Line 3. The only change is that the subpackage name follows the package name. After that, you can place an asterisk to import all of the classes in the subpackage or you can import a specific class in the subpackage.

You may also be wondering where the import statement fits into a Java program. Import statements are typically placed before the class declaration at the beginning of the program. Later in the chapter, we will be creating a Java program that takes in input from the user so we will use the import statement to import a class that will enable us to get user input.

3.4 Basics of a Java Program:

As we start to look at more and more Java programs, it would be helpful to know some of the basic requirements of a Java program so that it will be easier to understand. You may not understand some of these requirements until we dive deeper into Java but it's important to keep them in mind.

Firstly, as mentioned earlier, a Java program must have at least one class. The class usually contains a main method but remember that a class is required and a main method is not. Tracking back to the HelloWorld program, recall that it had a class called HelloWorld. A Java program does not exist with a class. Another concept to recall is the idea that Java is a high-level language and that a computer only understands machine language. To solve that problem, a compiler (built into Dr. Java) converts Java so that it can be interpreted by the computer. Finally, take a look at the code in Figure 3.8.

Figure 3.8

```
1   public static void main( String[] args )
2   {
3     // code
4     // code
5   }
```

The code seen above should be familiar to you. You saw it first in the HelloWorld program. Just in case you don't remember, this is a main method. Starting with Line 1, as we went over earlier, here a main method is being declaring. While looking at the declaration word by word, I mentioned that there were many words or phrases like String[] args would be explained later. Until we go over them, it's essential that you memorize this main method declaration because we will be using this declaration in almost every Java program we create in this book. Similarly, remember the left and right braces that open and close the body and that the body of the main method is indented.

3.5 Variables:

To understand variables, you have to look outside of computer science. In mathematics, a variable is a symbol that represents any particular value. For example, you know that x + 2 = 3. Based on that statement, you can determine that x = 1. x is a variable because it represents the value 1.

Likewise, in computer science, a variable also stores some arbitrary value. It also has a type, meaning that it can represent values like a number or some text. We will go over the various types for a variable in the next section. Another characteristic of a variable is that the value it stores can vary. If x has a value of 1, its value can change if 1 is added to x. Its new value would be 2. Variables are an integral part of Java and computer science in general. They are used in most computer programs so make sure you understand their purpose and characteristics.

3.6 Primitive Types and Strings:

As we discussed in the preceding section, variables can store many different types of values and that every variable has a specific type. Well, those various possible types are known as primitive types, or built-in types. There are a total of 8 primitive types in Java: **int**, **double**, **boolean**, char, byte, short, long, and float. We will be focusing on the 3 types that are in bold font: int, double, and boolean because they are the most commonly used types and are the types present in the AP Computer Science Java subset and exam.

The `int` Primitive Type

As you may have guessed, the int primitive type is short for integer. It's just like any integer that you may be accustomed to seeing in mathematics; it's a whole number that can be positive or negative. Some examples of an integer include 2, -600, 543, -2. However, in computer science, there is a slight restriction on the value of an integer. It can still be positive or negative but it must fall within a range of -2,147,483,648 to 2,147,483,647. Values beyond that range are considered to be long. It also makes sense that these other types for too large or too small values are not used much as the existing range encompasses most values that would come up in a Java program.

Finally, remember that variables that are of type int store numbers that are integers. Such variables are often used in programs to store values that represent an amount, total, or anything numerical. Because numbers make up such a big part of our daily lives and, hence, Java programs, int variables are fairly common.

The `double` Primitive Type

Once you understand the int primitive type, understanding the double primitive type is a walk in the park. Specifically, a double represents a double precision floating-point number. Although it sounds quite complicated, it's actually very simple; it's basically the same as an integer except it can be used as a decimal. Some examples of a double are 2.23, -3.567, -123.23, 345.545 and common uses for double variables are representing price, weight, height, and other numbers that are usually represented with a decimal and are not whole numbers.

The `boolean` Primitive Type

This primitive type is a little bit different from the types we have looked at so far. An int or double variable can essentially have an infinite amount of different values. On the other hand, a boolean variable can only have one of two values: true or false. This makes it one of the simplest primitive types to work with. You may be wondering where boolean variables fit into a Java program. There are often situations in Java programs where a variable represents the answer to a question like "Is the car working?" The answer to this question (true or false) can be represented using a boolean variable called isCarWorking and the value of the variable can be changed depending on what response to the question is. This primitive type will soon become extremely useful as we look at control structures and conditions later in this book.

Strings

Now that we have learned a bit about the major primitive types, let's talk about strings, which many people mistakenly assume to be a primitive type as well. A string is considered to be an object and we will discuss that in more depth down the road, but it's important to remember that a string is not a primitive type.

A String is just a set of characters, or text. You can identify a string in Java because it is enclosed by quotation marks ("). For example, in the `HelloWorld` program, we printed out a string ("HelloWorld!"). The double quotes around it tell the computer that it is a string. Strings are often used in our various Java programs because there is almost always text used when interacting with a user.

3.7 Declaring and Casting Variables

You now know the values that variables can store. The next step is to learn to tell the computer that we have a variable. In this section, we will learn how to declare a variable of any type and then will move onto to slightly more advanced topics of casting and final variables. You will see variable declarations come up in almost every Java program so make sure you understand how they are implemented.

Variable Declarations

Variable declarations are very similar to the class and method declarations that we have already looked at. They include the name of the variable and a keyword. In Figure 3.9, you can see two different variable declarations in Line 2 and 3.

Figure 3.9

```
1   // Variable Declarations
2   type variableName;
3   type variableName = value;
```

These declarations are relatively self-explanatory. For the declaration in Line 2, the `type` would be replaced by whatever primitive type, like `int`, that the variable represents. The `variableName` would logically contain whatever the name of the variable you would like it to be. A variable name is also an identifier so all of the rules for an identifier apply. Since a variable declaration is a statement, a semicolon (;) is used to conclude the line.

Line 3 is very similar to Line 2 because it contains everything in Line 2 along with = `value`. The purpose of the equal sign (=) is to assign a value to the variable. Following the equal sign, the `value` is whatever you'd like to variable to store as long as it is in correspondence with the primitive type that you have indicated in the beginning of the line.

You may have noticed that the variable declared in Line 2 did not have a value associated with it, unlike Like 3. In a regular Java program, you can later assign a value to the variable from Line 2. We will look into how we do that in the next subsection. As a recap, we use variable declarations to initialize, or create, variables and this forms the foundation of our Java programs.

Declaring Different Types of Variables

Figure 3.10

```
1   // Variable Declarations
2   int x = 2;
3   int y;
4   y = 5;
5   double pi = 3.14;
6   pi = 3.1415;
7   boolean isMokshCool;
8   isMokshCool = true;
9   String s = "This is a string!";
10  String s2 = new String("This is a string!");
```

Let's dive right into the code. Most of the code in Figure 3.10 should seem familiar to you based on the syntax we looked at in Figure 3.9.

Line 2 shows an int variable declaration. We know this because the line starts of with the word int in the spot where the primitive type of the variable should be. The name of the variable is x and it has a value of 2. That's how simple a variable declaration is - that's it!

Likewise, in Line 3 and 4, a variable called y is being assigned a value of 5 in a slightly different way. The variable is initialized in Line 3 but is not given a value. Then, in Line 4, the variable is set to a value of 5. Notice that in Line 4, the type is not indicated because it has already been declared when the variable was initialized.

Line 5 demonstrates another variable declaration of, in this case, a double variable. Since the variable is of type double, it can have a value of 3.14 (or any other decimal). If an int variable was assigned a value of 3.14, it would cause an error because integers can only be whole numbers. The variable declared in Line 5, pi, is then given a different value of 3.1415. The original value of 3.14 is replaced and longer represents "pi." In Java, you can easily change the value of variables by simply assigning a different value to them.

Lines 7 and 8 show a boolean variable being initialized and then set to a value of true. The only difference between these two lines and Lines 3 and 4 is that the primitive type of the variable being created is boolean rather than int.

Last but certainly not least, Lines 9 and 10 are also variable declarations, but they are different from other declarations. They are declarations for variables that are Strings. This difference is on account of a String not being a primitive type. Line 9 follows the typical structure for the declaration with String in the place of a primitive type but notice that the primitive types like int or double are not capitalized while String is. Otherwise, the value of the variable is "This is a string!" which is enclosed by quotation marks just like any other String. Despite accomplishing the same job as Line 9, Line 10 deviates a bit more from what you would expect. In Line 10, everything on the left side of the equal sign remains the same buts it the right side where things start to change. As you can see, there is additional new keyword and the String value of the variable is enclosed in parentheses. Just like the other variable declarations we have looked at, there is a specific syntax that you have to follow. As mentioned earlier, both Line 9 and 10 fulfill the same purpose and you would logically prefer to use the variable declaration in Line 9 because it's shorter and more similar to a traditional variable declaration. The reason the declaration in Line 10 specifically applies to Strings has to do with a String being an object rather than a primitive type, a concept we will go over in more detail later down the road

Casting Variables

Casting variables refers to the concept of changing the primitive type of a variable or assigning a value to a variable of a primitive type that doesn't correspond. Two such examples of casting variables are when you want to assign an int value to a double variable and vice versa. One occurs smoothly while the other requires precaution while coding and some extra text.

Figure 3.11

```
1   // Casting Variables
2   int x = 2;
3   double y = x; // Fine
4
5   double x = 3.87;
6   int y = x; // Error
7   int y = (int) x; // Fine
```

Let's start off with the easier one: assigning an int value to a double variable. You can see an example of this in Lines 2 and 3. In Line 2, a variable called "x" is initialized and assigned a value of 2. The same happens on Line 3 with a variable "y" getting the value of "x", or 2. The variable "y" is a double but it's being assigned a value from a int variable. Remember that even though a double variable is used usually for numbers with decimals, there is no restriction on storing a value that is just a whole number. Therefore, assigning an int value to variable y does not cause an error at all.

Alternatively, storing a double value to an int variable causes an error as seen in Lines 5 and 6. Unlike a double, an int is meant only for whole numbers and giving an int variable y a double variable of 3.87 causes an error. This is where casting variables comes into play. On Line 7, you can see a solution that utilizes a cast. By adding in (int) between the equal sign and x, the computer converts the value of the variable x to an int value so that it can be stored to the variable y. You would assume that the `double` value 3.87 would be rounded up to an `int` value of 4. However, the `double` value is truncated meaning that everyone to the right of the decimal is disregarded so 3.87 gets converted to an `int` value of 3 and is stored to the variable y. The (`int`) that we added is known as a cast and it enabled us to convert from a `double` value to an `int` one.

Figure 3.12

```
1   // Round Instead of Truncate
2   double x = 3.87;
3   int y = (int) (x + 0.5);
```

There are often situations in programs that require you to round, rather than truncate, the `double` value. In that case, add on 0.5 to the `double` value. The truncation will still happen but the truncated value of the `double` value plus 0.5 will be equivalent to rounding the `double` value. As you can see in the example above, the `double` value 3.87 has 0.5 added onto it so that it is 4.37 before it is truncated. After truncation, the new value is 4, making it correctly rounded. When working with negative `double` values, subtract 0.5 rather than add.

In conclusion, forgetting to cast is an error that throws off many Java programmers. It is essential so that we can merge values of different primitive types together. In this section, we looked at converting between `double` and `int` values but casting is not just limited to that. Casting can be used to turn numbers (`int`) into text (String) and so on. There are, however, some limitations such as the fact that you cannot convert a `boolean` value to an `int` value.

Final Variables

For the last part of this section, we will be looking at a different type of variable called a final variable. A final variable is also known as a constant. This means that once a value has been assigned to it, it cannot be changed. The variables we have encountered thus far can have their value modified later in the program but a final variable is different in that way.

Figure 3.13

```
1   final type variableName = value;
2   final int numOfPeople = 10;
```

The code above shows how we indicate that a variable is a final variable. We do so by putting the `final` keyword before we declare the primitive type of the variable; that's the only change that needs to be made. If we try to change the value of the `int` variable declared in Line 2 later in the program, there will be an error.

You are likely wondering why final variables are needed. Let's look at an example. Let's say that you are creating a Java program that is dependent on the number of people present and that number is 10. There may be many locations in the code where the 10 has to be referenced as that is the number of people. Instead of putting 10 everywhere, it would be much better to put a variable, like numOfPeople. This also makes it much easier if the number of people present change because then you just have to change the value of the variable rather than every instance of 10 in the Java program. Similarly, there are countless different scenarios where constants are needed to represent a value and final variables are the solution.

3.8 Input and Output

Getting User Input in Java Programs

Input is something that is used in practically all computer programs. Input refers to the concept of the user entering, or inputting, information. Most computer programs have some element of interaction between the computer and the user so that the user stays engaged. Although input is not part of the AP Computer Science Java Subset, meaning that it will not show up in the AP Computer Science exam, it is essential part of Java and will come in handy as you start to create your own Java programs.

Figure 3.14

```
1   // Using Input
2   import java.util.Scanner; // import Scanner class from Java Class Libraries
3
4   // in main method
5   Scanner input = new Scanner( System.in ); // Scanner object
6
7   System.out.println("Enter the first number: ");
8   int num1 = input.nextInt(); // get 1st number
```

There are a couple of different things that you have to do in order to enable input in your Java program as seen in Figure 3.14. Input is also perfect example for us to use the Java Class Libraries that we discussed in Chapter 2 and the import statement from earlier in the chapter. You can see the import statement used in Line 2. In order to enable input, we use a class called the Scanner class that is part of the java.util package. Remember that it's an import statement so you will see it before the class declaration in the first few lines of the Java program.

After importing the Scanner class, you need to create an object of the Scanner class once you are in the body of the main method. You can accomplish this using the code in Line 5 which looks fairly similar to a String variable declaration because both the String is an object just like the Scanner object. Essentially, we are declaring a variable called input that refers to a Scanner object, or an instance of the imported Scanner class. A variable like such is known as an object reference. This object reference declaration is something that you just have to remember because you will use it in your programs that involve input.

Now that we have instantiated an object of the Scanner class, we can call the methods within the Scanner class. The primary method within the class that we will be utilizing is the nextInt() method. The method name does a good job of explaining its purpose, or functionality. It essentially reads whatever int value the user inputs next. In Line 7, the user is prompted to enter in a number and then the nextInt() method is called in the following line. In addition, in Line 8, a variable is initialized and it stores whatever the nextInt() method returns, essentially what the user inputs. Pay close attention to how the method is called or run. The format for is object.methodName(). Whenever you call methods, this is the syntax to follow. In addition, there are many methods within this class, such as nextDouble() or nextLine(), that function similarly to nextInt(). We will use input for a Java program later in this chapter.

Outputting Text in Java Programs

Unlike input, output, rather than taking user input, display information for the user. Other differences include that it's included in the AP Computer Science Java subset and that we've already worked with it in the HelloWorld program. Just like input, output falls under the umbrella of keeping the user engaged and informed about what is happening in the computer program.

Figure 3.15

```
1  // Using Output
2  System.out.print("I love ");
3  System.out.print("AP Computer Science!");
4
5  System.out.println();
6  System.out.println("I love ");
7  System.out.println("AP Computer Science!");
```

Output

```
I love AP Computer Science!
I love
AP Computer Science!
```

Above, you can see an example of using some output methods to display text. You may notice that there is no import statement or object reference declaration in the code. Just as input relies on a Scanner object, output depends on a Standard Output Object. Fortunately, we don't have to import the Standard Output class or instantiate it because it is built-in due to its popularity.

There are two different methods in Standard Output class that are included in the Java subset and are most-used. These methods are `print()` and `println()`. You used the `println()` method in the `HelloWorld` program. Let's compare and contrast these two methods as they serve the same purpose with minimal differences. They are both methods of the `System.out` class. In addition, they both are used to print out, or display, text. As you saw in the `HelloWorld` program, a string or variable is put in between the parentheses to determine what will be printed out. The string or variable printed out is known as an argument that is passed to the method. The implementation of both methods is the same. There is only a slight difference between the two. You can see an example of the difference in the code above. If you look carefully, you will see that the `print()` method continues printing text on the same line while the `println()` method begins printing on a new line after it is executed. You can use either method depending on what your requirements for output are.

Escape Sequences

Printing out text also brings up another concept of escape sequences. An escape sequence is a combination of a backslash and a character and is used for formatting what is printed out by the computer program. When utilizing escape sequences, you tend to include them within the String that is being printed out and the computer automatically recognizes them. In the table below, you can see some widely-used escape sequences.

Common Escape Sequences | Figure 3.16

Escape Sequence	Purpose
\n	Continues printing on a new line
\\	Prints out a backslash
\"	Prints out a double quote
\t	Continues printing one tab to the right

Don't worry if this seems a bit overwhelming. Escape sequences are quite easy to use and we will see them being implemented in a bit. The \n and \t escape sequences are used for formatting what you print out and come in quite handy. The \\ and \", however, serve a slightly different purpose. Because the computer requires double quotes around Strings and does not print out the quotation marks, a programmer would be stuck in a tough situation if he or she actually needs to print out quotes. By inserting the \" escape sequence within the String and quotes, the computer will know that it needs to actually print out a quotation mark as well. Similarly, you could need to print out a backslash (\) but the computer may interpret it as part of an escape sequence (and, hence, not print it out). The \\\ escape sequence solves that problem. There are a countless amount of escape sequences and those are some of the common ones.

Figure 3.17 | EscSeq.java

```java
1   // Escape Sequences
2   public class EscSeq
3   {
4     public static void main( String[] args )
5     {
6       // \n escape sequence
7       System.out.println("I\nlove this book");
8
9       // \\ escape sequence
10      System.out.println("\\ is a backslash");
11
12      // \" escape sequence
13      System.out.println("\" is a quote");
14
15      // \t escape sequence
16      System.out.println("I\tlove this book");
17    }
18  }
```

Output

```
> run EscSeq
I
love this book
\ is a backslash
" is a quote
I       love this book
```

Figure 3.17 shows a Java program called EscSeq.java that demonstrates some escape sequences in action. As you compare the code and output, you can see the functionality of each escape sequence. In addition, the escape sequences are integrated within the quotes enclosing the String and are very simple to use. Overall, escape sequences are frequently used with output to format text and display special characters.

3.9 Arithmetic Operators

Arithmetic operators are something that we have been introduced to ever since we learned 1+1 at a very young age. They are used to represent arithmetic operations like addition. As you may know, computer science is based on a lot of mathematics and arithmetic operators are frequently used in Java programs to perform calculations.

Basic Arithmetic Operators

Most of the arithmetic operators that we will work with will be familiar to you and all of them should be very easy to use. Logically, arithmetic operators are used with numbers like an int or a double. In the table below, you can see the symbols for arithmetic operators, their corresponding operations, and examples of their use in both Java and algebra.

Arithmetic Operators | Figure 3.18

Symbol	Purpose	Algebraic Example	Java Example
+	Addition	$x = y + 2$	x = y + 2;
-	Subtraction	$x = y - 2$	x = y - 2;
*	Multiplication	$x = 5y$	x = 5 * y;
/	Division	$x = \frac{y}{5}$	x = y / 5;
%	Remainder	$x = y \bmod 5$	x = y % 5;

You should be familiar with the first four symbols, which just represent the basic arithmetic operations of addition, subtraction, multiplication, and division. As you may have noticed, arithmetic operations within Java are very similar to those in algebra. The primary difference is that an asterisk (*) represents multiplication and that a slash (/) does division. Speaking of division, division between integers works differently than you would imagine. For example, if you are doing 6 / 4, you would assume the answer to be 1.5. However, Java requires that dividing two integers should result in a quotient that is also an integer. The correct answer, 1.5, is then truncated and the answer results to 1. The simple solution to this to use the (double) cast as follows: (double) 6 / 4. This will return an answer of 1.5.

The last operator, called a modulus, is a percent sign (%) and is not as common as the other operators. The use of the modulus is quite simple and is somewhat related to division. It essentially returns the the remainder of division between two numbers. For example, 10 % 3 = 1. The modulus is particularly useful for determining divisibility because if a modulus returns a 0, you know that they are divisible.

Increment and Decrement Operators

The increment and decrement operators a very simple purpose: to add or subtract 1 from a number. The increment operator (++) can make the equation x = x + 1; much simpler as x++;. Similarly, the decrement operator(- -) can do the same when subtracting numbers. In the table below, you can see how the use of increment and decrement operators varies a bit.

Increment and Decrement Operators | Figure 3.19

Symbol	Name	Example	Explanation
++	Prefix increment operator	++x;	Increase x by 1 and then use its new value in the same expression
++	Postfix increment operator	x++;	Use the current value of x and then increase it by 1
− −	Prefix decrement operator	− −x;	Decrease x by 1 and then use its new value in the same expression
− −	Postfix decrement operator	x− −;	Use the current value of x and then decrease it by 1

Putting the operator in front or behind the increment or decrement operator can make a world of difference. Let's consider an example. Say you have a variable a that is equal to 3 and you want to print it out a number that is 1 greater than it. You can utilize an increment operator for that, but your placement of the operator can determine whether you successfully complete your objective or not. If you decide to type System.out.println(a++);, then the computer will output 3 because it will use the current value of a first and then add on the 1. So if you were to try to print out a again after this statement, the computer would print out 4. Alternatively, if you used System.out.println(++a);, 4 will be outputted because a is increased first and then it is printed out. The same goes for decrement operators.

Once we start using control structures, we will use increment and decrement operators more than ever. In addition, these operators come in handy when keeping count because you tend to increase or decrease by 1.

Addition Program

In this subsection, you will look at a basic Java program that applies a lot of what we have learned recently. This includes input, output, and arithmetic operators. Below, you can see the code for the Addition program filled with comments along with the output of the program. Take a look at the code and try to interpret it to the best of your abilities. Then, read the explanation of the code that follows.

Figure 3.20 | Addition.java

```java
1   // Addition.java
2
3   import java.util.Scanner; // import Scanner class from Java Class Libraries
4
5   public class Addition
6   {
7     public static void main(String[] args)
8     {
9       Scanner input = new Scanner( System.in ); // Scanner object
10
```

```
11      int num1; // first number
12      int num2; // second number
13      int sum; // sum of the first and second numbers
14
15      System.out.println("Enter the first number: ");
16      num1 = input.nextInt(); // get 1st number
17
18      System.out.println("Enter the second number: ");
19      num2 = input.nextInt(); // get 2nd number
20
21      sum = num1 + num2; // get sum by adding the 2 numbers
22
23      System.out.println("The sum is " + sum );
24   }
25 }
```

Output

```
> run Addition
Enter the first number:
2
Enter the second number:
3
The sum is 5
```

It definitely is a lot to take in. Don't be overwhelmed - we will work through this together part by part. By the time we finish, you will realize that creating a Java program and implementing the concepts you have learned is easier than you think. If we go over a concept and you don't remember much of it, track back to an earlier section in the back which will help you refresh your memory.

Line 1 - 3

Figure 3.21

```
1 // Addition.java
2
3 import java.util.Scanner; // import Scanner class from Java Class Libraries
```

The first 3 lines feature a few end-of-line comments that, as you know, don't affect the functionality of the program and simply keep us in the loop about what is going on. The most important part of this set of lines is the import statement in Line 3. We actually saw this line of code earlier in this very chapter when we went over input. Essentially, we are importing the Scanner class so that we can instantiate a Scanner object. We will then be able to call methods from the Scanner class that will enable us to read whatever the user inputs. Remember that import statements come before the class declaration at the beginning of the program.

Line 5 - 8

Figure 3.22

```
5   public class Addition
6   {
7     public static void main(String[] args)
8       {
```

We essentially looked at this set of code with the HelloWorld program. In Line 5, we have a class declaration for the Addition class and then the signature right brace to signify the start of the body of the class. Then, on Line 7 and 8, the main method is declared along with the right brace and we are ready to start typing up code to make this Addition program come to life.

Line 9

Figure 3.23

```
9     Scanner input = new Scanner( System.in ); // Scanner object
```

In Line 9, we are creating a Scanner object and creating an object reference (basically a variable) called input to it. Remember that we are able to instantiate this Scanner object because we imported the Scanner class earlier in the program. Now, with the Scanner object, we can call methods that we need from the Scanner class.

Line 11 - 13

Figure 3.24

```
11      int num1; // first number
12      int num2; // second number
13      int sum; // sum of the first and second numbers
```

This is the first time you are coming across variable declarations in an actual Java program and, as you can tell, they are relatively straightforward. With these 3 lines of code, we are initializing 3 int variables named num1, num2, and sum. Notice that the variables are not given a value yet and are defaulted to a null value. Later in the program, when the time is right, we will assign a value to each one. The end-of-line comments following each variable declaration help explain the purpose of each of the variables. The variables num1 and num2 represent the first and second number that the user inputs and sum depicts the sum of the two numbers given by the user. Now that all variables are initialized, we will move on and assign the appropriate values to them.

Line 15 - 19

Figure 3.25

```
15      System.out.println("Enter the first number: ");
16      num1 = input.nextInt(); // get 1st number
17
18      System.out.println("Enter the second number: ");
19      num2 = input.nextInt(); // get 2nd number
```

This is where a lot of the magic happens. First, in Line 15, we prompt the user to enter the first number. Then, using the nextInt() method, we can get whatever int value that the user inputs when prompted. Then, we can set the value of the num1 variable to whatever the user gives us. Similarly, we repeat the same process to obtain the second number from the user and then store it to the num2 variable. The user has now done his or her job of giving us two numbers to work with and it's up to us to turn those two numbers into one.

Line 21 - 25

Figure 3.26

```
21      sum = num1 + num2; // get sum by adding the 2 numbers
22
23      System.out.println("The sum is " + sum );
24    }
25  }
```

If you are given two numbers and asked to find their sum, you add them. Similarly, we need to have the computer do the same. We will accomplish this using the arithmetic operators. The num1 and num2 variables are added together using the + arithmetic operator and their sum is assigned to the sum variable.

At this stage, all of our variables have been assigned a value and we have the final answer, or the sum, that we need to return to the user. The only task left is to display it for the user, which we will do using the println() method. In Line 23, we print out what the sum is. Rather than just printing out the variable, we place some text before the number so that the user understands the concept. The + operator is used again but for a different purpose: to combine the variable and String so that they can be outputted. In the output, you can see that The sum is 5 is printed out.

Finally, there are two consecutive right braces to close the bodies of the main method and Addition class and that's it! We just walked through a Java program which interacts with the user and performs calculations. As you learn more concepts down the road, you will be able to add more functionality to create a better experience for the user.

3.10 Relational and Equality Operators

Although you may not know them by name, you always use relational operators when comparing different numbers. Examples of relational operators include the greater than sign (>) and the less than sign (<) and they are used in Java just as you are accustomed to using them.

Relational Operators

All of the relational operators that we will be working with will be entirely familiar to you and even more simpler to use in your Java programs. These operators are primarily used when you want to compare numbers like an int or a double. In the table below, you can see each relational operator along with its corresponding example Java condition and meaning.

Relational Operators | Figure 3.27

Operator	Name	Java Condition Example	Condition Meaning
>	Greater than	x > y	x is greater than y
<	Less than	x < y	x is less than y
>=	Greater than or equal to	x >= y	x is greater than or equal to y
<=	Less than or equal to	x <= y	x is less than or equal to y

The table does an adequate job of explaining the functionality of each operator and these are the very same operators that you use when working with inequalities in math. As you know, these operators are used based on the relationship between the two numbers and which is bigger or smaller. The only difference between the relational operators in Java and what you are used to is the way a few of them are represented. The greater than or equal to and less than or equal to operator are typically written as a greater than or less than sign with an underscore underneath them. However, in Java, they are written as >= or <=. Other than that, you can continue to use them in Java just as you have for the most of your life.

Equality Operators

Equality operators are actually very similar to relational operators and, as you can probably tell from the name, they are all about the equal sign. They are also used to compare numbers to each other but rather than checking if numbers are greater or less than each other, they check if numbers are equal to each other. Here is another table that explores the two equality operators that we will work with in this book.

Equality Operators | Figure 3.28

Operator	Name	Java Condition Example	Condition Meaning
==	Equal to	x == y	x is equal to y

Equality Operators | Figure 3.28

Operator	Name	Java Condition Example	Condition Meaning
!=	Not equal to	x != y	x is not equal to y

These 2 operators may seem a bit more unfamiliar to you. You may be used to seeing the not equal to operator (!=) as an equal sign with a slash through it but, because we do not have the ability to type characters with a slash through them on a computer, we use != as the alternative. Likewise, you are likely to the equal to operator consisting of only one equal sign rather than two. However, when you are trying to compare two different numbers you need to use two signs and when you are assigning values to variables use one. The == operator is an equality operator and the = operator is an assignment operator, which we will go over in the next section.

Use in Programs

You may be wondering where relational and equality operators fit into programs. These operators are used in a condition, or a boolean expression that can evaluate to true or false when comparing primitive types. In the two tables that we looked at earlier, the Java condition example column was filled with Java conditions that could evaluate to true or false depending on the values of x and y.

Figure 3.29

```
1  boolean x = ( 5 >= 4 ); // true
2  boolean y = ( 3 == 2 ); // false
```

In the figure above, the expressions enclosed within the 2 sets of parentheses are conditions because they evaluate to a boolean value. In the first line, the condition 5 >= 4 evaluates to true because 5 is indeed greater than 4. Hence, the boolean variable x is set to a value of true. Likewise, upon evaluation, the variable y is set to false. You can see that a relational operator and an equality operator are used in the condition. In addition, the single equal sign (=) is used to assign a value and the double equal sign (==) is used to compare values.

Comparison Program

Now we will apply what we have learned in this section but creating a Comparer program that prompts the user for 2 numbers and then tells the user if the first number is greater than the second number or not. You will use a relational operator to compare the numbers and print out the answer. Before you look at the code right below, think about how you would go about implementing such a program using what you have learned.

Figure 3.30 | Comparer.java

```
1   // Comparison.java
2
3   import java.util.Scanner; // import Scanner class
4
5   public class Comparer
6   {
7     public static void main( String[] args )
8     {
9       Scanner s = new Scanner( System.in); // Scanner object
10
11      int num1; // 1st number
12      int num2; // 2nd number
13
14      System.out.println( "Enter the first number: " );
15      num1 = s.nextInt(); // get 1st num
16
17      System.out.println( "Enter the second number: " );
18      num2 = s.nextInt(); // get 2nd num
19
20      System.out.println("1st number greater than 2nd number: " + (num1 > num2));
21    }
22  }
```

Output

```
> run Comparer
Enter the first number:
10
Enter the second number:
3
Is 1st number greater than the 2nd number: true
```

Line 1 - 18

The majority of this program is the same as what we saw in the Addition program so we are going to skip over it. Quickly glance over the first 18 lines and, if you come across anything that you don't understand, go back to the Addition program and check out the explanation.

Line 20

Figure 3.31

```
20      System.out.println("1st number greater than 2nd number: " + (num1 > num2));
```

Line 20 is really the only line in this program that contains something we haven't seen in a full-fledged program yet. At this point, we have 2 variables that store the int values that the user has inputted. Now, we need to tell the user if the first number is greater than the second number. We do this by using the greater than relational operator within a condition. The condition returns true or false which is then outputted by the computer to give the user the answer.

3.11 Logical and Assignment Operators

In the last section, we looked at relational and equality operators which are used when comparing numbers. Now, we will be working with logical and assignment operators which are another set of operators that are essentials to Java programs. We will be moving into control structures in the next chapter and you will find them to be especially useful.

Assignment Operators:

Assignment operators do exactly what they sound like: they assign values. We have already worked extensively with the most used assigned assignment operator - the equal sign. As you know, the equal sign is used so frequently because it is used whenever you are setting a value to a variable. The other assignment operators are similar to increment and decrement operators in the notion that you can live without them but they make life much easier. Check out this table below to learn more about the assignment operators.

Assignment Operators | Figure 3.32

Operator	Java Example	Explanation
=	x = 7	value of x is 7
+=	x += 5	x = x + 5
-=	x -= 3	x = x - 3
*=	x *= 9	x = x * 9
/=	x /= 2	x = x / 2
%=	x %= 4	x = x % 4

Because you already know the purpose of the equal sign (=) assignment operator, we will focus on the last 4 assignment operators. To understand their purpose, let's think of a situation where you have an int variable x and you want to add on 2 to it. You would have to add the expression x = x + 2; to your Java program. Instead, you can use the assignment operator += to simplify the expression to x += 2; and it accomplishes the same objective. Similarly, you can place any of the arithmetic operators we know before the equal sign and it will work. These assignment operators will become very useful as you start to create more advanced Java programs.

Logical Operators:

Recall that in the last section we worked with conditions and the relational operators within them. Well, as a programmer, you can often come across situations that require you to evaluate multiple conditions at once and return a single true or false value. You can use logical operators to link these various conditions together. This may sound very abstract and confusing so let's just dive right into these operators and you'll see their use as we use them in situations.

The 3 logical operators we will work with in Java are &&, | |, and !. First, let's look at the && operator, which is also known as the logical AND operator. This operator is used to combine conditions together and it returns only if both conditions individually evaluate to true. Basically, the following complex condition (3 > 2 && 2 <= 5) would evaluate to true because both conditions 3 > 2 and 2 <= 5 are true. If even one of the conditions had been false, the complex condition would have come out to be false. In the table below, you can see that you can only get a true value from a complex condition with the && operator if both conditions are true; otherwise, it evaluates to false.

&& Operator Truth Table | Figure 3.33

&&		
	T	F
T	T	F
F	F	F

With the && operator, only 1 of the 4 possible situations result in a true value, but, with the | | operator, 3 of 4 situations do. The | | operator is also known as the logical OR operator and it is used just like the && operator for complex conditions. The only difference lies in the notion that only 1 of the 2 conditions have to be true for the overall result to be true. This means that you can only get a false value from a complex condition with the | | operator if both conditions evaluate to false. The following complex condition (3 < 2 | | 4 > 1) would result in true because the second condition is true. Just as we saw a table for the possible outcomes with the && operator, there is a table below that shows the same for the | | operator.

| | Operator Truth Table | Figure 3.34

	T	F
T	T	T
F	T	F

The last logical operator is a little bit different from the ones we have looked at thus far, but it also has many applications within computer science. This is the logical NOT operator that is represented by !, an exclamation mark. It simply reverses the value of a `boolean` expression. For example, the following condition !(3 > 2) would return `false` because 3 is greater than 2 and ! operator results in the opposite of the value of the `boolean` expression. An exclamation point commonly represents opposite in computer science as we say with the does not equal operator (!=). You can see another table below for the outcomes with a logical NOT operator.

! Operator Truth Table | Figure 3.35

!	
T	T
F	F

These logical operators may not seem very relevant at this point, but, as soon as we hit the next chapter, they will become a commonplace in our programs. Keep them in mind and make sure you remember each one.

Short-Circuit Evaluation

Short-circuit evaluation is an issue that comes up as a product of using the logical AND and OR operators. To best understand short-circuit evaluation, let's pretend we have a complex condition that is (`false condition && true condition`). As you know, both conditions have to be `true` in this situation to get a `true` value. When the computer evaluates this condition, it goes from left to right and, after it realizes the first condition is `false`, it skips over the second condition because it is impossible to end up with anything other than a `false` value. Likewise, the computer could be working with a complex condition like (`true condition || false condition`) and the same thing would happen with the | | operator. Immediately after recognizing that the first condition was `true`, the computer would disregard the second condition because the overall result will definitely be `true`.

You may be wondering what's wrong with that. After all, all it does is help the computer evaluate a complex condition faster. However, it is possible that a condition that is skipped over by the computer actually impact the value of a variable. For example, let's say that the second condition of a complex condition is x++ < 8. Then, if it is disregarded by the computer due to short-circuit evaluation, x will never have 1 added on to it which can affect its overall value and create problems for later in the program. Yes, most conditions don't change values but short-circuit evaluation can create problems in certain conditions.

The solution to this is to use & and | instead of && and | |. By simply, only put one symbol instead of two, the computer knows to evaluate both conditions no matter what the result of the first condition is. For example, if you have a complex condition like (`false condition & true condition`), the computer knows that the overall condition will be false after evaluating the first one. But, because there is a single & rather than two, it checks the second condition anyway. The same goes for using | instead of | |. Short-circuit evaluation often catches programmers off guard and will definitely show up on the AP Computer Science exam.

3.12 Order of Operations

We've looked at so many different operators in this chapter and parts of our programs can become especially confusing when there are many types of operators used. The compiler follows a specific order of operators to interpret; it doesn't just go left to right. It's important to know the order of operations because your calculations could return answers that you would not expect. In the table below, you can see the precedence of each operator we've learned of thus far.

Operator Precedence | Figure 3.36

Priority	Operator(s)	Associativity
1	++, − −, !	right to left
2	*, /, %	left to right
3	+, -	left to right
4	>, >=, <, <=	left to right
5	==, !=	left to right
6	&&	left to right
7	||	left to right
8	=, +=, -=, *=, /=, %=	right to left

Let's quickly glance through this table together and then, later in the chapter, you will have the opportunity to evaluate some expressions with various operators to check your knowledge of the order of operations. Associativity is referred to as the order in which the operator is evaluated. You can see that the most and least important operators are the ones that are from right to left while the rest are left to right. Otherwise, the table is rather straightforward and you just have to remember this order because it will become very important when you make complex calculations with your Java programs. The types of operators from most to least precedent is increment/decrement and logical NOT operators, multiplication/division/remainder, addition/subtraction, relational operators, equality operators, logical AND operator, logical OR operator, and assignment operators.

3.13 Chapter Summary

Wow! This is one long chapter. We went over so much and it definitely is a lot to taken. However, soon all of these concepts will become second nature to you just as concepts from Chapter 2 have. We looked at operators, input/output, declaring variables of different primitive types, and so much more. It's amazing that we have created so many different programs throughout this chapter and start off unable to develop a single one. Here's to more chapters just like this one where you learn a lot!

Multiple Choice Questions

1) Which of the following class names is incorrect?

(A) APcs_2015_java

(B) Apcs_java_2015

(C) Java_APcs_2015

(D) 2015_java_APcs

2) Which of the following comments is incorrect?

(A) ///AP computer science java.

(B) // AP computer science java.

(C) ///AP computer science.

(D) /AP computer science/

3) Which of the following comments is correct?

(A) /*ABCD*/

(B) */ABCD*/

(C) /*ABCD/*

(D) **ABCD//

4) Which of the following `HelloWorld` programs is correct?

(A)
```
        public class HelloWorld
    {
      public static void main(String[] args)
      {
        System.out.println("Hello world");
      )
    }
```

(B)
```
public class HelloWorld
    {
      public static void main(String[] args)
      [
        System.out.println("Hello world");
      ]
    }
```

(C)
```
public class HelloWorld
    {
      public static void main(String[] args)
      {
        System.out.println("Hello world");
      }
    }
```

(D)
```
public class HelloWorld
    (
      public static void main(String[] args)
      {
        System.out.println("Hello world");
      }
    )
```

5) Do comments affect the functionality of the program?

(A) Yes, only while exectuing the class

(B) No, not at all

(C) Yes, only while executing the main method

(D) No, only the methods are affected

6) Which of the following main method declarations is correct?

(A) `public static void main(String() args);`

(B) `public static String main(String[] args);`

(C) `public static void main(String arg);`

(D) `public static void main(String[] args);`

7) Which of the following statement(s) is a valid variable declaration and assignment?

(A) `int x = 21.7;`

(B) `int x;`
`x = 21.7;`

(C) `int x = (int) 21.7;`

(D) `int x = (double) 21.7;`

8) What is the result of the following expression?

`int result = 2 - 6 / 3 * 4 + 2 % 5;`

(A) 4

(B) -4

(C) 3

(D) -3

9) What is the result of the following expression?

```
int result = 5 / 3 + 6 - 2 * 2;
```

(A) 4

(B) -4

(C) 3

(D) -3

10) Consider the following code segment.

```
public class Test
{
   public static void main(String[] args)
   {
      int result1 = 2 - 6 / 3 * 4 + 2 % 5;
      int result2 = (2 - 6) / 3 * (2 + 2);
      System.out.println(result1);
      System.out.println(result2);
   }
}
```

What numbers are printed as a result of executing the code segment?

(A) Both numbers are the same

(B) -4, -1

(C) 4, 1

(D) -3, -1

11) Which of the following code segments properly declares and assigns the variable x a value?

I. `int x = 2;`

II. `int x = 20000;`

III. `int x = 21.2;`

IV. `double x = "X";`

V. `String x = "X";`

(A) Only I

(B) Only I and II

(C) I, II, III, V

(D) I. II, V

B only 1 & II

12) If x is a `double` variable with a value of 654321 and y is a `double` variable with a value of 654321.0, what will result from the following expression?

`x == y`

(A) true

(B) false

(C) 0

(D) Compile time error

13) Consider the following code segment.

```
boolean x = true;
boolean y = false;
boolean z = !x;

System.out.println("Result 1: " + (x | y));
System.out.println("Result 2: " + (y & z));
System.out.println("Result 3: " + (!z));
```

What is printed as a result of executing the code segment?

(A) Result 1: true
     Result 2: true
     Result 3: true

(B) Result 1: true
     Result 2: false
     Result 3: true

(C) Result 1: true
     Result 2: false
     Result 3: false

(D) Result 1: false
     Result 2: false
     Result 3: true

14) What occurs if an attempt is made to compile and execute the following code segment?

```
double big = 45.67;
int small = 45;
boolean result = (big > small && small != 100);
System.out.println("The result is " + result);
```

(A) The result is true

(B) The result is false

(C) An error will occur at Line 3

(D) An error will occur at Line 4

15) Which of the following variable declarations will not compile successfully?

(A) String x = 5;

(B) double temperature = 15.24;

(C) boolean ok;

(D) String x = "5";

16) Upon execution of the code fragment below, what will the values the variables a, b, and c be?

```
int a;
int b = 5;
int c = 3;
int a = --b * c++;
```

(A) a = 16, b = 4, c = 4

(B) a = 42, b = 5, c = 8

(C) a = 48, b = 5, c = 8

(D) a = 12, b = 4, c = 4

17) Consider the following code segment.

```
int g = 3;
System.out.print(++g * 8);
```

What is printed as a result of executing the code segment?

(A) 24

(B) 12

(C) 32

(D) 16

18) Consider the following code segment.

```
int g = 3;
System.out.print(g++ * 8);
```

What is printed as a result of executing the code segment?

(A) 16

(B) 24

(C) 8

(D) 32

19) Upon execution of the code fragment below, what will the values the variables a, b, and c be?

```
int a;
int b = 5;
int c = 3;
int a = b-- * c++;
```

(A) a = 16, b = 4, c = 4

(B) a = 42, b = 5, c = 8

(C) a = 35, b = 6, c = 7

(D) a = 15, b = 4, c = 4

20) Which of the following statement(s) is an invalid variable declaration and assignment?

(A) `int a = 10;`

(B)
```
int a;
    a = 10;
```

(C) `a = 10;`

(D) `int a;`

Answers and Explanations

Answer Key

1. D
2. D
3. A
4. C
5. B
6. D
7. C
8. B
9. C
10. A
11. D
12. A
13. B
14. A
15. A
16. D
17. C
18. B
19. D
20. C

Explanations

1) **(D)** The name of a class is considered to be an identifier, meaning that it can consist of letters, numbers, underscores, and dollar signs and cannot have any spaces or begin with a digit. In addition, class names and word within them are usually capitalized (like HelloWorld). In this case, notice that all choices don't have any spaces and use the appropriate characters but Choice D starts with a digit, making it invalid.

2) **(D)** An end-of-line comment is a comment that begins with // and spans only one line. The contents of a comment do not matter since a comment does not affect a the functionality of a program. Since Choice D is does not begin with //, it is incorrect.

3) **(A)** A traditional comment is a comment that can span multiple lines and it is implemented by starting with /* and ending with a */. Choice A meets that requirement.

4) **(C)** All of the answer choices have the correct text and the only difference between them lies in how the bodies of the HelloWorld class and main method are enclosed. The bodies of a class and

method should be enclosed by braces, meaning that they start with { and end with }, which Choice C correctly does.

5) **(B)** Comments have no impact on the functionality of a program whatsoever and are there for the convenience of the programmer. They are essentially used as small notes so that a programmer can keep track of what is going on in any part of a program and are especially useful with large and complex programs.

6) **(D)** At this point, memorizing the main method declaration because it shows up in almost every program and we will understand its components soon, but, for now, know it by heart.

7) **(C)** Choices A, B, and D are incorrect because a double value (21.7) is being assigned to an int variable which causes an error. However, Choice C works because the (int) cast converts the double value to an int value so that it can be assigned.

8) **(B)** In order to do this question correctly, you must follow the order of operations. Therefore, you complete the division, multiplication, and modulus first going from left to right and are left with 2 - 8 + 2. This yields a final answer of -4.

9) **(C)** Just like the previous questions, you must correctly utilize the order of operations. Based on that, after completing the multiplication and division first, you are left with 1 + 6 - 4. Remember that 5 / 3 returns 1 because you are dividing integers so the remainder is truncated. Then, you end up with a final answer of 3.

10) **(A)** In this question, the focus of the code given is on the 4 lines in the body of the main method. We must evaluate the expressions that determine the values for the result1 and result2 variables to determine what numbers are printed out. We can achieve this using the order of operations. For result1, you complete the division, multiplication, and modulus first going from left to right and are left with 2 - 8 + 2. This yields a final answer of -4. For result2, the parantheses take precedence over everything else so you get -4 / 3 * 4 which returns -4. Remember that -4 / 3 returns -1 because you are dividing integers so the remainder is truncated.

11) **(D)** I and II are correct because x is being assigned an int value and that matches what is being declared. III is incorrect because a double value is assigned when an int is declared. IV is incorrect for the very same reason as a String value is being assigned to a double variable. V is correct because x is a String variable and is given a String value.

12) **(A)** Since an equality operator (a type of relational operator) is being used, we know that true or false will be returned. 654321 and 654321.0 represent the same numerical value which is what the == operator so true is returned.

13) **(B)** For the variables, x has a value of true and y has a value of false. z has a value that this opposite of the value of x because of the ! operator so it stores false. The first result is based on the expression (x | y) which is equivalent to true OR false. With the OR operator, if either of the values is true, the expression returns true, so result 1 is true. For result 2, the expression is (y & z) which translates to false AND false. With the AND operator, if either of the values is false, false is returned, making result 2 false. For our final result, !z is the experssion and can also be thought

of as NOT false. With the NOT operator, it returns the opposite of the original value so result 3 is true.

14) **(A)** First of all, no error will occur in this code segment as everything is properly declared, assigned, and evaluated. Since big is 45.67 and small is 45, we can go ahead and evaluate the expresion that determines the value fo the result and, hence, what is printed out. The boolean expression is (big > small && small != 100). Both halves of this expression, (big > small) and (small != 100), need to be true for this expression to eevaluate to true as we are working with the && operator. We know that (big > small) is true since 45.67 is greater than 45 and (small != 100) is true as well as 45 does not equal 100. Therefore, the variable result gets a value of true.

15) **(A)** For Choice A, the declared String value does not match the 5 that is assigned resulting in an unsuccessful compilation. For the remaining choices, there's no such error. For Choice D, "5" is considered to be a String value.

16) **(D)** Getting this question correct is entirely dependent on your understanding of ++ and -- operators. Remember that when these operators are used, if they are before their respective variables, their values are changed before the expression is evaluated. However, if they are after, the values are also increased or decreased after the expression is evaluated. In this case, a = --b * c++; is basically a = 4 * 3 which is 12 and b and c both finish with a value of 4.

17) **(C)** Getting this question correct is entirely dependent on your understanding of ++ and -- operators. Remember that when these operators are used, if they are before their respective variables, their values are changed before the expression is evaluated. However, if they are after, the values are also increased or decreased after the expression is evaluated. In this case, (++g * 8) is basically (4 * 8) which is 32.

18) **(B)** Getting this question correct is entirely dependent on your understanding of ++ and -- operators. Remember that when these operators are used, if they are before their respective variables, their values are changed before the expression is evaluated. However, if they are after, the values are also increased or decreased after the expression is evaluated. In this case, (g++ * 8) is basically (3 * 8) which is 24.

19) **(D)** Getting this question correct is entirely dependent on your understanding of ++ and -- operators. Remember that when these operators are used, if they are before their respective variables, their values are changed before the expression is evaluated. However, if they are after, the values are also increased or decreased after the expression is evaluated. In this case, a = b-- * c++; is basically a = 5 * 3 which is 15 and b and c both finish with a value of 4.

20) **(C)** Choice C is invalid because for the variable declaration, the variable type is not given, resulting in a compilation error. The rest of the choices are properly assigned and declared.

Chapter 4 - Control Structures

4.1 Chapter Overview:

We've learned a lot of the basics of the Java programming language. So far, we haven't interacted much with logic but control structures will change all of that. Control structures will enable our program to become exponentially more interesting because, each time we run it, we can have different code executed and, hence, a different outcome.

4.2 Introduction to Control Structures:

A control structure is a statement that supports repetition and conditional execution. Typically, our programs have simply been executed in order from the top to the bottom. But, with control structures, code within programs is executed in a nonsequential fashion. This means that some parts of the code could not be run or some others could be executed multiple times. This leads us to the two different branches, or types, of control structures.

The first type of control structures are decision-making control structures. They are also known as conditional statements and they usually involve checking for a specific condition and then executing a different snippet code depending on whether the condition returns `true` or `false`. If statements are the primary decision-making control structures that we will play around with.

The other type is an iterative control structure. This is associated with the repetitive end of control structures. With this type of control structure, you can execute the same code multiple times without having to type it out more than once. For example, you could print out a String like "I love this book!" 50 times using one line of code and a control structure. The repetitive control structures include the while and for loops and are immensely useful.

You also know that the repetition and conditional execution of control structures allow programs to be run in a nonsequential order. The primary purpose of control structures is to model the logic we encounter in our everyday lives. By this I mean that we often make a decision based on some information and control structures enable us to do the same with our Java programs. If you have found our computer programs thus far to be on the boring side, I don't blame you and control structures are definitely a solution to that boredom. Although we will just be looking at some simple use cases for control structures, the possibilities with them are infinite and you can extend the functionality of your programs in countless ways.

4.3 If Statements

If statements are often considered to be the most basic and useful of all control structures. With if statements, you will finally start making use of the conditions and relational operators we learned about last chapter. If statements can become a bit complicated as variations are added to them but they mostly involve the basic logic that you accustomed to using when you are making a decision. Without further ado, let's learn what an if statement is and where it's used.

If Statement

To learn these various control structures, including an if statement, we will first look at the syntax for the control structure, deduce its purpose, and attempt to implement it. After that, we will look at an actual example of the control structure in use and finally, at the end of a section, we will apply these control structures to create a Java program.

The if statement is used to add a decision-making functionality to a computer program. Up till now, the computer executes whatever code is in a program as long as it makes sense to the computer. However, with if statements, the computer program can check for a certain condition to decide whether to run the code or not. This adds yet another dimension to our computer programs.

Figure 4.1

```
1  if ( condition )
2  {
3      // body of code
4      // only executed if condition is true
5  }
```

The syntax of the if statement may remind you a lot of that of a method or a class because of the braces enclosing the code within the body and the indentation of that code. However, the true magic and excitement of this control structure lies in the first line of the example above. The first line is so simple yet so powerful. Let's look at it word by word - not that there are many! So the first word of the line, if, is a keyword and informs the computer that an if statement is starting. Next, there is a condition within a set of parentheses. Recall that a condition is a boolean expression that can evaluate to true or false. If the condition within the parentheses evaluates to true, the code within the body of the if statement is executed. And if it comes out to be false, the code is just skipped over. This is how the decision-making functionality comes into play; the computer decides to run the code depending on the value of the condition and it's possible that every time you run the program, you can end up with a different result depending on the values of such conditions.

Figure 4.2 | IfTest.java

```java
1   // IfTest.java
2
3   public class IfTest
4   {
5     public static void main( String[] args )
6     {
7       int x = 2;
8
9       if ( x == 2 )
10      {
11        System.out.println( "x is 2." );
12      }
13
14      if ( x == 3 )
15      {
16        System.out.println( "x is 3." );
17      }
18    }
19  }
```

Output

```
> run IfTest
x is 2.
```

With the IfTest.java example above, you can see how an if statement is used in a Java program and you may realize that it is quite easy to use. Let's quickly look through this example. For the sake of demonstration we initialize a variable called x that stores a value of 2. After that, we utilize our first if statement. The purpose of this if statement is to check whether the value of x is 2 and, if it is, to inform the user of that. The condition checks whether the x stores a value of 2 and the body of the statement prints that x is 2. The if statement from Line 9 to 12 is very easy to interpret. As we just discussed, in Line 9, we have the if keyword followed by a condition to determine if x is equal to 2. We are able to implement this condition using an equality operator (==). As you know, the body of the if statement is run when the condition returns a true value. Since x actually does have a value of 2, the condition is true and the computer runs the code within the body of the statement which prints out x is 2., as you can see in the output.

Following the first if statement, we have another one. However, it's just a little bit different. The condition checks to see if x has a value of 3 rather than 2 and, accordingly, the body of the statements prints out x is 3. if it is executed. The condition evaluates to false because, as you know, x has a value of 2 and the condition was determining if it was 3. With if statements, if the condition is `false`, the body is not executed and, hence, the computer does not print out anything, as reflected in the output.

This was a relatively simple look at some if statements and you got a hands-on look how you can add decision-making capabilities to your programs. You can do a lot with this like telling the computer what to do if a condition is `false` and we will explore that in the coming subsections.

If-Else Statement

Let's say that you have an if statement. Obviously, if its condition evaluates to `true`, the body of the statement will be executed. But what if it's `false`? The body will be disregarded. But what if you want to run some code if the condition is not met? That's where the if-else statement comes into play. The if-else statement adds another part to an ordinary if statement so that it has a separate body of code to execute if the condition is `false`.

Figure 4.3

```
1   if ( condition )
2   {
3     // body of code
4     // only executed if condition is true
5   }
6   else
7   {
8     // body of code
9     // only executed if condition is false
10  }
```

The if-else statement is awfully similar to the if statement with the only difference coming from a simple addition after the first body of code. You can see that the else keyword is added and then another body of code follows. The second body contains code that will be executed if the condition evaluates to `false`. If it comes out to `true`, everything goes as normal and the first body will be run. With if-else statements, there are two bodies of code and only one, not both, can be executed and that depends on what the condition evaluates to. Notice how you don't need a separate condition for the second body of code because it is only executed when the first condition is `false`.

Figure 4.4 | IfTest2.java

```
1    // IfTest2.java
2
3    public class IfTest2
4    {
5      public static void main( String[] args )
6      {
7        int x = 5;
8
9        if ( x < 4 )
10       {
11         System.out.println( "x is less than 4." );
12       }
13       else
14       {
15         System.out.println( "x is not less than 4." );
16       }
17     }
18   }
```

Output

```
> run IfTest2
x is not less than 4.
```

We will be able to go through IfTest2.java above because we have already gone through the original program in Figure 4.2. In this case, we have a variable x that has a value of 5 and the condition checks if x is less than 4. As you know, x is not less than 4 and the condition evaluates to false, meaning that the first body is not executed. With a normal if statement, that would mean that the body of code would be disregarded and the program would continue on after the if statement. But, in this case, we have an if-else statement. The code within the else block is executed and x is not less than 4. is printed out. It's that simple. Whenever you are developing a Java program and have two different bodies of code and only want to use one depending on a condition, utilize an if-else statement.

Extended If-Else Statement

Although an if-else statement is very useful, it can fall short in some situations. The extended if-else statement allows you to check for multiple conditions within the same if statement. Think of it as a way of adding on more if blocks before the else block. In many situations, you need to check for more than just one condition and the extended if-else statement is the solution.

Figure 4.5

It will execute the first true condition

```
1   if ( condition )
2   {
3       // body of code
4       // only executed if condition is true
5   }
6   else if ( condition2 )
7   {
8       // body of code
9       // only executed if condition2 is true
10  }
11  else if ( condition3 )
12  {
13      // body of code
14      // only executed if condition3 is true
15  else
16  {
17      // body of code
18      // executed if all conditions are false
19  }
```

As you can see in the figure above, the extended if-else statement has a couple of additions in between the if and else block. You are adding the else if blocks so that you can check for other conditions if the first condition is not met. For the first condition, you simply use if, but, use else if when you need to check for any other conditions following that. Adding in else if blocks is the same as any if block with the only difference coming from the addition of the word else at the beginning. The computer goes through the extended if-else statement systematically from top to bottom. This means that it checks the first condition and if it's false, it moves onto checking the second condition if there is one. It continues to do this until it encounters an else block. The else block is only used when all conditions that are checked for evaluate to false. However, if the second condition turns out to be true it executes the corresponding body of code and then skips the rest of the statement. This means that even if the third condition is true, it will be disregarded because the second condition was already true. Also note that there can be an unlimited amount of else if blocks.

Figure 4.6 | IfTest3.java

```
1    // IfTest3.java
2
3    public class IfTest3
4    {
5      public static void main( String[] args )
6      {
7        int x = 5;
8
9        if ( x < 4 )
10       {
11         System.out.println( "first" );
12       }
13       else if ( x == 5 )
14       {
15         System.out.println( "second" );
16       }
17       else if ( x > 2 )
18       {
19         System.out.println( "third" );
20       }
21       else
22       {
23         System.out.println( "none" );
24       }
25     }
26   }
```

Output

```
> run IfTest3
second
```

Working through the IfTest3 program will be relatively straightforward as you are quite familiar with if statements at this point. First, we initialize a variable x and assign it a value of 5. Then, we go right into the extended if-else statement. The first condition checks if x is less than 4, which it is not, and evaluates to false. The computer then moves onto the next condition which checks if x is equivalent to 5. In this case, it is and the computer returns true. This means that the corresponding body of code is executed which instructs the computer to print out second. The computer then disregards the remainder of the extended if-else statement as one condition has already been met and a body of code is executed. If you look carefully, you can see that the third condition would have returned true as well but its body was not executed because the second condition was checked first. If hypothetically, none of the 3 conditions were met, the else block would have been executed and none would have been printed out.

Nested If Statement

Sometimes you want to check for a condition but only after you have met another condition before that. You can use nested if statements in such situations. A nested if statement is simply an if statement inside of an if statement and the outer condition has to be true so that the inner condition can be checked. Take a look at the syntax example below to see how it works.

Figure 4.7

both statements must be true

```
1   if ( condition ) // outer
2   {
3     if ( condition2 ) // inner
4     {
5       // body of code
6       // only executed when
7       // both conditions met
8     }
9   }
10
11  if ( condition && condition2 )
12  {
13    // body of code
14    // only executed when
15    // both conditions met
16  }
```

In first 9 lines of figure above, you can see a nested if statement. Line 1 starts out with an outer if statement. If that statement's condition evaluates to true, it executes the body which contains the second if statement. If the second condition returns true, it will run the body of that statement and, if not, it finishes executing the body of the first if statement and nothing happens. Basically, in order for the body of code to be executed, both conditions have to be met.

Both conditions having to be met may remind you of the logical AND operator (&&) from last chapter that only returns true if both conditions are true, just like this situation. To make your life simpler, you could use the && operator to combine the conditions into one if statement and still achieve the same functionality. You can see an example of such an if statement in Lines 11 - 16.

Figure 4.8 | IfTest4.java

```java
1   // IfTest4.java
2
3   public class IfTest4
4   {
5     public static void main( String[] args )
6     {
7       int x = 5;
8
9       if ( x < 10 ) // outer
10      {
11        if ( x > 2 ) // inner
12        {
13          System.out.println( "Both conditions met." );
14        }
15      }
16    }
17  }
```

Output

```
> run IfTest4
Both conditions met.
```

The code above is a very simple example of a nested if statement. The objective of the program is to print something out if x is less than 10 AND greater than 2. We have a variable x with a value of 5. The first, and outer, condition checks if x is less than 10, which it is. It then proceeds to the second, and inner, conditions which determines whether x is greater than 2 and that returns true as well. It then executes the body which prints out Both conditions met. If either of the conditions were not met, the program wouldn't have printed anything out.

There are two things you should note regarding nested if statements and this program. Firstly, you can have an unlimited amount of nested if statements. This means that, technically, you can keep putting if statements inside each other to check for more and more conditions. Secondly, in this program as well, the && operator can simulate a nested if statement and you can combine the conditions into one condition so that you only have to use one if statement.

Grader Program

Now that we have learned all about if statements, we can finally apply these concepts to an actual program. We will be creating a Grader program. The purpose of this program is to prompt the user for their grade as a percentage and then inform the user what letter grade that percentage translates to. For example, a 95% is an 'A' and a 68% is a 'D'. The ranges we are using are 90 - 100 is an 'A', 80 - 89 is a 'B', 70 - 79 is a 'C', 60 - 69 is a 'D', and anything less than a 60 is a 'F'. As always, think about how you go about creating this program and attempt to do yourself before viewing the code below.

Figure 4.9 | Grader.java

```java
1   // Grader.java
2
3   import java.util.Scanner;
4
5   public class Grader
6   {
7     public static void main( String[] args )
8     {
9       Scanner input = new Scanner( System.in );
10
11      int grade; // grade of user
12
13      System.out.println("Enter your grade as a percentage: ");
14      grade = input.nextInt(); // setting user grade
15
16      if ( grade >= 90 ) // > 90
17      {
18        System.out.println( "You grade is an A" );
19      }
20      else if ( grade >= 80 ) // < 90 and > 80
21      {
22        System.out.println( "You grade is a B" );
23      }
24      else if ( grade >= 70 ) // < 80 and > 70
25      {
26        System.out.println( "You grade is a C" );
27      }
28      else if ( grade >= 60 ) // < 70 and > 60
29      {
30        System.out.println( "You grade is a D" );
31      }
32      else // < 60
33      {
34        System.out.println( "You grade is a F" );
35      }
36    }
37  }
```

Output

```
> run Grader
Enter your grade as a percentage:
72
You grade is a C
```

Rather than looking at this program line by line as we usually do, we will pay attention to the most important part of the program: the extended if-else statement. The first 15 lines of this program should be completely straightforward as we have already reviewed them multiple times and used them in countless programs. If you are having trouble comprehending any of it, check out the previous chapter. Essentially, after 15 lines, have a variable called grade which stores whatever percentage grade the user has provided. Now it is up to us to determine what letter grade that is equivalent to and to inform the user.

We will accomplish this using an extended if-else statement, which starts on Line 16. The first condition we check for is to see if x is greater than 90. If it is, we print out that the user has an A and disregard the rest of the statement. However, if it isn't, we move on to the the next condition, which determines if the x is greater than 80. At this point we know that x is definitely less than 90 since the first condition evaluated to false and if the second condition comes out to be true, we know that it falls within the 80 and 90 range and is hence a 'B.' This continues to even lower percentages if conditions come out to be false. However, once the grade is not even greater than 60, meaning that it is definitely less than 60, it is a definitely a 'F' no matter what so we can then use the else block. In the sample output, I outputted my grade as 72 so the first and second conditions evaluated to false but the third was true so the computer knew that my grade was in between 70 and 80, making it a 'C'.

As you can see, we were able to make decisions in a Java program using if statements and this is just the tip of the iceberg in terms of what you can do with control structures.

BigNumber Program

The BigNumber program is a very simple program that you should not have much trouble creating. It is also an excellent opportunity for you to see how much you have learnt and give creating your own program a shot. The BigNumber program simply prompts the user for a number and then prints out "You have a big number" if the number is greater than 100 and "You have a small number" if not. It's even easier to develop than the Grader program and here's a hint: use an if statement. Be sure to give this a shot so that you can see how you can create your own Java programs. Once you have finished, you can compare your work to the code below.

Figure 4.10 | BigNumber.java

```java
1   // BigNumber.java
2
3   import java.util.Scanner;
4
5   public class BigNumber
6   {
7     public static void main( String[] args )
8     {
9       Scanner s = new Scanner( System.in );
10
11      int number; // number given by user
12
13      System.out.println("Enter an integer: ");
14      number = s.nextInt(); // setting user number
15
16      if ( number > 100 ) // bigger than 100
17      {
18        System.out.println( "You have a big number" );
19      }
20      else // NOT bigger than 100
21      {
22        System.out.println( "You have a small number" );
23      }
24    }
25  }
```

Output

```
> run BigNumber
Enter an integer:
15
You have a small number
```

Here's a very quick walkthrough of the program just in case you weren't able to develop it yourself. The first 15 lines are the basics of a Java program that we are accustomed and we now have a variable that stores the user input and we need to tell the user if they have a large or small number. Then, we have a simple if statement that first checks if the number is greater than 100. If it is, it prints out You have a big number and if it's not, it prints out You have a small number. That's it. It's that simple. Hopefully, at this point, if statements are becoming second nature to you. As you can see in the sample output, the user inputted a value of 15 and that was not greater than 100 so You have a small number was printed out.

4.4 Iterative Control Structures

While the if statements allowed us to make decisions using our programs, iterative control structures allow us to repeat code for as many times as we would like. They also add another dimension to our programs and often times bring about a lot of convenience.

While Loop

The while loop is the first example of a iterative control structure that we will be working with. It is used to represent a real-life scenario in which you continue doing something until something else happens. For example, I will continue ignoring you until you say sorry so I am repeating the action of ignoring you while you refuse to apologize for your mistake. Similarly, in the programming world, you can have a condition and continue to execute the corresponding body until the condition becomes `false`. Without further ado, let's look at the syntax of a while loop right below.

Figure 4.11

```
1  while ( condition )
2  {
3      // body of code
4      // continues execution
5      // until condition
6      // becomes false
7  }
```

Firstly, there is one primary similarity between an if statement and a while loop. That is that they both have a condition which needs to be `true` for the body of code to be executed. But that is also where the difference comes. With an if statement, the code is only run once if the condition is `true`. However, with a while loop, the code is run over and over again until the condition becomes `false`. Let's say that you are working with a while loop and the condition is `true`. The body will be executed once and then the computer will check the condition again. If it is still `true`, the code will be run again and the condition checked again and so on and so forth. As you can probably tell, you have to do something within the body so the condition eventually becomes `false` or you will be stuck on the while loop infinitely.

On a syntax end, the while loop utilizes the while keyword and has a condition that is enclosed by parentheses, just like an if statement. In addition, it has a body of code that is indented and enclosed by braces. Now, let's look at an actual example of a while loop in action.

Figure 4.12 | WhileTest.java

```
1   // WhileTest.java
2
3   public class WhileTest
4   {
5     public static void main( String[] args )
6     {
7       int x = 1;
8
9       while ( x < 5 )
10      {
11        System.out.println( "x is " + x );
12        System.out.println( "x is less than 5." );
13        x++;
14      }
15    }
16  }
```

Output

```
> run WhileTest
x is 1
x is less than 5.
x is 2
x is less than 5.
x is 3
x is less than 5.
x is 4
x is less than 5.
```

Let's look through the WhileTest program so that we see how the while loop produced the shown output. First off, we have a variable called x which stores a value of 1. Then, the computer encounters the while loop on Line 9 and reads the condition checking whether x is less than 5. Since x is indeed less than 5, the condition returns true and the body of code is executed, resulting in x is 1 and x is less than 5. getting printed out, as you can see in the output. Then, using an increment operator in Line 13, x's value is increased from 1 to 2. Once the body is finished executing, the computer checks the original condition (x < 5) again. This time x has a different value but the condition still returns true and that body of code is executed once again. This time it prints out x is 2 and x is less than 5. and x's value increases to 3. However, the condition remains true and the code is run again and this continues until x is 4 and x is less than 5. are printed out and x's value becomes 5. This time when the condition is checked, it returns `false` and the computer moves past the while loop. That's basically what happens from a computer's standpoint in a while loop and we were able to show an increase in the value of x rather than having to write the same code again and again to continue printing out statements. The most important line in program is probably Line 13 because that is where x's value keeps getting increased so that it can eventually reach 5. Without this condition, the while loop would keep running and printing out text in the console infinitely and the user would be stuck in an infinite loop. In addition, you can now see how increment and decrement operators are used to increase value of variables so that they can eventually prevent a loop from executing.

For Loop

The for loop provides functionality very similar to that of the while loop but has a few key differences. As we look at the syntax of the for loop below, it will seem a lot more confusing than it actually is and that's just because it introduces some new terms. In actuality, it is quite simple and easy to use. Basically, the for loop also allows you to repeat some action(s) a certain amount of time.

Figure 4.13

```
1   for ( initialization; condition; updater )
2   {
3     // body of code that continues
4     // to run until the termination
5     // condition is not met
6   }
```

Let's look at the simpler part of the for loop first. The body is just like that of any control structure we have looked at so far; it is indented and enclosed by braces. The rest of the for loop will be new to you. With the for loop, logically, you will utilize the for keyword. Usually, we have simply put a condition within the parentheses that follow the keyword but things work a little bit differently with the for loop. There are 3 different things, rather than one, that you have to put inside of the parentheses. The initialization is an expression that starts the loop and it's the first thing executed when the loop begins. It usually is used to initialize a variable that will act as a counter for the loop. The condition is just like the condition that you are used to in control structures; the loop continues to run until the condition evaluates to `false`. Finally, the updater is an expression that continues to increase or decrease the counter variable so that the condition can eventually become `false` and the loop can terminate. The updater is just like the x++ in the `WhileTest` program. Although these different expressions may seem a bit confusing, looking at an example, like the one below, will help you get a better grasp of them.

Figure 4.14 | ForTest.java

```java
1   // ForTest.java
2
3   public class ForTest
4   {
5     public static void main( String[] args )
6     {
7       for ( int i = 1; i <= 3; i++ )
8       {
9         System.out.println( i );
10      }
11    }
12  }
```

Output

```
> run ForTest
1
2
3
```

The example above should definitely make for loops a lot clearer. The entire ForLoop program is made up of a single for loop, which starts on Line 7. Let's look at this from the perspective of the computer. By reading the for keyword, we know that we are encountering a for loop. Next, we execute the initialization expression first to start off the loop. In this case, the initialization expression is int i = 1 which creates a variable i with a value of 1. Next, we check the condition to see if comes out to true or false. If it's true, we execute the body once, but, if it's false, we skip the for loop and move on. In this case, the condition i <= 3 is indeed true and we run the body of the loop once. Executing the code causes the value of i, 1, to be printed out. Finally, the updater expression i++ is executed and the value of i increases from 1 to 2. Then we start all over again. We don't run the initialization expression again because that it is only run once at the beginning of the program so we check the condition again and it again evaluates to true. Next, we run the body again and print out 2 this time. The update expression then increases the value of i to 3 and we continue with this pattern until the time i's value become 4 and the condition evaluates to false. At that point, the for loop terminates and the computer moves on past it.

You will become more familiar with for loops as you interact with them more, but the paragraph gives a general explanation of how they function. As you can tell, they are extremely similar to while loops with the primary difference coming in the arrangement of the various components. The while loop's initialization expression is outside of the loop and its updater expression is within the body of the loop. Both allow you to repeat code to make both your and the user's life much easier. Another point is that you do not necessarily have to use the ++ operator. You can use other expressions like i += 2 or i-- -- to update the value of the counter variable. Just keep in mind that the purpose of the updater expression is to bring the condition closer and closer to false so that the for loop can eventually terminate.

OddNumber Program

The first program that we will be applying our newly learned control structures to is the OddNumber Program. The OddNumber program prompts the user for 2 integers and then it displays all of the odd numbers between the 2 numbers. For the purposes of focusing on the logic of the program, we assume that the second integer inputted is greater than the first integer inputted. Note that this is not a good programming practice and we are simply doing it for this example. Hint: round the even integers to odd integers and use a for loop to iterate through the numbers in between the two numbers. As always, try to deduce the logic of this program and develop it yourself before you look at the code below.

Figure 4.15 | OddNumber.java

```java
1   // OddNumber.java
2
3   import java.util.Scanner;
4
5   public class OddNumber
6   {
7     public static void main( String[] args )
8     {
9
10      Scanner s = new Scanner( System.in );
11
12      int num1; // 1st number from user
13      int num2; // 2nd number from user
14
15      System.out.println( "Enter 1st integer: " );
16      num1 = s.nextInt(); // assign value to num1
17
18      // assume num2 > num1
19      System.out.println( "Enter 2nd integer (bigger than 1st): " );
20      num2 = s.nextInt(); // assign value to num2
21
22      if ( num1 % 2 == 0 ) // if even
23      {
24        num1++; // make odd
25      }
```

```
26
27        if ( num2 % 2 == 0 ) // if even
28        {
29          num2--; // make odd
30        }
31
32        // num1 increase by 2 until greater than num 2
33        for ( num1 = num1; num1 <= num2; num1 += 2 )
34        {
35          System.out.println( num1 + " ");
36        }
37      }
38 }
```

Output

```
> run OddNumber
Enter 1st integer:
3
Enter 2nd integer (bigger than 1st):
12
3
5
7
9
11
```

The first 21 lines of the OddNumber program are straightforward and we have looked over similar code multiple times. At the end of these 21 lines, the user has inputted two integers and the code stores them as the variables num1 and num2. As mentioned earlier, for the purposes of this program, we can assume that num2 is bigger than num1.

The first thing that we want to do is to make sure that both of the numbers are odd so that we can later use a for loop to iterate through all the odd numbers in between by increasing by 2s. We can check if a number is divisible by 2 by using the % operator. As you can see on Line 22, we check to see if the smaller number, num1, is even based on whether it is divisible by 2. If it is, we increase its value by 1 so that it becomes odd. We do the same with the larger number, num2, on Line 27 and, since it is the bigger number, we decrease it by 1 if it turns out to be even. Following the two if statements from Line 22 - 30, we should have two numbers that are both odd and we are now ready to determine all of the odd numbers between them.

We can find the odd numbers by using a for loop. You can see the for loop that we utilize on Line 32. Typically, we use the initialization statement to initialize a counter variable but, in this case, we will use num1 as the counter variable so we simply fulfill the requirement with num1 = num1. The termination condition is num1 <= num2 so we want to keep iterating through the numbers in between num1 and num2 until we reach num2. Lastly, the updater expression increases the value of num1 by 2 each time because we only want the odd numbers which appear every other number. Every time the body is executed, the value of num1 is printed out and, since num1 ends up representing every odd number in the range at some point, each odd number is printed out. This functionality would definitely not be possible without the for loop and this program is a testament to its importance. The great thing about for loops is that they are very flexible so they can be used in many different situations and make the life of a programmer much simpler.

Average Program

The Average program is definitely one of the most realistic and useful programs that we will create. It utilizes the while loop and allows for a lot of flexibility on the user's side. Basically, the user can enter as many numbers as he or she wants and the program will output their average. This is a relatively simple program but the major part of it is that the user can choose to enter just 2 numbers or even 1,000,00 numbers and still get a correct answer.

Figure 4.16 | Average.java

```
1    // Average.java
2
3    import java.util.Scanner;
4
5    public class Average
6    {
7      public static void main( String[] args )
8      {
9        Scanner s = new Scanner( System.in );
10
11       int total = 0; // sum of values
12       int count = 0; // # of values entered
13       int number; // value given by user
14       double average; // average of the values
15
16       System.out.println( "Enter an integer or -1 to quit: " ); // for 1st # only
17       number = s.nextInt();
18
19       while ( number != -1 ) // -1 to finish adding #s
20       {
21         total += number; // total increases by # entered
22         count++; // increase count by 1 for each loop
23
```

```
24          System.out.println( "Enter an integer or -1 to quit: " );
25          number = s.nextInt(); // new assignment for number
26       }
27
28       if ( count != 0 ) // if no #s entered
29       {
30          average = (double) total / count; // calc average
31          System.out.println( "The average is " + average );
32       }
33       else // no #s entered
34       {
35          System.out.println( "Nothing was entered." );
36       }
37    }
38 }
```

Output

```
> run Average
Enter an integer or -1 to quit:
5
Enter an integer or -1 to quit:
7
Enter an integer or -1 to quit:
9
Enter an integer or -1 to quit:
-1
The average is 7.0
```

With the first 14 lines of code, we simply get the program going and initialize a couple of variables. The name of the variables and their corresponding comments make it easier to understand the purpose of each variable and note that the average variable is a double value because averages are often decimals.

On Line 16, we prompt the user to enter the first integer. Notice that we also give them the option to enter -1 to quit the program and get their final result. We store the int they input to the number variable.

Next, we encounter a while loop on Line 19. As you can see, we will continue to execute the body of the while loop until the number gets a value of -1 and that can only happen when the user inputs -1. This means that the user can enter as many integers as he or she wants and can enter -1 whenever he or she wants the final result. Within the commented body, you can see that the total keeps increasing the user adds on more values and the count goes up every time code is executed. At the end of the code, the user is again prompted to enter an integer and the number variable's new value becomes whatever the user inputs. This continues until the condition evaluates to `false` when the user enters -1.

Once the while loop is completeed, we have added in an if-else statement that starts on Line 28. This if statement checks to make sure that the count is not 0 because, if it is, that means the user did not enter anything and the else block is executed, printing out `Nothing was entered`. However, provided at least one number is entered, the if block is executed and the average is calculated by dividing the total sum by the number of values entered by the user. Notice that there is a `double` cast because the average variable is of type `double`. Finally, the computer prints out whatever the average is.

Although this program is a bit complicated, it also demonstrates what if statements, while loops, and for loops can do for your program. Control structures help add logic to our programs and make them a lot more powerful.

4.5 Chapter Summary

This was probably one of the most important chapters because it required you to understand the logic that goes into programming. Logic truly is the backbone of computer science and control structures enable us to model the logic we have in computer programs. It makes programs a lot smarter and more interactive. The control structures we went over were if statements (decision-making) and while and for loops (iteration). Thanks to control structures we were able to develop programs that could go on forever or display a different output every time and this was our first deviation from the typical top-to-bottom code execution.

Multiple Choice Questions

1) Consider the following code segment.

```java
int number = 100;

if (number == 100)
{
  System.out.print("equal");
}

if (number < 100)
{
  System.out.print("less than 100" );
}
else
{
  System.out.print("greater than 100");
}
```

What will be displayed upon execution of this code segment?

(A) The statements will not compile.

(B) greater than 100

(C) less than 100

(D) equalgreater than 100

2) Consider the following code segment.

```java
int a = 1;
int n = 0;
int result = a / n;

if (n == 0)
{
  System.out.println("divide by zero"); // statement1
}
else
{
  System.out.println(result); // statement2
}
```

Which of the following occur upon execution of the code segment?

(A) A syntax error

(B) statement1 is executed

(C) statement2 is executed

(D) Both statements are executed

Cannot divide by zero

3) Consider the following code segment.

```java
int x = 30;
int y = 10;
int z = 50;

if (x > y)
{
  if (z <= y)
  {
    System.out.print("x ");
  }
  else
  {
    System.out.print("x or z ");
    System.out.print("xyz ");
  }
}
else
{
  if (y > z)
  {
    System.out.print("y ");
  }
}
```

What will be displayed upon execution of this code segment?

(A) The statements will not compile.

(B) x y

(C) x or z y

(D) x or z xyz

4) Consider the following code segment.

```java
boolean x = false;

if (x)
{
  System.out.print("false");
}
System.out.print("true");
```

What will be displayed upon execution of this code segment?

(A) Nothing will be displayed.

(B) true

(C) false

(D) falsetrue

true end is printed

5) Consider the following code segment.

```java
for (int i = 0; i <= 1; i++)
{
  for (int j = 0; j < 2; j++)
  {
    if (i == j)
    {
      // nothing happens
    }
    else
    {
      System.out.println("i = " + i + " , j = " + j);
    }
  }
}
```

(handwritten annotation: "If they're equal nothing happens")

What will be displayed upon execution of this code segment?

(A) i = 0, j = 1
i = 1, j = 0

(B) i = 0, j = 1
i = 0, j = 2

(C) i = 0, j = 0
i = 1, j = 1

(D) i = 1, j = 2

6) Consider the following code segment.

```
for (int i = 2; i > 10; i--)
{
   System.out.print("i = " + i + " ");
}
```

b/c condition is not met

What will be displayed upon execution of this code segment?

(A) The statements will not compile.

(B) i = 3 i = 2

(C) i = 2 i = 1

(D) i = 1

(E) Nothing will be displayed

7) Consider the following code segment.

```
for (int x = 5; x <= 50; x += 5)
{
   System.out.print(" " + x);
}
```

Which of the following while loops are equivalent to the for loop above?

(A)
```
int x = 5;
while (x <= 50)
    {
       System.out.print(" " + x);
       x += 5;
    }
```

(B)
```
while (x <= 50)
    {
       int x = 5;
       System.out.print(" " + x);
       x += 5;
    }
```

(C)
```
while (int x = 5; x <= 50)
    {
       System.out.print(" " + x);
       x += 5;
    }
```

(D)
```
int x = 5;
    while (x <= 50; x += 5)
    {
       System.out.print(" " + x);
    }
```

8) Consider the following code segment.

```
int x = 0;
while (x <= 3)
{
  System.out.print(" " + x);
  x++;
}
```

0
1
2
3

(A) The statements will not compile.

(B) Nothing will be displayed.

(C) 0 1 2

(D) 0 1 2 3

(E) 0 1 2 3 4

9) Which of the following for loops can be used to iterate from 1 to 10?

(A)
```
for (i <= 10; i++)
    {
       System.out.println(i);
    }
```

(B)
```
for (int i = 1; i <= 10; i++)
    {
       System.out.println(i);
    }
```

(C)
```
for (int i = 1; i < 10; i++)
    {
       System.out.println(i);
    }
```

(D)
```
for (int i = 1; i <= 10; i--)
    {
       System.out.println(i);
    }
```

10) Consider the following code segment.

```
int i;
for (i = 1; i <= 10; i++)
{
    System.out.println(i);
}

int result = i;
System.out.println(result);
```

10 +1 = 11

What will be displayed upon execution of this code segment?

(A) 10

(B) 11

10

(C) 9

(D) The code will not compile.

11) Which of the following while loops can be used to iterate from 1 to 7?

```
(A) int i = 1;
    while (i < 7)
    {
      System.out.println(i);
      i++;
    }
```

```
(B) int i = 1;
    while (i <= 7)
    {
      System.out.println(i);
      i++;
    }
```

```
(C) int i = 1;
    while (i <= 7)
    {
      System.out.println(i);
    }
```

```
(D) int i = 1;
    while (i = 1; i < 7)
    {
      System.out.println(i);
      i++;
    }
```

12) Consider the following code segment.

```
int i = 1;
while (i < 10)
{
   System.out.print(i);
}
```

What will be displayed upon execution of this code segment?

(A) 123456789

(B) 1

(C) There will be an endless loop.

(D) 12345678910

13) Consider the following code segment.

```
for (int i = 0; i >= 0; i++)
{
   System.out.println("a");
}
```

What will be displayed upon execution of this code segment?

(A) a

(B) The code will not compile.

(C) There will be an endless loop.

(D) Nothing will be displayed.

14) Consider the following code segment.

```
int sum = 0;
for (int i = 0, j = 0; i < 5; ++i)
{
   sum += i;
}
System.out.println(sum);
```

What will be displayed upon execution of this code segment?

(A) 5

(B) 10

(C) 4

(D) 7

15) Which of the following code segments can be used to determine whether x is an odd number?

```java
(A) if ( x % 2 = 0 )
    {
       System.out.println("You entered an even number.");
    }
    else
    {
       System.out.println("You entered an odd number.");
    }
```

```java
(B) if ( x / 2 = 0 )
    {
       System.out.println("You entered an even number.");
    }
    else
    {
       System.out.println("You entered an odd number.");
    }
```

```java
(C) if ( x % 2 == 0 )
    {
       System.out.println("You entered an even number.");
    }
    else
    {
       System.out.println("You entered an odd number.");
    }
```

```java
(D) if ( x / 2 == 0 )
    {
       System.out.println("You entered an even number.");
    }
    else
    {
       System.out.println("You entered an odd number.");
    }
```

16) Which of the following code segments can be used to determine whether number is an prime number?

```
(A) for (int i = 2; i <= number / 2; i++)
    {
      if (number % i = 0)
      {
        return false;
      }
    }
```

```
(B) for (int i = 2; i <= number / 2; i++)
    {
      if (number / i == 0)
      {
        return false;
      }
    }
```

```
(C) for (int i = 2; i <= number / 2; i++)
    {
      if (number / i = 0)
      {
        return false;
      }
    }
```

```
(D) for (int i = 2; i <= number / 2; i++)
    {
      if (number % i == 0)
      {
        return false;
      }
    }
```

17) Consider the following code segment.

```
int x = 7;
int y = 6;
int z = 1234;
System.out.println(" " + x + y + z);
```

b/c of this they don't add

What will be displayed upon execution of this code segment?

(A) 761234

(B) 23

(C) 1247

(D) The code will not compile.

18) Which of the following code segments prints out all the multiples of from 3 to 36?

```
(A) for (int n = 3;  n < 36;  n++)
    {
       if (n % 3 == 0)
       {
         System.out.println( n );
       }
    }
```

```
(B) for (int n = 3;  n <= 36;  n++)
    {
       if (n % 3 == 0)
       {
         System.out.println(n);
       }
    }
```

```
(C) for( int n = 3;  n < 36;  n--)
    {
       if (n % 3 == 0)
       {
         System.out.println(n);
       }
    }
```

```
(D) for (int n = 3;  n <= 36;  n--)
    {
       if (n % 3 == 0)
       {
         System.out.println(n);
       }
    }
```

19) Consider the following code segment.

```
int x = 1;
while (x <= 32)
{
  x = 2 * x;
  System.out.print(x + " ");
}
```

What will be displayed upon execution of this code segment?

(A) 1 2 4 8 16 32 64

(B) 2 4 8 16 32 64

(C) 2 4 8 16 32

(D) 1 2 4 8 16 32

20) Consider the following code segment.

```
int x = 5;
int y = 1;
while (x >= 0)
{
  x = x - 1;
  y = y * x;
  System.out.print(y + " ");
}
```

What will be displayed upon execution of this code segment?

(A) 4 12 24 12 4 0

(B) 4 12 24 24 0

(C) 0 4 12 24 12 4 0

(D) 4 12 24

21) If x = 2 and y = 5 after executing the following code segment, what are the original values of x and y respectively?

```
int temp;
temp = x;
x = y;
y = temp;
```

(A) 2, 5

(B) 2, temp

(C) 5, 2

(D) temp, 5

22) Consider the following code segment.

```
int years;
int principal = 1000;
double interest;
double rate = 0.5;
for (years = 0;  years < 5;  years++)
{
   interest = principal * rate;
   principal += interest;
   System.out.println(principal);
}
```

What will be displayed after 1 iteration of the for loop?

(A) 1000

(B) 500

(C) 0

(D) 1500

23) Consider the following code segment.

```
int temperature = 50;
if (temperature < 50)
{
  System.out.println("It's cold."); // Line 1
}
else if (temperature < 80)
{
  System.out.println("It's nice."); // Line 2
}
else
{
  System.out.println("It's hot."); // Line 3
}
```

Which lines are displayed upon execution of this code segment?

(A) Line 1

(B) Line 1 and Line 2

(C) Line 2

(D) Line 2 and Line 3

(E) Line 3

24) Consider the following code segment.

```java
for (int d = 1; d <= n; d++)
{
  if (n % d == 0)
  {
    System.out.println(d);
  }
}
```

What will be displayed upon execution of this code segment?

(A) The quotients of n

(B) The remainders of n

(C) The remainders of d

(D) The divisors of n

Answers and Explanations

Answer Key

1. D
2. A
3. D
4. B
5. A
6. E
7. A
8. D
9. B
10. B
11. B
12. A
13. C
14. B
15. C
16. D
17. A
18. B
19. C
20. B
21. C
22. D
23. C
24. D

Explanations

1) (**D**) For the first if statement, the condition is `true` so `equal` is printed out. With the second if-else statement, the condition is `false` so the `greater than 100` is printed out.

2) (**A**) A error occurs because of `int result = a / n;` with n being equal to 0. You cannot divide by 0 and that leads to an error.

3) (**D**) The condition for the overall if statement is `true` so we move onto the if-else statement inside the if block. The second condition we evaluate is `false` so `x or x xyz` is printed out.

4) (**B**) Only `true` is printed out because the if statement does not produce anything as the condition is `false`.

5) **(A)** i and j iterate through 0 and 1 in their respective for loops and their values are only printed out when they are not equal to each other, which is at i = 0, j = 1 and i = 1, j = 0.

6) **(E)** Nothing is displayed because the for loop never ends up iterating as the initial condition of i > 2 is not met.

7) **(A)** Choice A is the only choice that accounts for the initial condition, termination condition, and the increment shown in the for loop.

8) **(D)** The while loop iterates through 0 to 3 for values of x that are printed out.

9) **(B)** Choice B is the only choice that follows the syntax of a for loop and iterates from 1 to 10.

10) **(B)** i continues to increase to 11 at which point it stops increasing because the for loop stops iterating and that's what's printed out.

11) **(B)** Choice B is the only choice that follows the syntax of a while loop and iterates from 1 to 7. x needs to be declared outside of the while loop.

12) **(A)** The while loop continues printing i when its values range from 1 to 9 and stops once i reaches 10.

13) **(C)** The for loop iterates infinitely because i needs to be greater than or equal to 0 and i just keeps on increasing with every iteration.

14) **(B)** The j = 0 is just there to throw you off. The j is not used in evaluating the loop. i has values of 1 through 4 during the iteration of the loop and that yields a sum of 10.

15) **(C)** The condition x % 2 is used to check if a number is divisible by 2, or even. That will also allow us to check if a number is odd. Remember to use the == operator when comparing values.

16) **(D)** Like the last question, use the % and == operators to determine the divisibility and, hence, whether number is prime.

17) **(A)** In this case, the + operator is being used to combine values into one String because of the empty String that is being printed out. If that empty String was not there, x, y, and z would have been added up and printed out as 1247 with the + serving as an arithmetic operator.

18) **(B)** The for loop should include n being equal to 36 because 36 is a multiple of 3. Obviously, the value of n needs to increase after every iteration of the for loop.

19) **(C)** The while loop allows x to increase and print out as multiples of 2 going all the way up to 32.

20) **(B)** y is multiplied by x every time the loop iterates and x's values keeps decreasing from 5 to 0.

21) **(C)** This is a tricky question. You need to think backwards. If x ends up as 2, that means that y's initial value had to be 2. Similarly, temp had to have been 5 when it gave x its initial value (5) so that y could end up as 5.

22) **(D)** At the first iteration of the for loop, interest becomes 500 and principal becomes 1500.

23) **(C)** The first condition becomes false and the second condition true so Line 2 is printed out and the if-else statement stops evaluating as soon as one block is executed.

24) **(D)** We are using the % operator to see which numbers (divisors) n is divisible by.

Chapter 5 - Classes, Objects, and Methods

5.1 Chapter Overview:

Chapter 5 will be a combination of a review and an introduction to some new ideas. It's an important chapter because it will shed some light on concepts that we have implemented but not fully understood. In addition and most importantly, you will learn to create your methods so that your classes can have more than a simple main method. This is a critical step that will allow you to make your programs even more extensible and exciting.

5.2 Review of Classes and Objects

This section serves primarily as a review of concepts that you are already familiar with. It also demonstrates the importance of classes and objects because they are, quite literally, the foundation of Java and having a good understanding is absolutely essential. Finally, this section will be a good buildup for the rest of, not only this chapter, but the book.

Classes

As we learned in Chapter 2, a Java program is made up of pieces called classes, which are composed of methods. Classes can be considered the "building blocks" of any Java computer program. A class is a template for creating an object.

Speaking of objects, let's understand what objects are. Objects are a huge part of Java, but, first, let's look at them outside of Java - or, for that matter, outside of software. Everything around you is an object. For example, let's take a pencil. It's yellow. It's thin. It's hard. It writes and it erases. I actually just listed some of the attributes and behaviors of the object with attributes being adjectives and behaviors verbs. The same goes for software objects, which make up computer programs. Every object, a software object or not, consists of attributes and behaviors.

So far, we have learned of objects and classes, both of which are important Java concepts. However, the relationship between the two is even more critical. Classes and objects complement each other and enable software reusability, a major factor in making Java a popular programming language.

The perfect analogy to describe the relationship between objects and classes is that classes are to objects as blueprints are to houses. Just as we build multiple houses with only one blueprint, we can create many objects using a single class. In addition, objects have the abilities (or behaviors) to perform functions that are needed for Java computer programs. For example, a house can cool itself but the blueprint for the house cannot cool itself. An object is considered to be an instance of a class, and when you create an object from a class, you instantiate an object.

Methods and Instance Variables

A method is a component of a class that performs tasks and returns information. Methods are like the functions, or abilities of a class. An object is an instance of a class. Going back to the pencil example from the last subsection, we listed some of the actions that a pencil can complete such as writing and erasing. These behaviors, or abilities, are called methods because they are "performing tasks." Note that the pencil object utilizes the writing method and that the blueprint, or sketch, of the pencil simply outlines the functionality, but does not actually perform it. In addition, objects, like the pencil, do not know the implementation of the method. This means that the pencil object can write but it does not know what type, shade, or size of lead is used to accomplish the task. That information is in the pencil class.

Next, let's examine instance variables. Instance variables are the fields, or attributes, of the class. Objects contain the instance variables defined in the class. Back to the pencil example, some attributes, or instance variables, of the pencil class are color and length. The actual value of these variables is defined within the object and leads to variability among objects comes about. For example, we could have one pencil object that is blue and 5 inches long and another one that is yellow and 8 inches long. Similarly, some instance variables can be predefined in the class and be different among objects. You could hypothetically have a YellowPencil class with an instance variable that is set to yellow so any YellowPencil object would be yellow no matter what. These concepts seem very abstract at this point, but as we start to implement them in our programs, they will start to make a lot more sense. At this point, remember that methods represent behaviors and instance variables attributes.

5.3 Keywords:

You may remember keywords from when we declared a class like `public class HelloWorld` one of the keywords was `public`. In previous sections, we would disregard these keywords because they would have been a little bit too complicated. But now we are at a point where you will be able to understand the significance of various keywords like `public`, `private`, and `static`.

Review of Keywords

A keyword, also known as a reserved word, is a word that already has a predefined meaning in a programming language. This means that when you use any keyword, the computer will assume that it is being using in the context of its predefined meaning rather than as the name of a class or any other identifier. We have interacted with numerous keywords. For example, the `if` keyword tells the computer that we are using an if statement, the `int` keyword informs the computer that we are defining a variable that is an integer, and so on and so forth. Similarly, there are some keywords that we have used but don't understand the purpose of and this section aims to solve that.

The `public` keyword

Figure 5.1

```
public class HelloWorld
```

As mentioned earlier, you were first introduced to the `public` keyword in the HelloWorld program when you were declaring the HelloWorld class, as you can see in Figure 5.1. We understood the purpose of the `class` keyword (telling the computer we are defining a class) and the "HelloWorld" (giving the class a name) but we had held off understanding the `public` keyword until now.

The `public` keyword is called an access modifier. As an access modifier, the `public` keyword can determine how much a program or class has access to any specific class, method, or variable. The implication of the `public` keyword is the same as that of the word "public" in the real world. It means that it is accessible by all. So, in the case of computer science, using the `public` keyword allows whatever is being declared to be accessible by any program or class. Tracking back to Figure 5.1, the HelloWorld class can be accessed by other classes as well. Similarly, you can use the `public` keyword while declaring a method or variable. We also use the `public` keyword when are declaring a main method within a class. Note that all of the classes that you work with in AP Computer Science will only be `public` so you don't have to worry about other types of classes.

You may be wondering what the purpose of limiting or extending the accessibility of a method is. Well, let's think of an example. Let's say that you have a Car class. There are likely a lot of methods within the Car class such as accelerate or reverse. These methods probably call other methods within them to do all of the technical work within the engine to actually move the car. Once you create a Car object, you want the object to be able to make the car move by calling the accelerate or reverse method, but you don't want the object calling methods for small tasks just within the engine because there's no reason to give the driver access to them. In that case, you only make the methods you want the object to call `public`.

The `private` keyword

We have not interacted with the `private` keyword ever before and this will be our first time working with it. Now that we understand the `public` keyword, working with the `private` keyword will be a walk in the park. Just like the `public` keyword, the `private` keyword is used for exactly for what you would expect it to be used for. As an access modifier as well, it restricts access to a class, method, or variable. The "private" word means "belonging to or for the use of one particular person or group of people only." Similarly, any method or variable that is `private` can only be accessed by some other methods or classes rather than any of them as with the `public` keyword.

Essentially, when you have private variables and methods, they can only be accessed by methods of the same class and not by other classes. Note that classes cannot be private because the entire purpose of a class is to work with other classes. Tracking back to the Car example from the previous subsection, we had some methods within the Car class that are related to the engine combustion and enable the drive method to function. However, we don't want these methods to be `public` because there is no reason for the driver to be able to access them. We will list these methods as `private`. By doing this, the methods of the Car class (such as the drive method) can access these `private` methods but the Car object cannot. This Car class is an example of a software engineering practice called *data hiding* which refers to the idea of only giving the object access to method it needs rather than all of them.

Figure 5.2

```
private void add()
```

The `static` keyword

We have only encountered the `static` keyword in one situation till now: the main method declaration. The `static` keyword is probably the hardest keyword to grasp just because we aren't familiar with it like the `public` or `private` keyword. The purpose of the `static` keyword is to help with memory management. To understand the use of the `static` keyword, let's look at static variables and methods. We will touch a bit on static methods before going over them in more depth later in the chapter.

Figure 5.3

```
public class StudentAtFSU
{
    static String collegeName = "FSU";
    String hairColor;
}
```

Take a few moments to look over the code snippet above in Figure 5.3. Most of the code should seem familiar with the exception of the `static` keyword in the third line within the variable declaration. Essentially, we have a class called `StudentAtFSU` which represents a student at a university called FSU and this student has two attribute, or instance variables. They are the `collegeName`, which is, obviously, FSU, and `hairColor` which is not defined.

A static variable is a variable that is associated with the class rather than the object. In our situations, we have two variables. The `hairColor` variable is associated with the object because every `StudentAtFSU` object will have a different color of hair so we have to let it be unique to each object. However, for the `collegeName` variable, it is associated with the class because every `StudentAtFSU` object will have the college name be FSU no matter what. Therefore, this variable is for the class because it relates directly to the class and every object will have it no matter what and, hence, it is defined as a static variable. We were able to initialize it as a `static` variable using the `static` keyword before we put the variable type. Everything within the variable declaration remained the same. You should utilize `static` variables whenever situations like this one come up where a variable should be specific to the class, not the object. The main purpose of the static variable is for memory management so that you don't have to use more memory for the variable every time it is created within an object and only have to store one variable which is used for an infinite amount of objects. As you start working with bigger programs, memory and speed of the program will become more important.

Figure 5.4

```
public static void main( String[] args )
```

Aside from static variables, we also have static methods and we will explore them in more detail a bit later in this chapter, but I'll give you a basic overview of them right now. Static methods are also known as class methods and are basically methods that you can execute from within a class without having to call the method from an instantiated object. As we have discussed briefly and will more in the future, we develop methods and then call them from the objects but with static methods we don't have to create an object. For example, we use the `static` keyword with our main method declaration so that we can run the program from within the class. If, hypothetically, the main method were not a static method, we would have to create an object of the class and then we would be able to execute the main method. Usually, you make methods that you want to call within the class static. Going back to the `Car` class example from the last subsection, some of the methods that are used for the internal engine of the car would be static because we would need to call these methods within the drive method in the class. As you can see in Figure 5.4, we added the `static` keyword to the main method declaration to indicate that a static method was being declared. We will get even more information about static methods in the next section.

5.4 Methods:

So far we have only worked with the main method. However, in Java, we usually tend to create our own methods and the main method is used to put everything together. This section is devoted to teaching you that as well as introducing you to the many types of methods. We will be utilizing many concepts we have already learned and will be able to create even more complex and powerful Java program. This section is very hands-on so you will be looking at many code examples.

Declaring Methods

Figure 5.5

```
accessModifier returnType methodName( parameters )
```

Above, you can see the syntax for a method declaration. Fortunately, we already know a lot of what goes into a method declaration. Let's look at the syntax example which is in the first line. It starts off with an access modifier, which can be a keyword like `public` or `private`. This will determine how accessible the method is. Next, we have the return type which is something that is unfamiliar to us. It represents what the method returns. For example, a method called `getName()` returns a `String` containing a name so the return type of the method is a `String` and you put `String` where the return type goes. Similarly, the return type is whatever object or primitive type that the method gives back when it is executed. There are also situations where a method does not return anything and you put the `void` keyword as the return type. For example, because the main method does not return anything, we use the `void` keyword in the method declaration. We will understand how to return values from methods works just a little bit later into the book. Note that if you were to use the `static` keyword for a static method, you would place `static` in between the `accessModifier` and `returnType`. Next, there's the `methodName`, which is relatively straightforward. You choose the name of the method and follow all the guidelines that you use to name classes and variables. Obviously, the method name should be relevant to the purpose and functionality of the method. Lastly, we have parameters which are enclosed within the parentheses following the `methodName`. There's a separate subsection for parameters, but let's go over them briefly. You can understand what a parameter is easily by thinking about them in terms of algebra. Let's say you know $f(x) = x + 2$. Then you call the function as follows: `f(2)`. You are substituting the value of x with 2 and get an output of 4. In this case, the x within the parentheses is the parameter. A parameter is any value you pass to a method so that it can do something with that value. This sounds vague, but we'll understand it as we look at more examples.

Figure 5.6

```
public void printName( String name )
```

Above, you can see an example of a method declaration that you would expect to see in a Java program. Before we look at the line of code word by word, let's understand what the purpose of this method is. This method prints out a name that it receive when it is called. Now, onto the actual code.

Based on the `public` keyword, you know that the method is `public` and completely accessible. Next, the `void` keyword in the location of the `returnType`, meaning that the method does not return any value. This makes sense because this method just prints out a `String` and does not need to return anything. The name of the method is `printName`, which is in accordance with the method purpose. At this moment, we have nailed most of the requirements for the method except that it does not have the ability to print out any `String` it is given when it is called. This can be achieved using a parameter, which goes in between the parentheses following the method name. We're going to hold off talking about method parameters until the next subsection, but notice how the parameter is used. Realistically, there would be the left and right braces along with the method body after the method declaration.

Method Parameters

Figure 5.7

```
1  methodName( type name, type name )
2
3  public void printName( String name )
4  {
5    System.out.println( name );
6  }
```

We already have a basic understanding of what a method parameter is. It is a value, of any type, that a method receives when it is executed. Usually, a method uses its parameter in some shape or form during the execution of the code. On Line 1, we can see the syntax for a method parameter. Notice that only the parameters and method names are included in the example and the keywords that come before the method name but are omitted for the sake of space and simplicity. There are 2 parameters within the parentheses. You first put the type of the parameter like int or double. Then, you place the name of the parameter. The name can be anything you would like and you will use that name to refer to the parameter, or value, in the body of the method. You can technically have an unlimited amount of method parameters, and all you have to do is make sure that they are separated by parentheses.

Now let's look at the example from Lines 3 - 6. You will notice that it is exactly the same method declaration from the last subsection. The only difference this time is that this method has an actual body as well. Let's just focus on the parameter part of the method declaration because we are already familiar with the rest. In this case, we have one parameter that goes by name and is a String. Remember that the purpose of this method is to print out whatever String it receives at the time of execution. The String that it receives is the parameter. In order fulfill this program's requirement, we have to print out the name variable which we can do using the println() method in the Line 5. The computer automatically recognizes that "name" refers to the parameter. Note that you cannot access the name parameter outside of this method because it is local to only this method. Now that we know how parameters work, you're likely wondering how you will be able give the method a String to print out. Check out the code ahead to get an answer.

Figure 5.8

```
// Calling Method
String myName = "Moksh";
printName(myName);
```

We will dive into more of the specifics of calling methods but the example does a good job of giving you an introduction. In fact, we have been calling a method every time we use the println() method or the nextInt() method. The above example is primarily meant to show you how to call a method when it has a parameter. In this case, the printName() has a String parameter so you have to make sure you put a String value inside of the parentheses or the method will not function. We have a String variable called myName with a value of "Moksh" so the printName() method receives that value and then proceeds to output it. The main takeaway from this example is how the parameter was accounted for by referring to the appropriate value within the parentheses of the method call.

PassFail Program

The PassFail program is a Java program that asks the user to give his or her AP test score and then informs the user if he or she has passed. A valid AP Score is any whole number in between 1 and 5. Scores of 3, 4, and 5 are considered passing and 2 or 3 is not. This program is probably very straightforward for you to implement but the twist comes from the fact that you must create a separate method (other than the main method) in the PassFail program to call within the main method. This method will be called checkPassed() and will take in one parameter, an int representing the score that the user received. In addition, the method should return a boolean value of true or false indicating whether the student passed. Hint: be sure to include the static keyword in the method declaration for checkPassed() because you are going to call the method from within the class. Check out a Java program that meets all of the requirements below and pay close attention to the checkPassed() method.

Figure 5.9 | PassFail.java

```
1  // PassFail.java
2
3  import java.util.Scanner;
4
5  public class PassFail
6  {
7    public static void main( String[] args )
8    {
9      Scanner s = new Scanner( System.in );
10
11     int score; // user score
```

```
12
13        System.out.println( "Enter your APCS Test Score: " );
14        score = s.nextInt(); // user input
15
16        // calling checkPassed method to get result
17        System.out.println( "Passed: " + checkPassed(score) );
18      }
19
20      private static boolean checkPassed( int apScore )
21      {
22        if ( apScore > 0 && apScore <= 5 )
23        {
24          if ( apScore == 1 || apScore == 2)
25          {
26            return false;
27          }
28          else
29          {
30            return true;
31          }
32        }
33        else
34        {
35          System.out.println("Enter a valid AP Score!");
36          return false;
37        }
38      }
39 }
```

Output

```
> run PassFail
Enter your APCS Test Score:
0
Enter a valid AP Score!
Passed: false

> run PassFail
Enter your APCS Test Score:
2
Passed: false
```

```
> run PassFail
Enter your APCS Test Score:
5
Passed: true
```

The primary focus of this program is adding a separate method and then calling it in the main method. The logic of the program is now in the checkPassed() method, unlike our previous programs in which it was in the main method. You should be relatively familiar with everything else, but we will quickly review it all.

Lines 1 - 15 consist of code you feel like you have seen a gazillion times by now. To quickly summarize what happens in these lines, the program is able to receive input from the user regarding what his or her AP test score was.

The fun and significance of this program really comes from Line 17 where the program calls the checkPassed() method to determine whether the user passed AP Computer Science.

The checkPassed() method is defined from Lines 20 - 38. Line 20 consists of the method declaration and it is essential that you are able to identify the purpose of every word in the declaration. The first word, private, indicates that the checkPassed() method is a private method. Although there is no harm in keeping it as a public method, we choose to make it private because only the main method and no other class needs to access it. Next up, we have the static keyword which allows us to call and execute the checkPassed() method within this class (as we do on Line 17) rather than having to instantiate an object and call it from there. Next, we determine whether the program will be returning a value or not. Remember that the purpose of this program is to tell us whether it is true or false that the user passed and since true and false are boolean values, the method returns a boolean. Following that you see the name of the method which is checkPassed. Finally, we have one of the most important components of the method declaration: the parameter. Since the checkPassed() method takes in an int value that represents the AP test score of the user, we have a parameter called apScore that is of the int type. This parameter requires us to include an int value in between the parentheses whenever we call the checkPassed() method. For example, on Line 17, we have have a reference to the score variable which represents an int value and the user's score. Since the parameter's name is apScore, we will use 'apScore' whenever we refer to the int value in the body of the method.

The body of this method is relatively straightforward. Our first objective when determining whether a score passes or not is to see if it even falls within the range of a valid AP score. A valid AP score is 1, 2, 3, 4, or 5. If any number is less than 1 or greater than 5, the method should return false because that value cannot pass. We are able to implement this using an if statement with a logical AND operator to make sure that the apScore value we are given is greater than 0 AND less than 5. If either of these conditions is false, the program will return false as you can see in the else block and it also prints out that the given score is not a valid score. A 1 or a 2 on the AP Computer Science test means that you did not pass and a 3, 4, or 5 means that you did. Within the original if statement, we have a nested if statement (Line 24) that checks if the score is equal to 1 OR 2 using the logical OR operator. If either condition evaluates to true, the body executed and false is returned since the value was equal to 1 or 2. However, if both conditions are `false` and the complex condition becomes `false`, the else block is executed as the value is either 3, 4, or 5. This means that the score was a passing score and results in a `true` value. Having covered all situations for values of the AP score, this method now completes its purpose of determining if a value represents a pass or a fail.

Back to Line 17, we know that `checkPassed(score)` will either return `true` or `false`. Depending on what it returns, `Passed: true` or `Passed: false` will be printed out. In this program, by having a separate method, we are able to keep our main method clean and concise while allocating different jobs and logic to methods.

DayName Program

Here is an opportunity for you to take what you learned in the previous subsection and create a program with multiple methods. Create a DayName program that prompts the user for an an integer that represents a day in the week with 1 representing Sunday, 2 representing Monday, and so on. It should include a `static getName()` method that takes in an integer as a parameter and returns a `String` which contains the name of the day. You should call this method in the main method and then print out the name of the day based on what is returned by the method. If the number the user enters is not between 1 and 7, inform the user that the number that he or she has entered is invalid. Before you look at the solution below, be sure to give this program a shot as it is very similar to the PassFail program.

Figure 5.10 | DayName.java

```
1   // DayName.java
2
3   import java.util.Scanner;
4
5   public class DayName
6   {
7     public static void main( String[] args )
8     {
9       Scanner s = new Scanner( System.in );
10      int dayNum;
11
12      System.out.println( "Enter the number of the day in a week (1-7): " );
13      dayNum = s.nextInt();
14
15      String result = getName( dayNum ); // using getName() method to find day name
16      System.out.println( result );
17    }
18    private static String getName( int dayNumber )
19    {
20      if ( dayNumber == 1 )
```

```
21        {
22          return "Sunday"; // day 1 is Sunday
23        }
24      else if ( dayNumber == 2 )
25        {
26          return "Monday"; // day 2 is Monday
27        }
28      else if ( dayNumber == 3 )
29        {
30          return "Tuesday"; // day 3 is Tuesday
31        }
32      else if ( dayNumber == 4 )
33        {
34          return "Wednesday"; // day 4 is Wednesday
35        }
36      else if ( dayNumber == 5 )
37        {
38          return "Thursday"; // day 5 is Thursday
39        }
40      else if ( dayNumber == 6 )
41        {
42          return "Friday"; // day 6 is Friday
43        }
44      else if ( dayNumber == 7 )
45        {
46          return "Saturday"; // day 7 is Saturday
47        }
48      else // not in range of 1 to 7
49        {
50          return "Not a Valid Day Number!";
51        }
52    }
53 }
```

Output

```
> run DayName
Enter the number of the day in a week (1-7):
2
Monday

> run DayName
Enter the number of the day in a week (1-7):
10
Not a Valid Day Number!
```

The DayName program follows the structure of the PassFail program: it calls another method in the class within the main method. This "other" method returns a value that is eventually printed out by the computer. You should be able to understand everything that goes on in this program, but I'll quickly go through it to make sure you're on the right page.

With the first 13 lines, we are able to obtain an int from the user that represents the day of week. Our job is to take that number, convert it to the corresponding weekday, and then display that for the user. In this program, we obtain the number and print the weekday within the main method and we do the conversion in a separate getName() method.

On Line 15, we create a variable that will store a String that represents the name of the day corresponding to the number the user has given us. Its value is set to whatever the getName() method call returns. We call the getName() method and give it an argument of the int that the user entered.

The getName() method starts on Line 18. I'm going to quickly run through the method declaration. We have the private keyword so the method won't be called outside of this class and the static keyword allows the getName() method to be called within the class. The method returns a String that we know represents the day of the week and takes in a parameter, int dayNumber, which is a number from 1 to 7 that will be converted to a day. The body of the method is relatively clear. Using a series of extended if-else statements, the method checks if the dayNumber is equal to any number in between 1 and 7. If it is, it returns the appropriate day name and, if not, it informs the user that the number entered is invalid.

No matter what String the method returns, it gets saved to the result variable and is eventually printed out in Line 16. You can look at the Output to see how the program responds to some different inputs. As you can see, this program was straightforward and you were able to create a separate method to complete a specific objective. Similarly, you should now be familiar with having more than one method in a program to be able to develop a program like this one on your own.

Constructor Methods

We've been talking about objects and classes for a while now and we know that we can instantiate, or create, an object from a class. However, we are not completely clear on how exactly that happens.

Well, constructor methods are methods within classes that allow us to create objects from classes. Constructor methods are immensely useful and will soon become a commonplace within ou classes.

In this paragraph, I will outline some of the features of constructor methods. First of all, in order to let the computer know that a method is a constructor method, the method must have the same name as the class. Secondly, there is no return type included in the method declaration of constructor methods. This will become more apparent in the example below but basically, so far, we either use the void keyword or a primitive type to indicate what, if anything, a method returns. However, with constructor methods, the return type is not present at all. The purpose and function of the constructor method is to initialize the class and give the instance variables of the class some initial values. You can have multiple constructor methods within one class and they would differ based on the number of parameters they have. Although this seems a bit complex, it becomes a lot simpler once you look at the examples below.

Figure 5.11 | Ferrari.java

```
1  public class Ferrari
2  {
3    String color;
4
5    public Ferrari()
6    {
7      color = "red";
8    }
9  }
```

ParkingLot.java

```
1  public class ParkingLot
2  {
3    public static void main( String[] args )
4    {
5      // We Have a Ferrari in the Lot
6      Ferrari f = new Ferrari();
7    }
8  }
```

Above you can see two different Java programs: Ferrari.java and ParkingLot.java. The Ferrari program represents a class that models, well, a Ferrari. In the ParkingLot program, we model a parking lot and one of the cars within our "parking lot" is a Ferrari. In order to demonstrate that a Ferrari is present, we need to create an object of the Ferrari class. To instantiate the class, we utilize constructor methods which we have included within the Ferrari class.

First, we're going to look at the Ferrari class and understand how a constructor method is implemented. Within the class, we have an instance variable called color that logically represents the color of the said Ferrari. Lines 5-8 contain the most important component of the class: the constructor method. We are able to identify it as a constructor method because it has the same name as that of the class and does not contain a return type. Recall that the purpose of the constructor method is to initialize the class, which includes assigning values to instance variables. In this case, we have an instance variable that needs a value assigned, so in the constructor method, we give it a String value to store. Thanks to this constructor method, whenever an object of the Ferrari class is created, its color will be defined as red.

Now that we have created a class with the appropriate constructor method, let's actually create an object of that class. We accomplish this goal in the ParkingLot.java program. Since we actually plan on using this program, we have a main method where we will be creating an instance of the Ferrari class. We instantiate a Ferrari object on Line 6. You may notice that the syntax is very similar to that of a String declaration. That's because both are object declarations as a String is an object as well. You have inadvertently become accustomed to declaring object references and, just as a recap, the new keyword is essential. Once the computer executes Line 6, we successfully instantiate a Ferrari object that, because of the nature of the constructor method, is the color red.

Let's explore how we can make constructor methods more useful. We can do this by adding parameters to our constructor methods so that we can customize our objects. Take a look at the example below to see how constructor methods with parameters can be utilized.

Figure 5.12 | Mustang.java

```
1    public class Mustang
2    {
3      String color;
4
5      public Mustang()
6      {
7        color = "yellow";
8      }
9
10     public Mustang( String c )
11     {
12       color = c;
13     }
14   }
```

ParkingLot2.java

```
1   public class ParkingLot2
2   {
3     public static void main( String[] args )
4     {
5       // We Have Mustangs in the Lot
6       Mustang m1 = new Mustang();
7       Mustang m2 = new Mustang("Black");
8     }
9   }
```

This time, instead of Ferraris, we will be working with Mustangs. You can see the Mustang class with one instance variable. However, what may stand out is that there are two methods with the same name as the class, which tells us that they both are constructor methods. The difference between the two method declarations (in Lines 5 and 10) is that one method doesn't have any parameters and the other has one. The method without a parameter (Lines 5 - 8) is just like the constructor method we looked at earlier; it gives the instance variable a default value. On the other hand, the method with a String parameter assigns the instance variable the value of the parameter. This means that the Mustang can end up with different colors depending on what color is assigned to it when its constructor method is called.

Within the ParkingLot, we have two different Mustang objects being instantiated on Lines 6 and 7. Both declarations are just like String declarations that we have seen earlier. The difference is that the declaration on Line 6 does not have an argument while the declaration on Line 7 does. When the computer interprets Line 6, it recognizes that there are no arguments and executes the constructor method in the Mustang class without parameters. Logically, when the computer interprets Line 7, it notices that it does have a String argument and knows to evoke the constructor method with a String parameter. Therefore, the m1 Mustang object is yellow and the m2 Mustang object is black.

As you may have noticed, you can have more than one constructor method in a class. You need to differentiate these constructor methods based on the number and type of parameters so, when objects of a class are created, the corresponding constructor methods are executed.

Getter Methods (Accessors)

Getter methods, also known as accessors, are methods that return information about an object without altering the object. Once you see an example, you will find them to be very simple. They are essential to keeping classes neat and organized. Programmers find them particularly useful because a user can access the value of a variable within an object but won't actually be able to modify the value. This is in line with a common software engineering practice called encapsulation that ensures users only access what they need and no more.

Figure 5.13 | Person.java

```
1   public class Person
2   {
3     private String name;
4
5     public Person()
6     {
7       name = "Sam";
8     }
9
10    public String getName()
11    {
12      return name;
13    }
14  }
```

Group.java

```
1   public class Group
2   {
3     public static void main( String[] args )
4     {
5       Person sam = new Person();
6       System.out.println( sam.getName() );
7     }
8   }
```

Output

```
> run Group
Sam
```

In this example, we have a Person class and then we create an object of the class in Group.java. You already familiar with most of the Person class as there is a private instance variable representing the name and a no-parameter constructor method that sets the name of the person to "Sam." Pay specific attention to the fact that the instance variable is private meaning it cannot be directly accessed by an object.

From Lines 10 - 13, you get your first look at an accessor method. Unlike a constructor method, the computer has no way of distinguishing it as a getter method; the computer considers it to be an ordinary method. Notice that the the method is `public`, which means that any object of the class can access it and that it returns a `String` value. In addition, it does not have any parameters because it's job is to just return an instance variable. The code within the method is very simple as well; it returns the instance variable representing the name.

Then, in the `Group` program, we create an object of the class called `sam` that has a name of "Sam" because of the constructor method. In Line 6 of the `Group` program, we call the getter method so that we can get the value of instance variable and print it out. We use the expression `sam.getName()` to call the method. The period in the middle is called a dot operator and it enables you to call methods from a specific class. The syntax of it is as follows: `object.method()` or `object.variable`. You may be wondering why we didn't just use `sam.name` and we could completely avoid using the accessor method. However, remember that the name instance variable is `private`. We have made it `private` because so that the user cannot do something like `sam.name` = "Bob"; because we want to make sure that the name stays the same. Therefore, we have a getter method that allows the user to access the instance variable but not change it and this makes getter methods so useful. As you can see in the output, the name of `sam` is printed out. Finally, when creating classes, it's usually ideal to have accessor methods for every `private` instance variable so that the object can access them whenever needed.

Setter Methods (Mutators)

Setter methods, also known as mutators, are methods that change the instance variables of an object. Essentially, they are the opposites of and complementary to the getter methods. Just like the getter methods, they are easy to implement so, without further ado, let's check out an example.

Figure 5.14 | Person2.java

```
1   public class Person2
2   {
3     private String name;
4
5     public Person2()
6     {
7       name = "Sam";
8     }
9
10    public String getName()
11    {
12      return name;
13    }
14
15    public void setName( String n )
16    {
17      name = n;
```

```
18      }
19    }
```

Group2.java

```
1   public class Group2
2   {
3     public static void main( String[] args )
4     {
5       Person2 sam = new Person2();
6       System.out.println( sam.getName() );
7       sam.setName("Bob");
8       System.out.println( sam.getName() );
9     }
10  }
```

Output

```
> run Group2
Sam
Bob
```

Most things have remained the same from the example on getter methods but there are a few notable changes. First and foremost, there is a new setter method in the Person2 class from Lines 15 to 18. It's implement just as you would expect: it doesn't return anything because it's changing a value and takes a parameter for what you want the new value to be. Within its body, it changes the instance variable to whatever value was requested when it was called.

In the Group2.java program, we can see the effectivenes of the setName() method. We start by creating an object called sam with a name of "Sam". However, then we decide that sam needs to have a new name "Bob." In Line 7, we call the setName() method and reset the name of sam. In order to ensure the method has done its job, we print out the name of sam once again and see that this time it is changed to "Bob." Just like the getter method, the greatness of a setter method lies in not allowing the object to have direct access to instance variables. Getter and setter methods usually go hand in hand and you can expect to see both of them for most instance variables in our future programs. Both types of methods follow the principles of object-oriented programming and encapsulation.

Static Methods

While discussing the static keyword earlier in this chapter, we explored static methods a bit and, in fact, we've already used them in some of our own programs. Let's review them to understand them in more depth.

Static methods, also known as class methods, are methods that can be run within a class without creating an object of the class. The main method in classes is static so that it can be run without instantiating the class. Another rule for static methods is that they do not modify the instance variables. Note that setter methods are not meant to be static methods because they change the value of the instance variables and are run by the object.

Some of the previous methods we looked at are called by the object of a class. These methods, setter, getter, and constructor methods, are known as instance methods because they are executed by an instance of a class. On the other hand, static methods are called class methods because they are specific to the class rather than the object. Static methods can be easily implemented by adding the `static` keyword to the method declaration and are essential for our future classes.

Overloaded Methods

Believe it or not, you've actually already worked with overloaded methods. Overloaded methods are two or more methods that have the same method name but have different parameters. This should ring a bell. While working with constructor methods, you learned that you could have more than one constructor method within a class if, for example, one didn't have any parameters and the other had one. That's exactly what overloaded methods are. Programmers like to use overloaded methods so that users or programs that utilize the objects of their classes have a lot more options and variety. Tracking back to the constructor example, the user could have created an object with a default value for the instance variable or set the value his or herself.

Figure 5.15

```
public int multiply( int x, int y )
{
   return x * y;
}


public int multiply( int x, int y, int z )
{
   return x * y * z;
}
```

As you can see in the example above, we have two methods which we assume to be in the same class. The method declarations are almost exactly the same with the only difference coming from the extra `int` parameter that the second method has. These methods are not the same because they have different method signatures and are, hence, overloaded methods. A method signature is the combination of the method name and method parameters. Now, an object has the luxury of being able to call the `multiply()` method with either 2 or 3 arguments depending on what fits the situation. If `object.multiply(2, 3)` is run, the computer will know to use the first method and will return 6. Similarly, if `object.multiply(2, 3, 2)` is executed, 12 will be returned and the second method executed. Overloaded methods are frequently used for constructors, add more options for objects, and make classes more functional and user-friendly.

The `this` Keyword

Figure 5.16

```
private String name;

public void setName( String name )
{
  this.name = name;
}
```

Let's take a look at the example right above. We show a few important components of the class: a private instance variable and a setter method for that variable. Notice that the instance variable is name and that the parameter is name as well. We want to set the instance variable to the value of the parameter and we can do with name = name; but a problem comes up: the computer cannot distinguish which name we are referring to. To solve this, we use the this keyword, as seen in the body of the setter method. The this keyword is a reference to the object whose method or constructor is being called and this enables the computer to know that we are trying to set the value of the instance variable of the current object to that of the parameter. The primary use for the this keyword is when it is indistinguishable next to a constructor or method parameter. Usually, it's better to not have to use the this keyword to avoid confusion, but sometimes there are situations that require it.

Course Program

We will looking at a Course program where we will create our very own Course class and instantiate into an object for the first time. The purpose of the Course class is to model the attributes and features of a course. It will contain one instance variable representing the name of the course, two constructors (zero and one parameter), setter and getter methods, and a printName() method to welcome student to the course. You can see the Course class, its instantiation, and the output ahead.

Figure 5.17 | Course.java

```
1   public class Course
2   {
3     private String name;
4
5     public Course()
6     {
7       name = " ";
8     }
9
10    public Course( String name )
11    {
12      this.name = name;
13    }
14
15    public String getName()
16    {
17      return name;
18    }
19
20    public void setName( String name )
21    {
22      this.name = name;
23    }
24
25    public void printName()
26    {
27      System.out.println( "Welcome to: " + name );
28    }
29  }
```

CourseTest.java

```
1   public class CourseTest
2   {
3     public static void main( String[] args )
4     {
5       Course algebra2 = new Course( "Geometry" );
6       algebra2.printName();
7       algebra2.setName( "Algebra 2" );
8       algebra2.printName();
```

```
 9     }
10   }
```

Output

```
> run CourseTest
Welcome to: Geometry
Welcome to: Algebra 2
```

The example above is just a compilation of all the different types of methods you've learned of so it should be straightforward. I'll go through it to make sure that you have a complete understanding of methods.

Looking at `Course.java`, it has a private instance variable that represents the name of the course. Following that, from Lines 5 - 13, are the two constructors for the class. The first constructor has no parameters and gives the name of the course a default value of a blank space. On the other hand, the second constructor takes in a parameter and sets the instance variable to the value of the parameter. Note the use of the `this` keyword to indicate the instance variable of the current object is receiving the new value. After that, we have our setter and getter methods which are simple and just like what we are used to. Finally, we have the `printName()` method which prints out a statement welcoming the user to whatever course. This will be our way of making sure that the course name is what we want it to be.

Moving on to `CourseTest.java`, we instantiate an object called `algebra2` and, ironically, give it a name a "Geometry." We print out the name using the `printName()` method to make sure that the one-parameter constructor has done its job. Next we use the setter method to change the name to a more appropriate "Algebra 2." Finally, we print out the introduction and observe the change in the name, as seen in the output. Notice that we had a getter method and no-parameter constructor in the Course class that we didn't use. It's important to still have them available because they provide more options for the object and would be useful in other situations.

Overall, this Course program was really simple and demonstrates how classes are organized, how objects are instantiated, and methods are used. The Course program is an excellent introductory framework that ensures you understand the various types of methods that go into making a usable class and soon you will be able to do even more with such methods and classes.

5.5 Chapter Summary:

This definitely has been quite an eventful chapters and we've learned a lot. Namely, we were able to review classes and objects, learn the various keywords, understand methods completely, and work with some of the different types of methods. Now that we have an in-depth knowledge of methods, we will be able to make our programs exponentially more powerful and useful. Without methods, our programs are essentially nothing so be sure to have a good grasp of them.

Multiple Choice Questions

1) What's wrong with the following program?

```
public class Shapes
{
  public static void main(String[] args)
  {
    Rectangle rect;
    rect.width = 40;
    rect.height = 50;
    System.out.println("The rectangle's area is " + rect.area());
  }
}
```

(A) Width is not defined

(B) Height is not defined

(C) No object is created

(D) None of the above

2) Which of the following statements will create an instance of the `NumberHolder` class?

(A) `NumberHolder aNumberHolder;`

(B) `NumberHolder aNumberHolder = new();`

(C) `NumberHolder aNumberHolder = new NumberHolder;`

(D) `NumberHolder aNumberHolder = new NumberHolder();`

3) Consider the following code segment.

```
public class Change
{
  public static void changer( int a, int b )
  {
    a -= b;
    b *= a;
    System.out.println(a + " " + b);
  }

  public static void main(String[] args)
  {
    int x = 2;
    int y = 4;
    changer(x, y);
  }
}
```

What will be displayed upon execution of this code segment?

(A) 2 8

(B) -2 8

(C) 2 -8

(D) -2 -8

For Questions 4 - 6, consider the following code.

```
public class Identify
{
  public static int x = 7;
  public int y = 3;
}
```

4) Which of the following is/are the class variable(s)?

(A) x

(B) y

(C) x and y

(D) None of the above

5) Which of the following is/are the instance variable(s)?

(A) x

(B) y

(C) x and y

(D) None of the above

6) What is the output of the following?

```
Identify a = new Identify();
Identify b = new Identify();
a.y = 5;
b.y = 6;
a.x = 1;
b.x = 2;
System.out.print(a.y + " ");
System.out.print(b.y + " ");
System.out.print(a.x + " ");
System.out.print(b.x + " ");
System.out.print(a.x + b.x);
```

(A) 5 6 1 2 3

(B) 6 5 2 1 3

(C) 5 5 2 2 1

(D) Compile time error

7) Consider the following code segment.

```
public class Test
{
  public static void changer( int a, int b )
  {
    a /= b;
    b %= a;
    System.out.println(a + " " + b);
  }

  public static void main(String[] args)
  {
    int x = 6;
    int y = 5;
    changer(x, y);
  }
}
```

What will be displayed upon execution of this code segment?

(A) 1 0

(B) 1.2 0.2

(C) 1.2 5

(D) 1 5

8) What is wrong in the following code?

```
public class A
{
  public static void main(String[] args)
  {
    System.out.println(i);
    int i = 10;
  }
}
```

(A) No error

(B) Variable i is not defined

(C) Variable i is not public

(D) Variable i is not inside the quotations.

9) Consider the following code segment.

```
public class Moksh
{
  public void Moksh() // line 2
  {
    System.out.println("Ap computers");
  }
  // more code
}
```

What does Line 2 contain?

(A) A constructor

(B) A method

(C) An invalid statement

(D) A and B

10) Generally, the compiler generates one default constructor for class. What is the access modifier of this default constructor?

(A) `default`

(B) `public`

(C) `private`

(D) `protected`

11) Would you be able to instantiate the following class in another class?

```
public class A
{
  private A()
  {
    System.out.println("This is a constructor!");
  }
}
```

(A) Yes, the class is public

(B) No, the class is public

(C) No, the constructor is private

(D) Yes, the constructor does not matter in this case

12) Can you overload constructors in Java?

(A) No, there should only be one way of instantiating a class

(B) Yes, for multiple ways of instantiating a class

(C) No, constructors are different from ordinary methods

(D) None of the above

13) Consider the following code.

```
public class A
{
   final A()
   {
      System.out.println("This is a constructor!");
   }
}
```

What will be displayed upon execution of this code segment?

(A) This is a constructor!

(B) Compile time error

(C) Warning

(D) None of the above

14) Consider the following code.

```
public class ClassOne
{
  String c;

  public ClassOne(String c)
  {
    this.c = c;
  }
}



public class ClassTwo
{
  public static void main(String[] args)
  {
    ClassOne one = new ClassOne("Z");
    ClassOne two = new ClassOne("A");

    System.out.println(two.c);
  }
}
```

What will be displayed upon execution of this code segment?

(A) Z

(B) A

(C) Runtime error

(D) Compile time error

Answers and Explanations

Answer Key

1. C
2. D
3. D
4. A
5. B
6. A
7. A
8. B
9. D
10. B
11. C
12. B
13. B
14. B

Explanations

1) **(C)** The `rect` object gets declared but not instantiated.

2) **(D)** Only Choice D follows the syntax for instantiating an object.

3) **(D)** Evaluating the method, `a = 2 - 4 = -2` and `b = 4 * -2 = -8`. Remember to use the updated value of `a` for calculating `b`.

4) **(A)** A static variable is a class variable.

5) **(B)** Instance variables are all other variables that are not static.

6) **(A)** Simply printing out the `xs` and `ys` of the `Identify` objects.

7) **(A)** Evaluating the method, `a = 6 / 5 = 1` and `b = 5 % 1 = 0`. Remember to use the updated value of `a` for calculating `b` and integer division for calculating `a`.

8) **(B)** We attempt to print `i` before we declare and initialize it.

9) **(d)** It is a constructor method because it has the same name as the class. A constructor is a type of method.

10) **(B)** Default constructors are `public`.

11) **(C)** We would be unable to instantiate the class in another class because we can't call the constructor as it's private.

12) **(B)** Yes, this allows for the user to have a different number of arguments depending on the situation when instantiating a class.

13) **(B)** The `final` keyword should not be in the constructor method declaration.

14) **(B)** With `two.c` we are accessing the `c` instance variable of the `ClassOne` object.

Chapter 6 - Standard Classes

6.1 Chapter Overview:

The last few chapters were a lot to take in so, fortunately, this chapter will be a lot easier. In this chapter, as you can probably tell, we will learn more about the standard classes. Standard classes are a set of classes that contain methods that are immensely useful for our Java programs. Each class that we will be looking at (Object, String, Integer, Double, and Math Class) has its unique advantages. This chapter does not involve much logic at all and is mostly about knowing the various methods available to you to make your life easier.

6.2 The Object Class:

The Object class is the universal superclass of Java and has a direct or indirect relationship with every other class. We'll explore what superclasses and class relationships are in another chapter, but all you need to know is that the Object class is essentially at the top of pyramid of classes in Java. The Object class is part of the java.lang package and, to put its importance in context, the Object class is automatically imported into your Java programs without you having to import it because it's that useful. Last but not least, the Object class contains many methods that we will find immensely handy for our programs.

The toString Method

Essentially, the toString() method converts an Object to a String. Understandably, that may be an idea that is difficult to visualize or understand. How can you convert an object into just a set of characters? Let's take a look at an example.

Figure 6.1 | CourseTest2.java

```java
public class CourseTest2
{
  public static void main( String[] args )
  {
    Course algebra2 = new Course( "Algebra 2" );
    System.out.println( algebra2 );
  }
}
```

Output

```
> run CourseTest2
Course@29cb2795
```

The toString() method is a built-in method that is automatically invoked whenever you try to print out an object because you can only print out strings, not objects. In the example above, you can see that we instantiated a Course object and then we try to print it out. This is when the method is executed and the output comes out to be something that's completely unexpected: it is the name of the class followed an obscure and seemingly arbitrary alphanumeric set of characters. The letters and numbers correspond to the memory allocation of the object, but, more importantly, the output is of no use for the user. To solve this problem, we need to change the functionality of the built-in toString() method and we can achieve this by overriding the method. This will allow us to modify the toString() method to do what we want it to do so we can output something more understandable, like what the course name is, for the user. Below, you can see how we will accomplish that.

Figure 6.2

```
public class Course
{
  public String toString()
  {
    return "Course Name is " + name;
    // name is String representing course name
  }
  // rest of the Course class is same
}
```

Output

```
> run CourseTest2
Course Name is Algebra 2
```

With the code above, we were able to achieve the desired output. Remember that the toString() method is part of the Object class and has a method declaration and body. We override the body of the toString() method by using the same method declaration and having a different body. Upon seeing the exact same method signature, the computer knows that it should follow our code for the toString() method when it is invoked. Therefore, the output comes out as we want and we are able to convert the object to a String the way we'd like. Method overriding is a very important concept that we will be going into more depth in a later chapter. You should understand overriding but you will not need to actually override code for the AP test.

The `equals` **Method**

The `equals` method is another built-in method and it is used to compare objects. We are familiar with all the different operators like == and › but they are used to compare primitive types. The `equals` method returns `true` if the two objects being compared refer to the same object rather than having the same contents. The example below will help you understand that as well as how the `equals` method is utilized.

Figure 6.3 | CourseTest3.java

```
1   public class CourseTest3
2   {
3     public static void main( String[] args )
4     {
5       Course c1 = new Course( "Algebra 2" );
6       Course c2 = c1;
7       Course c3 = new Course( "Algebra 2" );
8       System.out.println(c1.equals(c2));
9       System.out.println(c1.equals(c3));
10    }
11  }
```

Output

```
> run CourseTest3
true
false
```

The `equals` method is used as follows: `obj1.equals(obj2)` where `obj1` and `obj2` are the two objects being compared. The locations of the two objects are interchangeable. In the code above, we instantiate 3 objects with all 3 having the exact same contents (course name) with the first 2 being equal to each other. As you can see, the `equals` method returns `true` for the first 2 objects but not for the first and third. This confirms that referring to the same object is needed for the method to return `true`. If you want to have an `equals` based its output on contents or anything else, you will need to override the method.

As we discussed earlier, the `equals` method is just like the == operator except it is meant for objects rather than primitive types. Remember that since a String is technically an Object, we use the `equals` method to compare them.

Polygon Program

Let's use the knowledge we have gained in this section to create our own program. The program we will develop is the `Polygon` program. Just as we have worked with the Course class, we will now code our own `Polygon` class. The `Polygon` class should have at least 1 instance variable which will be an `int` named `numSides`. The class should also have overloaded constructors with one having 0 parameters and the other having 1. There should also be a getter (accessor) and setter (mutator) method to modify the instance variable. The most important component of this class is the `toString()` method which, when invoked, returns a `String` indicating the number of sides in the polygon.

After you have completed the `Polygon` class, create a `PolygonTest.java` file to test out your Polygon class and make sure it is working correctly. Within the main method, type the following lines of code:

```
Polygon square = new Polygon(4);

System.out.println(square);
```

Then, run the program and the output should be a String indicating that the polygon has 4 sides. Be sure to give a determined effort at developing this program. After that, you can check the code and explanation below to see how you fared.

Figure 6.4 | Polygon.java

```
1   public class Polygon
2   {
3     private int numSides;
4
5     public Polygon()
6     {
7       numSides = 1;
8     }
9
10    public Polygon( int n )
11    {
12      numSides = n;
13    }
14
15    public int getNumSides()
16    {
17      return numSides;
18    }
19
20    public void setNumSides( int n )
21    {
22      numSides = n;
```

```
23    }
24
25    public String toString()
26    {
27      return "Number of Sides: " + numSides;
28    }
29  }
```

PolygonTest.java

```
1  public class PolygonTest
2  {
3    public static void main( String[] args )
4    {
5      Polygon square = new Polygon(4);
6      System.out.println(square);
7    }
8  }
```

Output

```
> run PolygonTest
Number of Sides: 4
```

The above code is actually quite similar to what we worked with for the extensions of the Course program. You should be relatively familiar with declaring a private instance variable and coding overloaded constructors, getter, and setter methods, which are Lines 3 - 23. If not, go to the end of the Chapter 5 to review them. In Lines 25 - 28, we override the toString method to print out the number of sides when the method is called instead of an obscure alphanumeric phrase.

Once we have done this, we can look at the PolygonTest.java file where we have the 2 lines of code given in the instructions. These lines instantiate a polygon object and print out the object, thereby executing the toString method. The output then reflects the successful execution of the program.

Overall, developing this program should not have been much of a task. You should already be comfortable with instance variables and the various types of methods. Overriding is understandably a confusing concept but it will become second-nature to you with more practice.

6.3 The String Class:

A String object is literally just a set, or sequence, of characters. Any time you see multiple characters together, they are just an instance of the String class. Recall that a String can be distinguished by the set of double quotes around it, which are not a part of the actual object but allow the computer to recognize it. Although we will be focusing primarily on the methods in the String class, we will also quickly go over actually declaring a String.

Instantiating String **Objects**

We have actually gone over constructing String objects very early in this book. This subsection will serve as a simmple review.

Figure 6.5

```
String name = new String("Bob);
name = "happy";
name = name + "man";
```

Above, you can see the two ways to declare a String. The first declaration is just like that of an object. Since Strings are used so often, you can also declare a String by directly assigning it to a string literal. Finally, on the third line, we use the concatenation operator (+) to combine the original String with "man". This operator allows us to put two different strings together and that's why the finally value of name is "happyman".

String **Class Methods**

There are a lot of class methods within the String class, but this book will only be outlining the important ones and those that appear on the AP test. All of the methods are straightforward and extremely useful as well.

Figure 6.6

```
String s = "I love APCS";
System.out.println( s.length() );
System.out.println( s.substring(3) );
System.out.println( s.substring(3, 8) );
System.out.println( s.indexOf("lo") );
Sysetm.out.println( s.indexOf("b") );
```

Output

```
> run Figure 6.6
11
ove APCS
ove A
2
-1
```

In the example, we have a String that we will be manipulating with the various String methods to see what each one does. The String has a value of "I love APCS".

The first method we look at is the length() method. The length method has a simple function: it returns an int representing the number of characters in the String, which in this case is 11. The total adds up to 11 because blank spaces count as characters as well.

The next method is the substring() method which enables us to pick out specific parts of a String. This method is an overloaded method, meaning that you can call the method with various numbers of parameters. In the third line, we execute the method with one parameter, the start index. The first character of a String is at index zero, the second at index one, and so on and so forth. It's important to remember that counting in computer science starts with 0 rather than 1 as we are typically accustomed to. The substring method returns a String that goes from the character at the start index to the end of the String. In our example, the character at index three is the fourth character which means that it is the "o". Therefore, the String returned and printed out is "o" followed by all of the characters after it. However, sometimes you don't want the end to be a part of the substring. In that case, you use the substring method with 2 parameters. The first parameter is still the start index but the last parameter is the end index, which logically is the index where you want to stop printing out the String. The end index is the first character that you do not want so the returned String goes from the start index to the end index - 1. On the fourth line, we call the substring method and give it an end index of 8 so the String that is returned is "ove A".

The last String method we will learn is the indexOf(String st) method. This method returns the index of the first appearance of st (the parameter) within the String. If st cannot be found within the String, this method returns -1. On the fifth line, we look for "lo" within our String and find it at index two so 2 is printed out. However, when we look for the character "b", we cannot find it at all and -1 is returned.

Comparing String Objects

There are two different methods we can use to compare strings. Since a String is an Object, we have the equals() method and the other method is the compareTo() method.

Figure 6.7

```
String s1 = "Moksh";
String s2 = "Jawa";
String s3 = "Moksh";
s1.equals(s2) // returns false
s1.equals(s3) // returns true
s1.compareTo(s2) // returns 3 (> 0)
s2.compareTo(s1) // returns -3 (< 0)
s1.compareTo(s3) // returns 0
```

Recall that the equals() method in the Object class only returns true if the two objects refer to the same object. The String class overrides the equals() method so that it returns true whenever the two strings are identical, or have the same contents. As you can see in the example above, when s1 and s2 are checked for equality, false is returned because they are two different strings. However, when s1 and s3 are compared, the method returns true even though they don't refer to the same object. This makes the equals() method equal to the == operator for strings.

The compareTo() is used to compare strings based on how they would be arranged in alphabetical order. The statement s1.compareTo(s2) returns a value less than 0 if s1 comes before s2 in the dictionary, a value greater than 0 if s1 comes after s2, and 0 if s1 and s2 have the same location. You can use if statements to check if comparisons return values less than, greater than, or equal to 0 to determine the location of strings relative to each other. The compareTo() method returning 0 means that using the equals() method will return true. Lastly, Java is case-sensitive so "Bob" is not the same as "bob".

Testing Out String Class Methods

String methods are functions that you should be familiar and comfortable with. I recommend playing around with them a little bit to make sure you understand the parameters and purposes of each method.

6.4 The Wrapper Classes:

Wrapper classes solve a problem that programmers often come across: they want to manipulate the value of primitive type but the method, or function, they are using require the value to be an object. A wrapper classes "wraps", or "boxes", a primitive type into an object so that it can be used in a specific method and then also allows you to "unwrap" the object back to a primitive type so that you can continue on with your program. In Java, every primitive type has a wrapper class, but the only two wrapper classes you need to know for the AP test are the Integer and Double classes.

The `Integer` Class and its Methods

An `Integer` object is essentially an object that only has one instance variable which is of type `int`. The `Integer` class takes an `int` value and turns it into an object. There are a couple of methods within the `Integer` class that you should be familiar with for the AP test.

Figure 6.8

```
int a = 5;
Integer b = new Integer(a); //boxing
System.out.println( "The value is " + b );
a = b.intValue(); // unboxing
Integer c = new Integer(2);
Integer d = new Integer(5);
b.compareTo(c) // returns 1 ( > 0 )
b.equals(d) // returns true
```

Since we are working with an `Integer` object, you declare it like any other object, as you see in Line 2. The constructor in the `Integer` class enables us to "box" the `int` value into an object. In Line 3, we attempt to print out the `Integer` object and the `toString()` method is automatically invoked and converts the `int` value in the `Integer` object to a `String`. To complement the "boxing" method, there is an "unboxing" method called `intValue()` that converts the `Integer` object to an `int` value, as seen in the fourth line. Last but not least, the `compareTo()` and `equals()` methods still apply to the `Integer` class. The `equals()` method is overridden so it returns `true` whenever the values are the same.The `compareTo()` method returns a negative value if the first `Integer` object is less than the second, 0 is they're the same, and a positive value if the first is greater than the second.

The `Double` Class and its Methods

A `Double` object is just like `Integer` object with the only difference coming in the fact that everything, like the instance variable, is of type `double` rather than `int`. This means that all of the methods as well have their names, parameters, and return values changed to correspond with `double`. The `toString()`, `equals()`, and `compareTo()` methods arepractically the same. In addition, the boxing and unboxing methods logically become `Double()` and `doubleValue()`.

Figure 6.9

```
double a = 5;
Double b = new Double(a); //boxing
System.out.println( "The value is " + b );
a = b.doubleValue(); // unboxing
Double c = new Double(2);
Double d = new Double(5);
b.compareTo(c) // returns 1 ( > 0 )
b.equals(d) // returns true
```

6.5 The Math Class:

While creating computer science programs, you often have to conduct mathematical operations. A lot of them like addition and subtraction are easy to utilize. However, there are other operations like exponents, absolute value, and square root that are not as commonly used but are still important. This is where the Math class comes into play. The Math class contains many methods that can be used to model these operations and it has only static methods and variables. This means that there are no instance of the Math class and its methods and variables are called with Math.method() or Math.variable. There is no need to import the math class to call its methods or variables.

Math Class Methods

The methods within the Math class are straightforward and easy to use. The methods that you need know for the AP exam are the abs(), pow(), and sqrt() methods.

Figure 6.10

```
Math.sqrt(4); // returns 2.0
Math.pow( 2, 2 ); // returns 4.0
Math.abs(-1); // returns 1
Math.abs(-2.3); // returns 2.3
```

```
static double sqrt( double d )
```

The first method is the square root method, which returns the square root of a number. Note that it returns a double so that's why the first statement returns 2.0 rather than 2.

```
static double pow( double base, double exp)
```

The next method is the power function which returns a double representing the base to the power of the exp.

```
static int abs( int i )
```

The abs( ) method returns the absolute value of int i.

```
static double abs( double d )
```

The abs( ) method returns the absolute value of double d.

Constants

There are many mathematical constants such as e and pi that are often needed for our Java programs. The math class contains these constants in the form of instance variables. You only need to know one for the AP Computer Science test.

Figure 6.11

```
System.out.println( Math.PI ); // returns 3.14159...
```

Math.PI

It's a constant representing π that is used to calculate the area of a circle and much more.

Circle Area Program

Now, use the methods and constants in the Math class to develop the Circle Area program. In this program, you will create a method to calculate the area of a circle. Within the CircleArea class, create a static method called calcArea that is public, returns a doublev, and takes anint(radius) as a parameter. Note: this method should bestatic" so that we can invoke it in the main method of the CircleArea class. This method takes the radius and return the area. As you may know, the formula to calculate the area of a circle is π multiplied by the square of r. Therefore, this method should take the parameter, square it, multiply it by π, and return it. Note: Use the Math.PI constant to represent π. Once you have created and coded the method, move over to the main method to test out this method. In the main method, type the following line of code:

```
System.out.println(calcArea(3));
```

Then, check out the code, explanation, and output that follows to see how you fared.

Figure 6.12 | CircleArea.java

```
1   public class CircleArea
2   {
3     public static void main( String[] args )
4     {
5       System.out.println(calcArea(3));
6     }
7
8     public static double calcArea( int r )
9     {
10      return ( Math.pow( r, 2 ) * Math.PI );
11    }
12  }
```

Output

```
> run CircleArea
28.274333882308138
```

The answer you should have received from your program is 9π, or 28.274. Developing this program should have been a simple task. You should have set up the calcArea() method as instructed and then utilized Math.pow() to square the radius and then Math.PI to multiply it by π. After returning the final value, it would have been printed out by the main method. If you had trouble with this program, see if you can develop a program to find the circumference of a circle with the radius given.

Math.random()

There is one final Math class method that we are yet to discuss. This method is extremely useful and a bit confusing to use so it deserves a subsection of its own.

```
static double random()
```

This method returns a randomly-generated double value that is greater than or equal to 0.0 and less than 1.0. The random() method comes in very handy when you need to add an element of chance to your programs.

Figure 6.13

```
double a = Math.random(); // 0.0 <= a < 1.0
double b = 10 * Math.random(); // 0.0 <= b < 10.0
double c = Math.random() + 3; // 3.0 <= c < 4.0
double d = 5 * Math.random() + 3; // 3.0 <= d < 8.0
int e = (int) (Math.random() * 100); // 0 <= e <= 99
int f = (int) (Math.random() * 100) + 1; // 1 <= f <= 100
int g = (int) (Math.random() * 20) + 30; // 30 <= g <= 49
```

The above example exemplifies the complexities that can come with using the random() method. The first statement is an example of the basic use of the random() method. For the next three statements, there is a formula you can follow that will help you generate random values within any range using this method. To set a range of low <= a < high, use (high - low) \ Math.random() + low;".

Sometimes, you want an integer value rather than a real one. In that case, you can use (int) cast to convert all values generated to integers. The formula to follow for random integers is (int) (Math.random() \ a) + b;will generate random integers in the rangeb, b+1,...,b+(a-1)". You can see this formula applied in the last three statements of the example.

Rolling Dice Program

Let's use this newfound "ability" to randomize results to create the Rolling Dice program. The purpose of this program is to simulate a dice. In order to achieve this, we will be utilizing the Math.random() method. Basically, what this program should do is output: "The dice shows #" with # representing a randomly generated integer between 1 and 6. This should be a quick test and the primary purpose of this exercise is to ensure you know how to use Math.random() method.

Figure 6.14 | RollingDice.java

```
1  public class RollingDice
2  {
3    public static void main( String[] args )
4    {
5      System.out.println( "The dice shows " + ( (int) (Math.random() * 6) + 1 ));
6    }
7  }
```

Output

```
> run RollingDice
The dice shows 6
> run RollingDice
The dice shows 1
> run RollingDice
The dice shows 2
```

We only need one line of important code for this program because all we are doing is using the (int) cast and Math.random() method to randomly generate integers in between 1 and 6, which fulfills our requirement. As you can see in the output, the result is completely random and within the range.

6.6 Chapter Summary:

This was a simple yet very important chapter. We explored various standard classes such as the Object, String, Integer, Double, and Math classes. There was more understanding than logic in this chapter and it is very important that you remember the methods and variables of each class because they will be very useful in the future.

Multiple Choice Questions

1) Which of these classes is a superclass of all other classes?

(A) Math

(B) Process

(C) System

(D) Object

2) What is the value of double constant 'PI' defined in Math class?

(A) approximately 3

(B) approximately 3.14

(C) approximately 2.72

(D) approximately 0

3) Which of these methods is a function of Math class?

(A) max()

(B) min()

(C) abs()

(D) All of the above

4) What is the value of double constant 'E' defined in Math class?

(A) approximately 3

(B) approximately 3.14

(C) approximately 2.72

(D) approximately 0

5) What will be displayed upon execution of this code segment?

```
double x = 3.14;
int y = (int) Math.abs(x);
System.out.print(y);
```

(A) 0

(B) 3

(C) 3.0

(D) 3.1

6) What will be displayed upon execution of this code segment?

```
double x = 3.1;
double y = 4.5;
double z = Math.max( x, y );
System.out.print(z);
```

(A) True

(B) False

(C) 3.1

(D) 4.5

7) What will be displayed upon execution of this code segment?

```
double x = 2.0;
double y = 3.0;
double z = Math.pow( x, y );
System.out.print(z);
```

(A) 9

(B) 8

(C) 8.0

(D) 9.0

8) Which of these methods returns a random number?

(A) `rand()`

(B) `random()`

(C) `randomNumber()`

(D) `randGenerator()`

9) Consider the following code. Will this generate same output if executed twice?

```
int y = Math.random();
System.out.print(y);
```

(A) Yes

(B) No

(C) Depends on the compiler

(D) Depends on the operating system

10) Which of the following code segments will successfully compile?

I. `System.out.println(Math.max(x));`

II. `System.out.println(Math.random());`

III. `System.out.println(Math.abs(10));`

IV. `System.out.println(Math.random(10,3));`

V. `System.out.println(Math.abs(10,3));`

(A) I and II

(B) I, III, and V

(C) II and III

(D) III and IV

11) Which of these is a wrapper for data type `int`?

(A) `Integer`

(B) `Long`

(C) `Byte`

(D) `Double`

12) What is the output of this program?

```
Integer i = new Integer(257);
int x = i.intValue();
System.out.print(x);
```

(A) `0`

(B) `1`

(C) `256`

(D) `257`

13) Which of the following methods returns the value as a `double`?

(A) `doubleValue()`

(B) `converDouble()`

(C) `getDouble()`

(D) `getDoubleValue()`

14) What will be displayed upon execution of this code segment?

```
Double i = new Double(257.578);
int x = i.intValue();
System.out.print(x);
```

(A) 0

(B) 1

(C) 258

(D) 257

15) Which of these methods of the String class can be used to test to strings for equality?

(A) isequal()

(B) isequals()

(C) equal()

(D) equals()

16) What will be displayed upon execution of this code segment?

```
String obj = "I" + "like" + "Java";
System.out.println(obj);
```

(A) I

(B) Like

(C) Java

(D) IlikeJava

17) What will be displayed upon execution of this code segment?

```
String obj = "I LIKE JAVA";
System.out.println(obj.length());
```

(A) 9

(B) 10

(C) 11

(D) 12

18) What will be displayed upon execution of this code segment?

```
String obj = "hello";
String obj1 = "world";
String obj2 = "hello";
System.out.println(obj.equals(obj1) + " " + obj.equals(obj2));
```

(A) false false

(B) true true

(C) true false

(D) false true

19) Which of these methods of the String class is used to extract a substring from a String object?

(A) substring()

(B) Substring()

(C) SubString()

(D) None of the above

20) What will be displayed upon execution of this code segment?

```
String s1 = "Hello World";
String s2 = s1.substring(0 , 4);
System.out.println(s2);
```

(A) `Hell`

(B) `Hello`

(C) `Worl`

(D) `World`

21) What will be displayed upon execution of this code segment?

```
String s = "Hello World";
int i = s.indexOf('o');
int j = s.lastIndexOf('l');
System.out.print(i + " " + j);
```

(A) 4 8

(B) 5 9

(C) 4 9

(D) 5 8

22) What will be displayed upon execution of this code segment?

```
String s1 = "Moksh";
String s2 = "Moksh";
String s3 = "Jawa";
System.out.print(s1.compareTo(s2) + " ");
System.out.print(s1.compareTo(s3) + " ");
System.out.print(s3.compareTo(s1));
```

(A) 0 0 0

(B) 0 3 3

(C) 0 -3 -3

(D) 0 3 -3

Answers and Explanations

Answer Key

1. D
2. B
3. D
4. C
5. B
6. D
7. C
8. B
9. B
10. C
11. A
12. D
13. A
14. D
15. D
16. D
17. C
18. D
19. A
20. A
21. C
22. D

Explanations

1) (D) The `Object` class is the superclass of all other classes. It is like the first human being - every human being today is indirectly related to it.

2) (B) It represents 3.1415....

3) (D) All three functions are frequently used functions of the `Math` class.

4) (C) It represents 2.7183....

5) (B) 3.14 becomes 3 after you take the absolute value of it and truncate it by converting it to an `int`.

6) (D) y is the larger value so z receives y's value.

7) **(C)** z is equal to 2.0 to the power of 3.0 = 8.0.

8) **(B)** The `random()` method randomly generates a `double` value in between 0.0 and 1.0.

9) **(B)** The `Math.random()` randomly generates a unique value every time it is executed.

10) **(C)** The `max` method should have 2 parameters. The `random` method should 0 parameters. The `abs` method should have 1 parameter.

11) **(A)** The `Integer` class is the wrapper class for the primitive type `int`.

12) **(D)** The `intValue()` method returns the value of the `Integer` object as an `int`.

13) **(A)** The `doubleValue()` method returns the value of the `Double` object as a `double`.

14) **(D)** The `intValue()` method automatically truncates the value of the `Double` object so that it becomes 258.

15) **(D)** The `equals()` method is used to test for equality among Strings.

16) **(D)** The + serves as a concatenation operator and combines the Strings together.

17) **(C)** The `String` contains 11 characters. Spaces count as characters.

18) **(D)** The `equals()` method for the `String` class is the equivalent of the == operator and tests to see if two Strings have the same contents.

19) **(A)** Method names are case sensitive. The `substring()` method is used to create substrings of `String` objects.

20) **(A)** The substring of `s1` is from index 0 to index 3.

21) **(C)** The first occurrence of "o" in `s` is at index 4 and it's index 9 for l.

22) **(D)** Since `s1` and `s2` are the same, the `compareTo()` method returns 0. Since `s1` comes after `s3`, -3 and 3 are outputted depending on which `String` called the method.

Chapter 7 Arrays and ArrayLists

7.1 Chapter Overview:

This chapter marks a very important transition away from predominantly basic concepts. The first of these topics is arrays and ArrayLists. They are data structures that are used to store a list of anything. They are particularly handy when you have many items of the same type and you need to organize them as one rather than individuals items. In addition, once you get the hang of them, you can use loops to analyze these lists and much more.

7.2 Reference Types:

The simple way to explain a reference type is that it is a non primitive type. Essentially, everything that isn't a primitive type is considered to be a reference type. Recall that the some of the primitive types that we are familiar with are `int`, `double`, and `boolean`. A few examples of reference types are classes and objects. A `String` is an object rather than a primitive type so it is also considered to be a reference type. At the beginning of this book, we learned that variables that represent objects are called object references. The "reference" part comes from the fact that an object is a reference type.

Reference Types vs. Primitive Types

Primitive and reference types are never the same as each other and are like opposites. In terms of using them in our programs, the true difference between them arises from their difference in storage. The code sample below will help you see that.

Figure 7.1

```
int x = 4;
int y = x;
x = 5; // y is still 4

Course a = new Course("a");
Course b = a;
b.setName("b"); // affects a and b
a.getName(); // "b"
b.getName(); // "b"
```

With primitive types, as you can see on the first 3 lines, we set the int variables x and y equal to each other to initialize them. Then, we change the value of x to 5 but that value of y still remains 4, the original value, as expected.

However, the same does not occur when working with reference types. In the last 5 lines, we initialize two Course objects called a and b and set them equal to each other. Unlike primitive types, this has a different significance. By setting the two object references as equal to each other, they then refer to the very same object. This means that memory is allocated for only one object and both a and b refer to that memory. Logically, this also means that changing one object reference will inadvertently modify the other as well. This concept is known as *aliasing*, a bad programming technique that should be avoided. It can be avoided by instantiating two different objects.

Storage is the only, but important, factor that separates reference and primitive types from each other and it most definitely influences how you work with variable and objects.

Null Reference

Occasionally with our programs, there comes a situation where we want to have an object reference but we don't want to it to refer to any object temporarily. Unlike int or double, you can't assign a value of 0 to an object. The equivalent of 0 in the reference type world is null.

Figure 7.2

```
Course x;
x = null;
(x == null); // conditional to check if null
```

In the first line, you can see how you can initialize an object reference but not give it an object to refer to. In that very moment, the x object reference is considered to be a null reference and have a null value. Alternatively, you could need to set an object reference to null after it's assigned to an object and you can achieve that using the = operator, as seen on Line 2. Last but not least, if you attempt to print out a null object reference, a NullPointerException will pop up and prevent your program from functioning at all. We will go over errors and exceptions but know that you should avoid them to allow your programs to complete their tasks. You can solve this by checking if an object is null using the == operator (see the conditional on the third line) and an if statement.

7.3 Introduction to Arrays:

An array is a group or collection of variables or values of the same type. It is a type of data structure and is the computer science way of modeling a list. In Java, an array is considered to be and treated like an object so that also means that it is a reference type. The list can contain primitive or reference type values along as all values are the same type. A use case is an array of int values which could be used to store a set of math grade scores that a student received for a semester. Or you can make an array of Course objects to represent a college student's schedule for a quarter. The possibilities with arrays are limitless and they are extremely useful for managing large groups.

Another important term to remember is that the values or variables in arrays are called *elements*. Just as you learned in the previous chapter, counting in computer science begins with 0. For an array of 5 elements, you would assume the first element to, well, be the first element in the real world. However, in the computer science world, that very element would actually be considered the 0th element. In this array, we would have a 0th, 1st, 2nd, 3rd, and 4th element. For an array of n elements, the index values of the elements go from 0 to (n - 1). Overall, arrays help make the lives of programmers much more efficient and allow them to do things like model a deck of cards or a class of students easily with a Java program. They are very extensible and fit into many different programming situations.

7.4 Implementing Arrays

Now that we have a basic understanding of arrays, let's see how we can use them in our programs and where they fit in. We will also go over a sample program that demonstrates how useful arrays are.

Initializing Arrays

There are quite a few ways of declaring and initializing arrays that can be seen below.

Figure 7.3

```
type[] arrayName = new type[N]; // syntax

int[] a = new int[10]; // array with 10 ints

int b[] = new int[10]; // same

int[] c;
c = new int[10];

String[] d = new String[20]; // array with 20 Strings
```

The code sample above shows the syntax for declaring an array on the first line and follows it with multiple valid ways of using arrays. Looking at the syntax, an array is declared a lot like a String as both are objects. For example, the new keyword is used in both. When declaring the array type, it is important to use brackets, [ ], so that the computer knows you are using an array. On the right hand side of the declaration, n represents the number of elements that the declared array has. One of the disadvantages of an array is that the number of elements is fixed and cannot be modified at any point in time. In the second example, you can see the array a is declared to have 10 int elements. Notice that the second and third examples both accomplish the same thing because the placing the brackets, [ ], on the right hand side of the declaration, after the type or arrayName does not matter. In the fourth initialization, we declare the array on one separate line and then initialize it with a specific amount of elements on another, just like we are used to with any variable or primitive type. The last declaration shows an example of the initializing an array with elements of the String type and it demonstrates that an array of any reference or primitive type can exist.

Giving Elements Values

The logical next step to arrays is understanding how we can assign values to individual elements and, hence, unleash the powers of arrays. Tracking back to the last subsection, we can now initialize an array and set it to have 10 int elements. When the array is initialized, every element is given a default value until one is assigned to it. For numerical primitive types (int, double, etc), that value is 0. For the boolean type, it's false and, for all reference types, it's null. In the figure below, you can see how we modify the value of the elements from their default value.

Figure 7.4

```java
int[] a = new int[3]; // array with 3 ints
a[0] = -2; // index 0
a[1] = -1; // index 1
a[2] = 20; // index 2

int[] b = {2, 45, 34, 56, 76, 33, 65, 67, 78, 9}; // 10 elements
b[0]; // 2
b[4]; // 76
b[9]; // 9
b[5]; // 33
```

As you can see, there are two primary ways of assigning values to the elements of arrays. The first is to take an initialized array like the one on the first line and then refer to each elements using arrayName[index] and assign each a value. The index values of the array go from 0 to n - 1. As you can see, we assigned values of -2, -1, and 20 to the three elements in array a using this method. However, this can become extremely tedious when you have large arrays and need to assign values to each element.

The solution to this is an initializer list which you can see in the second half of the code sample. Initializer lists are an easy and efficient way to both initialize an array and assign values to its elements. For example, with array b, we are able to initialize an array with 10 int elements and give them values at the same time. The change is the right hand side of the declaration contains all of the elements, separated by commas and enclosed by braces. The number of elements within the braces is based on the number of elements the array has. You can refer to each element within the array by combining the array's name and its index number, just as you did in the first half of this figure.

Array Length

The length of an array is the number of elements that an array contains, also referred to as n. Every array has a final variable for the length so that it can keep the amount of the elements within it fixed. This will come in especially handy when we use loops to go through arrays and need to know how many elements an array has. Fortunately, it is very easy to get the length of an array and use it.

Figure 7.5

```
int[] a = new int[3]; // array of length 3
System.out.println( a.length ); // 3
```

You can simply get the length of an array with arrayName.length as you can see above. This is just like the length() method that we used to find the number of characters in a String. However, that method should not be confused with the length of array. An array's length is a constant and there are no parentheses around it when it's accessed while the length of a String is method so there are parentheses.

Iterating through an Array

Here, we will talk briefly about using a for loop to go, or iterate, through an array. There is no direct way to access all the elements of an array at once so a for loop becomes very useful. You can use the for loop to access the elements themselves, get their indices, or replace some of them.

Figure 7.6

```
int[] a = {1, 2, 3};
for ( int i = 0; i < a.length; i++ )
{
  System.out.println( a[i] );
}
```

Output

1

2

3

The code above allows us to print out every element within an array. Thanks to the for loop, we are able to access every element in the array and, hence, print each out. This is a perfect example of where the length of an array has come in useful, as we are able to set the terminating condition based on it. The reason that the condition is i < a.length rather than i <= a.length is because of the index of the last element of the array is a.length - 1.

Figure 7.7

```
int[] a = {1, 2, 3, 7, 3};
for ( int i = 0; i < a.length; i++ )
{
  if ( a[i] == 3 )
  {
    System.out.println(i);
  }
}
```

Output

2

4

This code segment let's us find the elements that have a specific value, in this case, 3, and print out their index. We use the same for loop as the last figure and the only change we make this time is that we nest an if statement within the for loop so that we can check which elements have the right value. In this way, the possibilities are really limitless with for loops and arrays.

Passing Arrays to Methods

Since the computer treats arrays as objects, this means that everything that refers to an array is an object reference, and that there is only one array stored in memory there are no copies made of that array. Therefore, when an array is passed as a parameter for a method, no copy of the array is made and the elements within the array can be directly accessed and changed by the method.

To demonstrate the ability to change arrays that are parameters, look at the program below where we are able to double the values of all of the elements within any given int[] array.

Figure 7.8 | DoubleArray.java

```java
1  public class DoubleArray
2  {
3    public static void main( String[] args )
4    {
5      int[] a = {1, 2, 3};
6      System.out.println( "Original Array: " );
7      printArray(a);
8      doubleArray(a);
9      System.out.println( "Doubled Array: " );
10     printArray(a);
11   }
12
13   public static void doubleArray( int[] b )
14   {
15     for ( int i = 0; i < b.length; i++ )
16     {
17       b[i] *= 2;
18     }
19   }
20
21   public static void printArray( int[] c )
22   {
23     for ( int i = 0; i < c.length; i++ )
24     {
25       System.out.println( c[i] + " " );
26     }
27   }
28 }
```

Output

```
> run DoubleArray
Original Array:
1
2
3
Doubled Array:
2
4
6
```

You should focus on the doubleArray() method within this program. What this method does is it takes in an int[] array as a parameter and then uses a for loop to iterate through each element within the array and double it, or multiply it by two. By printing the array before and after the method is called, we can see that we were, as expected, able to modify the elements of an array in an external method. This is something that you can use to your advantage but it can also lead unexpected errors and should be accounted for it at all times.

What will happen if we try to use a method to double an array's element? Will the array get changed or not? Think of an answer and reasoning in your mind before looking at this next program.

Figure 7.9 | DoubleElement.java

```
1   public class DoubleElement
2   {
3     public static void main( String[] args )
4     {
5       int[] a = {1, 2, 3};
6       System.out.println( "Original Array: " );
7       printArray(a);
8       doubleElement(a[1]);
9       System.out.println( "Doubled Array: " );
10      printArray(a);
11    }
12
13    public static void doubleElement( int b )
14    {
15      b *= 2;
16    }
17
18    public static void printArray( int[] c )
19    {
20      for ( int i = 0; i < c.length; i++ )
21      {
22        System.out.println( c[i] + " " );
23      }
24    }
25  }
```

Output

```
> run DoubleElement
Original Array:
1
2
3
Doubled Array:
1
2
3
```

If you predicted that the array wouldn't change, you're right! Remember that the array as a whole is treated as an object but each individual element isn't. Each individual element in this case is an int so it's considered a primitive type. For that reason, the array isn't modified at all even though we supposedly doubled its second element.

Let's explore the extensiveness of what we can do with a for loop within an array. The program below allows you to identify the element within an array that has the maximum value. The logic for such a program is a bit confusing but it truly exemplifies the beauty of computer science and the logic that goes into it.

Figure 7.10 | MaxElement.java

```java
1  public class MaxElement
2  {
3    public static void main( String[] args )
4    {
5      int[] a = {1, 2, 3, 6, 4, 5};
6
7      int maxValue = a[0]; // initial max value
8      for ( int i = 1; i < a.length; i++ )
9      {
10       if ( a[i] > maxValue ) // value greater than max
11       {
12         maxValue = a[i]; // new max
13       }
14     }
15     System.out.println( maxValue );
16   }
17 }
```

Output

```
> run MaxElement
6
```

Again, we are using a for loop. In this case, we temporarily assign the first element to be the one with the max value and then execute a for loop going through the second to last elements to see if any of them have higher values. If they do, they become the new max value and, if they don't, the max value remains the same. This continues until the loop finishes and then the final max value is printed out.

Bag of Marbles Program

At this point, you should feel relatively comfortable with arrays and developing this program should be a breeze. The purpose of this program is to simulate a bag of marbles using an array. The job of this program is very simple. All you have to do within this program is create a `String` array called bag which contains `Strings` that represent the colors of the different marbles. Some of the `Strings` in this array could be "Maroon" or "Red". This is just a test to make sure that you know the basic of arrays and that you know how to use them.

Figure 7.11 | Marbles.java

```
1   // Marbles.java
2
3   public class Marbles
4   {
5     public static void main( String[] args )
6     {
7       String[] bag = { "Red", "Blue", "White", "Yellow" };
8     }
9   }
```

As you can see, the program was extremely simple and basically a one-liner. If you were unable to do it, I recommend rereading this chapter as this is as easy as arrays will get.

7.5 Enhanced For Statements:

As you've probably realized by now, the for loops is a concept that goes hand-in-hand with arrays and it's somewhat tedious to essentially put the same conditions every time. The enhanced for statement, also known as the for-each loop, is a simpler for loop that is geared specifically for parsing through arrays. Just like the for loops we have worked with, the enhanced for statement allows us to easily access all of the elements in an array.

Figure 7.12

```
for ( parameter : arrayName )
{
  statements;
}
```

Above, you can see the syntax for the enhanced for statement. It may seem a bit odd at first but it's actually very easy to get used to, especially when you recognize how the different parts of the enhanced for statement correspond to those of the for loop. The parameter is each element so it's like saying for every element in arrayName, execute these statements;. I understand that the explanation seems a bit confusing but looking at these examples will help you understand how for loops translate to for-each loops.

Figure 7.13

```
int[] a = {1, 2, 3};
int total = 0;

for ( int i = 0, i < a.length; i++ )
{
  total += a[i];
}

for ( int num : a )
{
  total += num;
}
```

The code sample above gets the total sum of the array, which is 6 using the enhanced for statement. The words int num refer to each number within array a and each of these elements is added to the total to get a final sum. The for loop and the enhanced for statement do the same thing and yield the same result. You can know clearly see how the enhanced for statement is much simpler as well as how the parts of the for loop correspond to those of the enhanced for statement.

Figure 7.14

```
int[] a = {1, 2, 3};

for ( int i = 0; i < a.length; i++ )
{
  System.out.println( a[i] );
}

for ( int i : a )
{
  System.out.println(i);
}
```

Output

```
1
2
3
```

In the figure above, we look at one of the first examples we saw using the for loop with arrays and see how much easier it is to implement it with an enhanced for statement. Both loops yield the exact same result with one doing it in a much simpler way. Note that the simplicity of the enhanced for statement becomes even more evident as you work with more complicated programs and arrays.

Figure 7.15 | MaxElement2.java

```
1  public class MaxElement2
2  {
3    public static void main( String[] args )
4    {
5      int[] a = {1, 2, 3, 6, 4, 5};
6
7      int maxValue = a[0]; // initial max value
8      for ( int i : a )
9      {
10       if ( i > maxValue ) // value greater than max
11       {
12         maxValue = i; // new max
13       }
14     }
15     System.out.println( maxValue );
16   }
17 }
```

Output

```
> run MaxElement2
6
```

Here we take the MaxElement program from the past section and we are able to simply achieve the exact same functionality with the for-each loop, further evidence to the extensibility of the enhanced for statement.

Enhanced For Statement vs. For Loop

Figure 7.16 | DoubleArray2.java

```java
1  public class DoubleArray2
2  {
3    public static void main( String[] args )
4    {
5      int[] a = {1, 2, 3};
6      System.out.println( "Original Array: " );
7      printArray(a);
8      doubleArray(a);
9      System.out.println( "Doubled Array: " );
10     printArray(a);
11   }
12
13   public static void doubleArray( int[] b )
14   {
15     for ( int i : b )
16     {
17       i *= 2;
18     }
19   }
20
21   public static void printArray( int[] c )
22   {
23     for ( int i = 0; i < c.length; i++ )
24     {
25       System.out.println( c[i] + " " );
26     }
27   }
28 }
```

Output

```
> run DoubleArray2
Original Array:
1
2
3
Doubled Array:
2
4
6
```

Of all the examples we've looked at so far, we have seen that we can easily use the enhanced for statement in place of the for loop. However, in this case, when we try to switch to the enhanced for statement, we see we do not get the intended functionality out of the program and that the elements of the array are not actually doubled. This is one of the of downsides of using the enhanced for statement. You cannot use an enhanced for statement to remove or replace elements in an array. For that, you just need to use a for loop. Other than that, both the enhanced for statement and the for loop have the exact same functionality and abilities with the enhanced for statement being the more convenient one.

Sum and Average of an Array Program

In this program, we will utilize the enhanced for statement to find the sum and average of the `int` elements within an array. Make sure that you remember that the average variable should be a `double` and to use the `double` cast when calculating the average. For reference, when an `int[]` array consists of [3, 5, 6, 8, 8, 10, 22], the sum should be 62 and the average should be 8.857142857142858.

Figure 7.17 | SumArray.java

```
1   public class SumArray
2   {
3     public static void main( String[] args )
4     {
5       int[] numArray = { 3, 5, 6, 8, 8, 10, 22 };
6       int sum = 0;
7       double avg;
8
9       for ( int n : numArray )
10      {
11        sum += n;
12      }
```

```
13
14      avg = (double) sum / numArray.length;
15
16      System.out.println("Sum: " + sum);
17      System.out.println("Average: " + avg);
18    }
19  }
```

Output

```
> run SumArray
Sum: 62
Average: 8.857142857142858
```

After initializing variables for the sum and average, we use an enhanced for statement to find their values. Just as you saw at the beginning of this section, you calculate the sum by adding onto the sum variable as you iterate through every element in the array. Then, you can calculate the average by dividing the sum by the length of the array. Be sure to use the double cast so that integer division is not conducted and you get an accurate answer.

7.6 Two-Dimensional Arrays:

Introduction to Two-Dimensional Arrays

A two-dimensional array is the computer science equivalent of a matrix. For example, check out this 2 x 5 matrix below.

```
3  5  9  0  8
4  1  7  2  6
```

Technically, speaking, a one-dimensional array also models a mtrix, but only one that has one row, like this 1 x 5 one.

```
3  5  9  0  8
```

With two-dimensional arrays, you can have a matrix with any number of rows and columns. These arrays are data structures that are often used to model things like board games (chess, checkers, etc), seating arrangements, or anything that can be arranged as a matrix.

```
3  5  9  0  8
4  1  7  2  6
9  2  5  1  5
```

Let's take a look at this 3 x 5 matrix to understand how two-dimensional arrays functions. Let's say that this matrix is a two-dimensional array called `arr`. In that case, `arr[1][2] = 7`. The 1 represents the row with index 1 and the 2 represents the column with index 2, or the second row and third column. Going to the second row and third column, you find the value 7. The syntax for accessing elements is `arrayName[rowIndex][columnIndex]`. Try to determine how you would access the element with value 0 from this array. You should come up with `arr[0][3]`.

Intializing Two-Dimensional Arrays

Declaring a two-dimensional array is actually quite like a one-dimensional array except it has another set of brackets for the extra dimension it has. Other than that, the ways of declaring a two-dimensional array are just like those of a one-dimensional one.

Figure 7.18

```
type[][] arrayName = new type[#r][#c]; // syntax

int[][] a = new int[3][5]; // int array with 3 rows, 5 columns

int[][] b;
b = new int[3][5];
```

Firstly, notice syntax for the declaration of a two-dimensional array and that there's an extra pair of brackets and the numbers that go in between the brackets represent the number of rows and columns the array has. Based on that, array `a` has 3 rows and 5 columns of `int` elements. As you can see with array b, you can initialize and define the number of rows and columns at separate times.

Figure 7.19

```
int[][] a = new int[2][2];
a[0][0] = 1;
a[0][1] = 2;
a[1][0] = 3;
a[1][1] = 4;

int[][] b = { {1, 2}, {3, 4} };
```

There are two different ways of declaring an two-dimensional array and assigning values to its elements, just like one-dimensional arrays. For the first method, you individually assign values to elements by referencing the index of their row and column with `arrayName[rowIndex][columnIndex]`. However, a more convenient option, especially when you have a lot of rows and columns, is to use an initializer lists as seen in the last line. If you think of a two-dimensional array as just multiple one-dimensional arrays, it becomes easy to understand. Pretend that you need to use an initializer list for multiple one-dimensional arrays and then combine those lists together. Basically, within the outer set of braces, have a set of braces for each row of the array. Both methods produce the same matrix that you can see below and it is clear that the latter is more efficient.

```
1   2
3   4
```

Two-Dimensional Array Length

There is a length variable for two-dimensional arrays as well but using it is a bit different from a one-dimensional array.

Figure 7.20

```
int[][] a = new int[2][2];
a.length // # of rows
a[0].length // # of columns
```

With the two-dimensional arrays, length is based on the number of rows and columns. `array-Name.length` is equal to the number of rows while `arrayName[i].length` is the number of columns within the row `i`. Note that, in the Java subset, we only look at rectangular arrays where each row has the same number of columns so it doesn't matter what row you check for the number of columns as long as it exists.

For Loops with Two-Dimensional Arrays

```
3   6   10   1
2   5   20   6
```

Let's say that you want to find the sum of all of the elements in this two-dimensional array. The approach to is to think of this array as being made up of multiple one-dimensional arrays with each row representing a single-dimension array. If you can calculate the sum of the elements of each row, you can add up all of those sums to get a final sum. With a Java program, this can be accomplished using nested for loops, or one for loop inside of another.

Figure 7.21

```
int[][] a = { {3, 6, 10, 1}, {2, 5, 20, 6} };

int sum = 0;
for ( int i = 0; i < a.length; i++ ) // each row
{
  for ( int j = 0; j < a[i].length; j++ ) // each column
  {
    sum += a[i][j];
  }
}
```

This code segment calculates the sum of the matrix, which is 53, using nested for loops. The outer for loop goes through each row and the inner for loop iterates through each column of every row. As the i in the outer for loop increases, the sum of each row continues to be added on sum variable. You can accomplish the same thing using nested enhanced for statements as well (see below).

Figure 7.22

```
for ( int[] row : a ) // each row
{
  for ( int col : row ) // each column
  {
    sum += col;
  }
}
```

Keep in mind we can only use the enhanced for statements because none of the elements are being removed or replaced. Just like with one-dimensional arrays, for-each loops are easier to use and more efficient.

Using for loops with arrays is all about intuition and understanding how exactly you are iterating through any array. Below, you can see a for loop that doubles all of the values in the second column of an array.

Figure 7.23

```
int[][] a = { {3, 6, 10, 1}, {2, 5, 20, 6} };

for ( int i = 0; i < a.length; i++ ) // every row
{
  a[i][1] *= 2; // on 2nd column of rows
}
```

Since we want to double the second elements of every row in the element, we need to use a for loop to iterate through every row. Since it's only the second column elements, we can keep its index of 1 constant for whenever we are doubling an element. Two-dimensional arrays are where things become complicated and understanding how you are going to iterate through a matrix is key to achieve what you're aiming for.

7.7 Introduction to ArrayLists:

What is an ArrayList?

An ArrayList is a method, or way, of storing is a list of objects. Keep in mind that it can only store objects and not primitive types like int or double. The ArrayList class is part of the Collections API, or Application Programming Interface. This means that the class is part of a package in the Java libraries. Therefore, in order to use an ArrayList, you must import the class. You can import the package that contains the ArrayList class with the following import statement: import java.util.ArrayList;. Most of the functionality and purpose of the ArrayList is very similar to that of an array but there are some notable differences as well, as outlined in the next subsection.

ArrayList vs. Array

You already know one of the differences between the two: an ArrayList only contains objects while an array takes in primitive values as well. Another very significant difference is that length of an ArrayList is flexible. Recall that once you set the number of elements for an array, it can't be changed. ArrayLists allow you to change the number and you can insert or delete elements and have the indices of the elements be automatically updated. This makes ArrayLists much easier to use in programs and you can always keep track of the last index as well. For similarities, both strive to do the same thing, which is to arrange a list of something and each has its unique advantages and disadvantages.

Declaring ArrayLists

Figure 7.24

```
import java.util.ArrayList; // important!

ArrayList<Type> name = new ArrayList<Type>(); // syntax

ArrayList<int> wrong = new ArrayList<int>();
ArrayList<Integer> right = new ArrayList<Integer>();

ArrayList<Card> myDeck = new ArrayList<Card>();
```

Above you can see some examples, correct and incorrect, of declaring ArrayLists. In the first line, we have the all-important import statement without which we wouldn't be able to use ArrayLists much less declare them. Remember that the import statement goes before even the class declaration in a program; it's the first thing in a program. In the third line, you can see the syntax of the declaration, similar to what you're used to. The Type is replaced with whatever object you are generating an ArrayList of. In the fifth line, we have an invalid declaration as int is not an object. The solution to that is to use the Integer object which comes from the wrapper class of the int primitive type, as you can see on Line 6. Finally, on Line 8, we have a realistic ArrayList declaration for a deck of cards with each element within the ArrayList being a Card object.

7.8 ArrayList<E> Methods:

We know that an ArrayList has a lot of enhanced functionality so it's only fitting that we learn about the methods that we can use with an ArrayList.

```
int size()
```

The first method is the size method. It returns the number of elements in the ArrayList and is equivalent to the length variable in an array.

```
E remove( int index )
```

The remove method removes the element at the specified index and returns it. The indices of the remaining elements are all updated and the size of the ArrayList decreases by 1.

```
boolean add( E obj )
```

The add method with one parameter appends obj to the end of the ArrayList and always returns true. The size increases by 1.

```
void add( int index, E obj )
```

The add method with two parameters inserts obj at the specified index. Elements at or after the index have their indices increased by 1 to adjust and the size of the ArrayList increases by 1 as well. This method doesn't return anything.

```
E get( int index )
```

The get method returns the element at the specified index. This is the ArrayList equivalent of getting the value at an index in an array.

```
E set( int index, E obj )
```

The set method replaces the element at the specified index with obj. It also returns the object that was originally at the index and was replaced.

Figure 7.25 | ArrayListMethods.java

```java
1   import java.util.ArrayList;
2
3   public class ArrayListMethods
4   {
5     public static void main( String[] args )
6     {
7       ArrayList<Integer> x = new ArrayList<Integer>();
8       x.add(5);
9       x.add(21);
10      x.add(34);
11      x.add(454);
12      x.add(12);
13      // [ 5, 21, 34, 454, 12 ]
14      // Size: 5
15
16      System.out.println( x.get(2) ); // 34
17      System.out.println( x.size() ); // 5
18
19      x.set( 2, 64 );
20      // [ 5, 21, 64, 454, 12 ]
21      System.out.println( x.get(2) ); // 64
22
23      x.add( 1, 82 );
24      // [ 5, 82, 21, 64, 454, 12 ]
25      System.out.println( x.size() ); // 6
26
27      x.remove( 2 );
28      // [ 5, 82, 64, 454, 12 ]
29      System.out.println( x.size() ); // 5
30    }
31  }
```

Above, you can see an example of generating an ArrayList and then using its methods to modify it. On Lines 7 - 12, we initialize the ArrayList and give it 5 elements. We use the get( ) and size( ) methods to find the element at index 2 and the general size. We replace the element at index 2, insert an element at index 1 and remove an element at index 2. As we complete those actions, you can see how the ArrayList is updated and modified. You would be unable to do a lot of these things if this was an array.

Positive or Negative Program

With this program, the objective is to create an ArrayList of Integers and determine and output the number of negative Integers present within the ArrayList. Use a for loop to complete this. For example if you had an ArrayList made up of [3, -5, 10, -10, 13], 2 should be outputted since that is the number of negative Integers in the ArrayList.

Figure 7.26 | PositiveNegative.java

```
1   import java.util.ArrayList; // IMPORTANT! DON'T FORGET!
2
3   public class PositiveNegative
4   {
5     public static void main( String[] args )
6     {
7       ArrayList<Integer> list = new ArrayList<Integer>();
8       list.add(3);
9       list.add(-5);
10      list.add(10);
11      list.add(-10);
12      list.add(13);
13
14      int numNeg = 0;
15
16      for ( int i = 0; i < list.size(); i++ )
17      {
18        if ( list.get(i) < 0 )
19        {
20          numNeg++;
21        }
22      }
23
24      System.out.println(numNeg); // 2
25    }
26  }
```

This is your first time using the for loop with an `ArrayList` so it's understandable if you got confused. However, this is exactly what computer science is about. It's about solving problems that you're not accustomed to using logic. With this program, just pretend that you're working with an array when planning the for loop and replace `length` with `size()` and access the elements with the `get()` method. Remember to use `Integers` not `ints`.

7.9 Chapter Summary:

Wow, this was definitely a long chapter and you were introduced to two extremely important data structures, arrays and ArrayLists. You can expect a lot of questions about them on the AP Computer Science exam, but don't worry because you can get the hang of them quite easily. Be sure to know how to use for loops with both and know when to use each one. Other than that, practice will help you become comfortable with them so give the practice questions your all!

Multiple Choice Questions

1) Which one of the following array declarations is incorrect?

(A) `int[] a = {1, 2, 3, 4, 5};`

(B) `int[] a = new int[5];`

(C) `int[] a = {"1", "2", "3", "4", "5"};`

(D) `int[] a = new int [5];`

2) What will be displayed upon execution of this code segment?

```
int[] myarr = new int[10];
for (int i = 0 ; i < myarr.length; i++)
{
  myarr[i] = i + 1;
}
for (int i = 0; i < myarr.length; i++)
{
  System.out.print(myarr[i]);
}
```

(A) `0 1 2 3 4 5 6 7 8 9`

(B) `12345678910`

(C) `1 2 3 4 5 6 7 8 9 10`

(D) `myarr 1 2 3 4 5 6 7 8 9 10`

3) Consider the following code segment. Which of the following will occur upon execution of this code segment?

```
for (int j = 0;j > a.length; j++)
{
   System.out.println(a[i]);
}
```

(A) Compile time error

(B) Run time error

(C) No error

(D) Infinity loop run

4) What will be displayed upon execution of this code segment?

```
int[] a = {1, 2, 3, 4, 5, 6, 7, 8, 9, 10};
int sum = 0;
for (int i = 0; i < a.length; i++)
{
   if (i % 2 == 0)
   {
      sum += a[i];
   }
}
System.out.println("Sum:" + sum);
```

(A) Sum:25

(B) Sum:30

(C) Sum:10

(D) Sum:40

5) Which one of the following `ArrayList` declarations is correct?

(A) `ArrayList<> al = new ArrayList<>();`

(B) `ArrayList<Integer> al = new ArrayList<Integer>();`

(C) `ArrayList[] al = new [];`

(D) `ArrayList<> al = new ArrayList<>;`

6) Which of the following are correct?

I. `List<> l = new ArrayList<>();`

II. `List<Integer> al = new ArrayList<Integer>();`

III. `ArrayList<Integer> al = new ArrayList<Integer>();`

(A) I and II

(B) II and III

(C) III and I

(D) II only

(E) I, II, and III

7) Consider the following code segment.

```
ArrayList<String> mem = new ArrayList<String>();
```

Which of the following is an appropriate way to add values to the `ArrayList`?

(A) `mem.add("XYZ");`

(B) `mem[0] = "XYZ";`

(C) `mem = {"XYZ"};`

(D) None of the above

8) Which of the following are valid `ArrayList` declarations?

I. `List<Integer> al = new ArrayList<Integer>();`

II. `ArrayList<Double> al = new ArrayList<Double>();`

III. `ArrayList<Integer> al = new ArrayList<Integer>();`

Which of the above are correct?

(A) I and II

(B) II and III

(C) I and III

(D) I, II, and III

For Questions 9-10, consider following code segment.

```
ArrayList<Integer> mem = new ArrayList();
int length = 10;
for (int i = 0; i < length; i++)
{
  mem.add(i * 20);
}
```

9) Which of the following code segments can be used to print out the elements at index 5 and 9?

```
(A) System.out.println(mem.get(5));
    System.out.println(mem.get(9));
```

```
(B) System.out.println(mem[5]);
    System.out.println(mem[6]);
```

```
(C) System.out.println(mem.get(5) && mem.get(9));
```

(D) Both A and C

10) Which of the following code segments can be used to print out the sum of all of the elements in the ArrayList?

(A)
```
int sum = 0;
for (int i = 0; i > length; i++)
{
   sum += mem.get(i);
}
System.out.println("Sum is: " + sum);
```

(B)
```
int sum = 0;
for (int i = 0; i < length; i++)
{
   sum += mem.get(i);
}
System.out.println("Sum is: " + sum);
```

(C)
```
for (int i = 0; i < length; i++)
{
   int sum = 0;
   sum += mem.get(i);
}
System.out.println("Sum is: " + sum);
```

(D) None of the above

11) Which one of the following statements is true?

(A) The size of an array is dynamic.

(B) The size of an `ArrayList` and an array is static.

(C) The size of an `ArrayList` is dynamic.

(D) None of the above

For Questions 12 - 14, refer to the following code.

```
public class Customer
{
  private String name;
  private String SSN;
  private int Age;

  public Customer(String name, String SSN, int Age)
  {
    this.name = name;
    this.SSN = SSN;
    this.Age = Age
  }
  public String getName()
  {
    return name;
  }
  public String getSSN()
  {
    return SSN;
  }
  public String getAge()
  {
    return Age;
  }
}
```

```
Customer[] Cust = new Customer[100];
```

12) Which of the following code segments to print the names of customers who are older greater than 50?

I.

```
for (int i = 0; i < Cust.length; i++)
{
  if (Cust[i].getAge() > 50)
  {
    System.out.println(Cust[i].getName());
  }
}
```

II.

```
String name = " ";
for (int i = 0; i < Cust.length; i++)
{
  if (Cust[i].getAge() > 50)
  {
    name = Cust[i].getName();
    System.out.println(name);
  }
}
```

III.

```
System.out.println(Cust[i].getName());
```

Which of the above code segment gives the correct output?

(A) I only

(B) II only

(C) I, II, and III

(D) III only

13) Which of the following code segments will print all of the details of the customer?

```
Customer[] Cust = new Customer[];
```

```
(A) System.out.println(Cust.getName());
    System.out.println(Cust.getSSN());
    System.out.println(Cust.getAge());
```

```
(B) for (int i = 0; i < 100; i++)
    {
       System.out.println(Cust[i].getName());
       System.out.println(Cust[i].getSSN());
       System.out.println(Cust[i].getAge());
    }
```

```
(C) for (i = 0; i < 100; i++)
    {
       System.out.println(Cust);
    }
```

(D) None of the above

14) Which of the following code segments will print the SSN and name of customers with "Edison" as their names?

```
(A) for (Customer c : Cust)
    {
      if ((c.getName()).equals("Edson"))
      {
        System.out.println(c.getSSN() + "," + c.getName());
      }
    }
```

```
(B) System.out.println(c.getSSN());
    System.out.println(c.getName());
```

```
(C) for (int i = 0 ; i < Cust.length; i++)
    {
      System.out.println(Cust.getName()+ ", " + Cust.getSSN());
    }
```

(D) None of the above

For Questions 15 - 16, refer to the following code.

```java
public class Employee
{
  private String EmpId;
  private String Name;
  private double Salary;

  public Employee(String EmpId, String Name, double Salary)
  {
    this.EmpId = EmpId;
    this.Name = Name;
    this.Salary = Salary;
  }
  // Setter and Getter methods
}
```

```java
Employee[] emp = new Employee[50];
```

15) Which of the following code segments can be used to print the maximum salary?

```java
(A) for (int i = 0; i < emp.length; i++)
    {
      int max = 0;
      if (emp.getSalary() > max)
      {
        max = emp.getSalary();
      }
    }
    System.out.println(max);
```

```
(B) int max = Employee[0];
    for (Employee e : emp)
    {
      if (e.getSalary() > max)
      {
        max = e.getSalary();
      }
    }
    System.out.println(max);
```

```
(C) if(emp[i].getSalary > emp[i+1].getSalary())
    {
      max = emp[i].getSalary();
    }
    System.out.println(max);
```

(D) None of the above

16) Which of the following code segments represents the total salary of all the employees?

```
(A) double total_sal = 0.0;
    for (Employee e : Emp)
    {
       total_sal = e.getSalary();
    }
```

```
(B) double total_sal = 0.0;
    for (Employee e : Emp)
    {
       total_sal = e[i].getSalary();
    }
```

```
(C) double total_sal = 0.0;
    for (Employee e : Emp)
    {
       total_sal += e.getSalary();
    }
```

```
(D) double total_sal = 0.0;
    for (Employee e : Emp)
    {
       total_sal += Emp.getSalary();
    }
```

17) What will be displayed upon execution of this code segment?

```
int [] a = {1, 2, 3, 4, 5, 6, 7, 8, 9, 10};
for (int i = 0; i < a.length; i++)
{
  if (a[i] % 2 == 0)
  {
    System.out.print(a[i] + " ");
  }
}
```

(A) 1 3 4 5 6 7

(B) 2 4 6 8 10

(C) 1 2 3 4 5

(D) 2 4 5 6 7

18) Refer to following code segment.

```
ArrayList<String> al = new ArrayList<String>();
```

Which of the following code statements is the correct way of adding a value to the `ArrayList`?

(A) `al.add(1);`

(B) `al.add(new Integer(1));`

(C) `al.add("xyz");`

(D) `al.add('ch');`

For Questions 19 - 21, refer to the following code.

```
ArrayList<String> gaints = new ArrayList<String>();
gaints.add("Peter");
gaints.add("Edward");
gaints.add("Tommy");
gaints.add("Cruise");
gaints.add("Richard");
gaints.add("TOM");

ArrayList<String> royals = new ArrayList<String>();
royals.add("Jimmy");
royals.add("James");
royals.add("Johny");
royals.add("Paul");
royals.add("Christopher");
royals.add("TOM");
```

19) What will be displayed upon execution of this code segment?

```
for (String g : gaints)
{
  System.out.print(g + " ");
}
```

(A) `Peter Edward Tommy Cruise Richard TOM`

(B) `Johnny TOM`

(C) `TOM`

(D) `Jimmy Johnny Paul Christopher TOM`

20) What will be displayed upon execution of this code segment?

```
ArrayList<String> G = new ArrayList<String>(gaints);
for (String gaint : G)
{
  System.out.println(gaint + " ");
}
```

(A) Johnny Paul Christopher TOM

(B) Johnny TOM

(C) Peter Edward Tommy Cruise Richard TOM

(D) Jimmy Johnny Paul Christopher TOM

21) What will be returned upon execution of `royalsCheck(royals)`?

```
public boolean royalsCheck(ArrayList<String> royals)
{
  for (String r : royals)
  {
    if (r.equals("Tommy"))
    {
      return true;
    }
    else
    {
      return false;
    }
  }
}
```

(A) `true`

(B) `false`

(C) `0`

(D) None of the above

22) Which of the following code segments correctly define a two-dimensional array?

I. `int[][] A = new int[3][2];`

II. `int[][] A = new int[3][];`

III. `int[][] A = new int [][];`

(A) I only

(B) I and II

(C) III only

(D) II and III

23) Which of the following code segments populates a two-dimensional with 0 as each element?

```
int[][] matr = new int[3][4];
```

```
(A) for (int r = 0; r < 3; r++)
    {
       for (int c = 0; c < 4; c++)
       {
          matr[r][c] = 0;
       }
    }
```

```
(B) for (int r = 0, c = 0; r < 3, c < 4; r++)
    {
       matr[r][c]=0;
    }
```

```
(C) for ( int r = 0, c = 0; r < 3, c < 4; r++, c--)
    {
       matr[r][c] = 0;
    }
```

(D) None of the above

24) What will be displayed upon execution of this code segment?

```
int[][] M = new int[4][4];
for (int r = 0, c = 0; r < 4, c > 4; r++, c--)
{
  M[r][c] = 0;
}
```

(A) Compile time error

(B) Run time error

(C) No Error

(D) None of the above

25) What will be returned upon execution of `matrfun(m);`?

```
int[][] m = {{1, 2, 3}, {4, 5, 6}};
```

```
public int[][] matrfun(int[][] matr)
{
  int[][] result = new int[matr.length][matr[0].length];
  for(int r = 0; r < matr.length; r++)
  {
    for(int c = 0; c < matr[0].length; c++)
    {
      result[r][c] = matr[r][c] * 2;
    }
  }
  return result;
}
```

(A) 1 2 3
    4 5 6

(B) 2 4 6
    8 10 12

(C) 1 4 9
    16 25 36

(D) None of the above

26) The following method replaces the diagonal elements in an array with 5.

```
public void diagonal(int[][] arr)
{
  // Method body
}
```

Which of the following code segments is the appropriate method body?

```
(A) for (int r = 0; r < arr.length; r++)
    {
       for (int c = 0; c < arr[0].length; c++)
       {
         System.out.println(arr[r][c]);
       }
    }
```

```
(B) for (int r = 0; r < arr.length; r++)
    {
       for (int c = 0; c < arr[0].length; c++)
       {
         arr[r][c] = 5;
       }
    }
```

```
(C) for (int r = 0; r < arr.length; r++)
    {
       for (int c = 0; c < arr[0].length; c++)
       {
         if (r == c)
           arr[r][c] = 5;
       }
    }
```

(D) None of the above.

For Questions 27 - 28, consider the following code.

```
public class Student
{
  private int id;
  private int gpa;

  public Student(int id,int gpa)
  {
    this.id = id;
    this.gpa = gpa;
  }
  public int getId()
  {
    return id;
  }
  public int getGpa()
  {
    return gpa;
  }
}
```

27) The method `indexele()` prints out the element at [4][5] in an array.

```
public void indexele(Student[][] x)
{
  // Method body
}
```

Which of the following code segments is is the appropriate method body?

```
(A) for (int r = 0; r < x.length; r++)
    {
      for (int c = 0; c < x[0].length; c++)
      {
        if (r == 4 && c == 5)
          System.out.println(x);
      }
    }
```

```
(B) for (int r = 0; r < x.length; r++)
    {
        for (int c = 0; c < x[0].length; c++)
        {
            if(r == 4 && c == 5)
                System.out.println(x[r][c].getId()+ " " + x[r][c].getGpa());
        }
    }
```

```
(C) for (int r = 0; r < x.length; r++)
    {
        for (int c = 0; c < x[0].length; c++)
        {
            if(r == 4 && c == 5)
                System.out.println(x.getId() + " " + x.getGpa());
        }
    }
```

(D) None of the above

28) The method `highestGpa()` finds the highest GPA.

```
public int highestGpa(Student [][]x)
{
  // Method body
}
```

Which of the following code segments is is the appropriate method body?

```
(A) for (int r = 0; r < x.length; r++)
    {
      for (int c = 0; c < x[0].length; c++)
      {
        int max_gpa = 0;
        max_gpa = x[r][c];
      }
    }
```

```
(B) for (int r = 0; r < x.length; r++)
    {
      for (int c = 0; c < x[0].length; c++)
      {
        max_gpa = x[r][c];
      }
    }
```

```
(C) int max_gpa =0;
    for (int r = 0; r < x.length; r++)
    {
      for(int c = 0; c < x[0].length; c++)
      {
        if(x[r][c].getGpa() > max_gpa)
        {
          max_gpa = x[r][c];
        }
      }
    }
    return max_gpa;
```

(D) None of the above

29) What will be returned upon execution of `matrixfun(m, n);`?

```
int[][] m = {{1, 2, 3}, {1, 2, 2}, {3, 2, 1}};
int[][] n = {{1, 1, 1}, {1, 2, 1}, {1, 1, 1}};
```

```
public static int[][] matrixfun(int[][] a, int[][] b)
{
  int[][] c = new int[3][3];
  for (int i = 0; i < 3; i++)
  {
    for (int j = 0; j < 3; j++)
    {
      for (int l = 0; l < 3; l++)
      {
        c[i][j] = c[i][j] + a[i][l] * b[l][j];
      }
    }
  }
  return c;
}
```

(A) 2 4 6
    4 5 6
    4 5 6

(B) 2 4 6
    4 5 7
    4 5 8

(C) 6 8 6
    5 7 5
    6 8 6

(D) 4 4 6
   4 5 6
   4 5 6

Answers and Explanations

Answer Key

1. C
2. B
3. B
4. A
5. B
6. B
7. A
8. D
9. A
10. B
11. C
12. C
13. B
14. A
15. B
16. C
17. B
18. C
19. A
20. C
21. B
22. B
23. A
24. E
25. B
26. C
27. B
28. C
29. C

Explanations

1) **(D)** The elements of an `int` array cannot be Strings.

2) **(B)** An array of the 10 `int` elements are all given a default value of 0 and then each element's value systematically increases to its index + 1. A for loop prints out all of the elements, without spaces.

3) **(A)** `i` is not defined.

4) **(A)** Every element with an even index is added to the `sum`.

5) **(B)** Only Choice B has all of the aspects of an `ArrayList` declaration.

6) **(B)** Only II and III follow the rules for an `ArrayList` declaration.

7) **(A)** The `add()` method is used to add elements to an `ArrayList`.

8) **(D)** All 3 options follow the rules for an `ArrayList` declaration.

9) **(A)** Use the `get()` method to access elements of an `ArrayList`.

10) **(B)** An ordinary for loop and the `get()` method allow you to calculate the `sum`.

11) **(C)** One of the advantages of an `ArrayList` is that its size can be modified.

12) **(C)** III does not iterate through the array or check the age of its elements.

13) **(B)** Choice B correctly accesses the elements of the array and calls methods to access the attributes of the elements.

14) **(A)** Only Choice A checks if the name of the customer is "Edison".

15) **(B)** Choice B correctly iterates through the array and updates the maximum value as it checks values.

16) **(C)** Choice C increases the total salary and appropriately access the salaries of each employee.

17) **(B)** The for loop prints out the even elements in the array.

18) **(C)** The `add()` method is used to add elements to an `ArrayList`.

19) **(A)** The enhanced for statements prints out the elements of `gaints`.

20) **(C)** The enhanced for statements prints out the elements of `gaints` after copying it to a new `ArrayList`.

21) **(B)** The code checks if "Tommy" is an element of the `royals` and returns `false` accordingly.

22) **(B)** III incorrectly spaces the array declaration.

23) **(A)** Only Choice A correctly uses nested for loops to access all elements in the array.

24) **(E)** Nothing is displayed; the `c > 4` condition is not met.

25) **(B)** The methods doubles the values of all of the elements.

26) **(C)** Choice C checks if `r == c` to make sure it is modifying a diagonal element.

27) **(B)** Choice B calls methods to print out the element because it is an object.

28) **(C)** Choice C correctly iterates through the array and determines the max value.

29) **(C)** Every element of the final array is equal to the element in the same position of array a and b multiplied together.

Chapter 8 Inheritance and Polymorphism

8.1 Chapter Overview:

Inheritance and polymorphism are two concepts that are key components of object-oriented programming. Both relate to the idea of connecting classes and objects to each other. Inheritance and polymorphism can seem a bit complicated but as you get an understanding of their significance and relate them to the real world, they become simple and easy to use. The programs that we have developed so far usually have one class but now we will learn to create programs that use multiple classes and link them all together.

8.2 Introduction to Inheritance:

Understanding Inheritance

Inheritance is an object-oriented programming concept that promotes software reusability. The best way to explain inheritance is to draw an analogy to the daily routine of the average human being. Inheritance is like a father-son relationship because it is a relationship in which "characteristics" are based down from a "father" to a "son." This is exactly what inheritance is all about. With inheritance in computer science, the "father" and the "son" become classes and the "characteristics" passed down are the methods and attributes of the class. This allows us to connect different classes to each other the way family members are connected to one another. Inheritance is useful because you can create one "father" class and have four "son" classes that have a lot of traits of the "father" class but also have their own unique characteristics.

Subclasses and Superclasses

We know that in the father-son relationship for inheritance, both the "father" and the "son" represent classes. There is actually some specific terminology for the "father" class and the "son" class that you will see used a lot in the programming field. The "father" class is known as a *superclass* and the "son" class is known as a *subclass.*

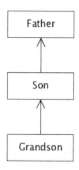

Figure 8.1

Since the father is the superclass, the "father" is the one with all of the characteristics and the "son", being the subclass that it is, the one who inherits all of the characteristics. One mantra to keep in mind is that the subclass inherits characteristics from the superclass.

Taking a look at Figure 8.1 above, we have a relationship between three different classes. However, for now, let's pretend that the Grandson class doesn't exist and focus on the Father and Son class. There is a superclass-subclass relationship between the Father and Son. The arrow represents the subclass inheriting from the superclass. Logically, the subclass goes on the bottom and the superclass on the top. Add in the Grandson class and we add another relationship, one that consists of the Grandson as a subclass and the Son as a superclass.

There are 2 different types of superclasses. A superclass can be either indirect or direct. The Son class is a direct superclass to the Grandson class because the Grandson class directly inherits from the Son class. However, on the other hand, the Father class is an indirect superclass to the Grandson class because its features are inherited through the Son class. Basically, if two classes are connected only by an arrow, the superclass is a direct superclass and, if something comes in between the two, the superclass is an indirect superclass.

The Java programming language supports single inheritance. This basically means that a class can only inherit characteristics from one class. Essentially, every class can only have a maximum of one superclass. Note that this does not mean that a superclass cannot have multiple subclasses. On a quick sidenote, the figure that we have been looking at can be called a class hierarchy and represents inheritance.

Relationships

Let's consider some of the relationships associated with inheritance. To consider these relationships, we will assume that we have two classes, the Creature class and the Reptile class. In addition, the Creature class will be the superclass and the Reptile class the subclass.

The first relationship is the IS-A relationship. This relationship is used to represent the inheritance relationship. A Reptile IS-A Creature. Basically, within any inheritance hierarchy, the subclass IS-A superclass. The next relationship is the HAS-A relationship, which represents composition.

Composition refers to the instance variables within a class. For example, let's say that the Creature class has the FaceColor variable. We can then say a Creature HAS-A FaceColor. Through inheritance, the Reptile class receives the FaceColor variable from the Creature class which means that a Reptile HAS-A FaceColor as well

Inheritance refers to the idea of passing down characteristics from one class to another. The term "characteristics" refers to methods and variables within a class. Let's say that the Creature class has a jump method and it is a general method to define the way that the average creature would jump. Since the Reptile class is a subclass, it will inherit the jump method. However, the Reptile is meant to jump in a different way specific to a reptile. In that case, you need to *override* the method so that you can change its implementation to something that is appropriate for the subclass. The notion of overriding methods is very common within inheritance as there are always some characteristics of superclasses that the subclasses don't want to have.

8.3 Using Subclasses:

We've learnt a bit about inheritance to the point where we have a decent understanding of its purpose and use case. However, inheritance is only so useful until you learn to implement it so that you can use its magic in your next Java programs.

Inheritance Rules

There are a few rules associated with inheritance that you need to familiarize yourself with so that you stay within the scope of inheritance abilities.

Inheritance Rules

1) A subclass does not inherit constructors from the superclass and must define its own.

At this point, we know that subclasses receive methods and variables from their superclasses. However, one set of methods that the subclass does not inherit are the constructor methods. Since every class needs to have a constructor, the subclass is required to implement its own constructor.

2) A subclass can override methods from its superclass as long as the methods are not static methods.

We have already discussed overriding a bit. Often times, subclasses end up overriding methods from their superclasses just so that they are custom to the job of the subclasses. For example, let's say we have a Vehicle class, which is the superclass, and the Car class, which is the subclass. The Vehicle class has a drive method which is defined to have the Vehicle move at 10 mph. The Car class inherits the drive method, but the problem is that the Car is meant to go at 20 mph, rather than the 10 mph that is already implemented for it. In the case, the Car class would override the drive method by using its same method signature from the superclass so that the compiler knows that it's being redefined. As long as the method isn't static, it can be overridden by the subclasses.

3) A subclass can add its own methods and variables.

This rule is pretty straightforward. The purpose of having a subclass is so that you can have an existing foundation from your superclass and build upon it. This is just like the father-son relationship. The son gets a lot from his father genetically but the son also seeks to add his touch and improve on what he got from his father. Not only can a subclass add its own methods and variables, but it is also highly expected that it does.

4) A subclass cannot access the private method and variables of its superclass.

Remember when we talked about the keywords used in method and variable declarations? Well, this is where these keywords come into play. The *private* keyword is used to restrict other classes from accessing the method or variable it is used with. Therefore, subclasses cannot access the private methods or variables because they are restricted from it. However, for example, a superclass could have a private instance variable but public accessor (getter) and mutator (setter) methods so the subclass can modify the variable without directly accessing the private variable.

How to Inherit

Now that we know the rules and reasoning for inheritance, it is time to figure out how we can implement it using code in our Java programs. Our solution is the `extends` keyword, which fits in a as a part of the class declaration. To show inheritance, the declaration of a subclass would be `public class subclassName extends superclassName`. Below, you can see an example using the Vehicle class (superclass) and the Car class (subclass).

Figure 8.2A

```
public class Vehicle
```

Figure 8.2B

```
public class Car extends Vehicle
```

As you can see in Figure 8.2, the declaration for the superclass remains the same as long as it is not inheriting a superclass as well. For the Car subclass, you see that it uses the `extends` keyword to let the compiler know that it is a subclass of the Vehicle class. Remember, that the private methods and variables of the Vehicle superclass will not be inherited by the Car subclass.

super Keyword

Although overriding is useful, it also has a disadvantage: the entire method is overridden which means that the subclass doesn't get any of the functionality of the superclass method. However, you can do partial overriding which is taking an existing method and adding onto its functionality.

It is used in situations where we like the superclass method but need some more functionality for the subclass method equivalent. We can implement this using the super keyword. For the example below, let's say our superclass has the calcTax() method and the subclass wants to use it as well but needs to add on some functionality to the calcTax() method.

Figure 8.3A

```
public void calcTax() // superclass method
```

Figure 8.3B

```
public void calcTax() // inherited subclass method
{
  super.calcTax(); // invokes superclass method
  // more statements for additional functionality
}
```

As you can see above, we have the calcTax() method that the subclass is overriding because it has the same method signature as that of the method in the superclass. Then, in the first line of the method body, the super keyword is utilized. The syntax for using the super keyword is super.methodName();. In the second line, super.calcTax() makes sure that the calcTax() superclass method is invoked so its functionality is used. After that, the subclass method will have statements that will add on to the subclass calcTax() method. One important rule about the super class method is that it must be used in the first line of the method body. If you plan on using the super keyword, make sure the first thing you do is use it. Overall, the super keyword comes in really useful for building on top of the superclass functionality.

super Keyword with Constructors

One of the rules of inheritance was that the constructors of the superclass are not inherited by the subclass. The super keyword is a workaround for when you want to use the constructor of the superclass. Let's track back to the example with the Vehicle superclass and Car subclass and, ahead, you can see how the Car subclass uses the Vehicle constructor as its own constructor.

Figure 8.4A

```
public class Vehicle // superclass
{
  public Vehicle() // constructor
  {
    // constructor body
  }
}
```

Figure 8.4B

```
public class Car extends Vehicle
{
  public Car()
  {
    super();
  }
}
```

Let's look directly at the code for the Car subclass. We know that it is a subclass of the Vehicle class because of the extends keyword. In the Car class constructor, super(); allows us to call the constructor we see in the Vehicle class. It's just that simple. The super keyword can be used very easily to call the constructor of a subclass and this can enable us to workaround one of the rules of inheritance. Note that if you have a superclass constructor with two parameters, you can call it in the subclass with super(parameter1, parameter2);. The same rules apply for the super keyword which means that it still has to be used in the first line of the constructor body.

Using Inheritance with the Bicycle and Mountain Bike Classes

For this example, we will be using all of the features of inheritance that we have learned about. Our superclass will be the Bicycle class and our subclass the MountainBike class. Check out the code ahead and look out for some of the keywords to understand what's going on and how the inheritance between the two is being implemented.

Figure 8.5A | Bicycle.java

```java
1   public class Bicycle
2   {
3     private int gear;
4     private int speed;
5
6     public Bicycle()
7     {
8       gear = 0;
9       speed = 0;
10    }
11
12    public Bicycle( int startGear, int startSpeed )
13    {
14      gear = startGear;
15      speed = startSpeed;
16    }
17
18    public int getGear()
19    {
20      return gear;
21    }
22
23    public void setGear( int g )
24    {
25      gear = g;
26    }
27
28    public int getSpeed()
29    {
30      return speed;
31    }
32
33    public void setSpeed( int s )
34    {
35      speed = s;
36    }
37
38    public void slowDown( int decrement )
39    {
40      speed -= decrement;
41    }
```

```
42
43    public void speedUp( int increment )
44    {
45      speed += increment;
46    }
47  }
```

Figure 8.5B | MountainBike.java

```
1   public class MountainBike extends Bicycle
2   {
3     private int seatHeight;
4
5     public MountainBike()
6     {
7       super();
8       seatHeight = 0;
9     }
10
11    public MountainBike( int startGear, int startSpeed, int startHeight )
12    {
13      super( startGear, startSpeed );
14      seatHeight = startHeight;
15    }
16
17    public int getHeight()
18    {
19      return seatHeight;
20    }
21
22    public void setHeight( int h )
23    {
24      seatHeight = h;
25    }
26  }
```

Let's start off by looking at the Bicycle class. It has two private instance variables, two constructor methods, getter and setter methods for its variables, and two more methods to modify the speed. Note that because the instance variables are private, the subclass will not inherit them. However, it will still inherit the setter and getter methods so the subclass will still be able to make the changes to the variables. All of the methods are public so that means the subclass will have access to all of them, with the exception of the constructor methods of course.

You'll notice that the MountainBike class is much smaller. That's because it inherits most of its components from the Bicycle class. Pay attention to the extends keyword because that's what enables this inheritance relationship. The big change going from the Bicycle class to the MountainBike class is that it adds on another instance variable, the seatHeight variable. This means that the constructors need to be modified to account for the new variable and a setter and getter method needs to be added.

For the constructors of the MountainBike to achieve their desired functionality, they need to define all three of the variables, the gear and speed variables from the superclass along with the newly-defined seatHeight variable. For the constructor without any parameters, we can use the super() statement to call the constructor without any parameters from the Bicycle class so that the first two variables have default values assigned. Then, we add on one more line to the constructor body to give the seatHeight variable a default value as well. We do the same for the other constructor with multiple parameters.

Finally, we add the standard setter and getter methods so that potential subclasses of the MountainBike program can access the new private instance variable seatHeight. And that's it! With that, we have successfully implemented an inheritance relationship and now you hopefully have a much better understanding of how it works. You should also be able to recognize the situations where the extends and super keywords were used.

Using Inheritance with the Circle and Cylinder Class

Now it's your chance to develop a program showing inheritance. Give it your best shot! We will have a superclass Circle and a subclass Cylinder. The Circle class will have a private instance variable of double type representing the radius. It will also have a constructor without any parameters that sets the radius variable's value to 1.0. There will also be a getRadius() and setRadius() method. Last but not least, the Circle superclass should have the findArea() method that returns a double representing the area of the circle. The formula for the area of a circle is $\pi \times (r^2)$.

The Cylinder subclass will inherit the methods and variables from the Circle superclass so remember to use the extends keyword. The Cylinder class will add on a private instance variable height that is a double. Remember that the Circle class constructor is not inherited so add a constructor without parameters for the Cylinder class. The constructor should give the radius and height a default value of 1.0 and note that the Cylinder subclass cannot access the private instance variable radius so the super keyword must be used to invoke the Circle class constructor. In addition, add a setHeight() and getHeight() method. Finally, add a findVolume() method that returns a double. The method should return a value equal to the area (accessed using the findArea() method) multiplied by the height. Once you are done, match your code with the following code.

Figure 8.6A | Circle.java

```
1   public class Circle
2   {
3     private double radius;
4
5     public Circle()
6     {
7       radius = 1.0;
8     }
9
10    public double getRadius()
11    {
12      return radius;
13    }
14
15    public void setRadius( double r )
16    {
17      radius = r;
18    }
19
20    public double findArea()
21    {
22      return radius * radius * Math.PI;
23    }
24  }
```

Figure 8.6B | Cylinder.java

```
1   public class Cylinder extends Circle
2   {
3     private double height;
4
5     public Cylinder()
6     {
7       super();
8       height = 1.0;
9     }
10
11    public double getHeight()
12    {
13      return height;
```

```
14      }
15
16      public void setHeight( double h )
17      {
18        height = h;
19      }
20
21      public double findVolume()
22      {
23        return findArea() * height;
24      }
25    }
26
```

Hopefully, you were able successfully develop the program. If not, don't worry, you'll get the hang of it very soon. Let's go through some of the key components of the program. Firstly, pay attention to the extends keyword in the Cylinder class declaration; it's really easy to forget. Next, you can see that the new height instance variable is declared and that we use the super keyword to use the constructor from the superclass. Otherwise, it's pretty straightforward and we have been familiar with the other elements of the program for quite a while.

8.4 Introduction to Polymorphism:

Understanding Polymorphism

To understand what polymorphism is, let's break it up into two pieces. The first piece "poly", means many and the second piece, "morphism", behaviors. Literally speaking, polymorphism directly means many behaviors. This literal definition provides a lot of insight into what polymorphism all about. Polymorphism is an object-oriented programming concept that is about the ability to process methods, classes, and objects differently depending on their situations.

Polymorphism may sound a bit complicated but it's actually easy to understand once you see an example. Let's presume that we have a Shape superclass and it has calcArea() method. In addition, there's a Rectangle subclass that wants to calculate area in a different way so it overrides the calcArea() method. Then, we create an object of the Rectangle class and call it rectObj. Next, we execute the following code: rectObj.calcArea();. Will the method body from the Shape class or the method body from the Rectangle class be executed? We know that the one from the Rectangle class will be run because we are working with the Rectangle object. However, if we had shapeObject.calcArea();, then the method from the Shape class would have been executed. That's basically what polymorphism is. In both cases, we are calling the calcArea() method but we are getting different results depending on the situation.

Method Overloading

The first example of polymorphism is method overloading. We've already gone over method overloading but, to quickly review it, it's the idea of having two methods with same name but different parameters. We are able to do this because the two methods have different method signatures. You can see an example of it in Figures 8.7A and 8.7B.

Figure 8.7A | Rectangle.java

```
1  public class Rectangle
2  {
3    private int length;
4    private int width;
5
6    public Rectangle()
7    {
8      length = 1;
9      width = 1;
10   }
11   public Rectangle( int l, int w )
12   {
13     length = l;
14     width = w;
15   }
16 }
```

Figure 8.7B | RectangleTest.java

```
1  public class RectangleTest
2  {
3    public static void main( String[] args )
4    {
5      Rectangle rectObj = new Rectangle();
6      Rectangle rectObj2 = new Rectangle( 2, 4);
7    }
8  }
```

The Rectangle class has overloaded constructors because it has two constructors, one with 0 parameters and one with 2 parameters. In RectangleTest.java, we create two different objects and are able to do so with different constructors because we give each constructor call a different number of arguments. The compiler tracks how many arguments there are when it is compiling the program and determines which method is appropriate to use. This is known as static binding, or early binding because the compiler picks the correct method before the program is run. Method overloading exemplifies polymorphism because we call the same method in both cases and, depending on the situation, the fitting method is run.

Method Overriding

We've looked at method overriding examples a couple of times within this chapter. The example with the calcArea() method and Shape and Rectangle classes is a perfect example of how method overriding functions. Unlike method overloading, method overriding follows dynamic binding. Dynamic binding, also known as late binding, is when the compiler decides which method to use when the program is being run rather than when it is being compiled. In this case, when the method is compiling, the compiler identifies that the calcArea() method will be called and, upon runtime, it determines which one to run. Below, you can see the calcArea() example implemented for reference.

Figure 8.8A

```java
public class Shape
{
  public int calcArea()
  {
    // code
  }
}
```

Figure 8.8B

```java
public class Rectangle extends Shape
{
  public int calcArea()
  {
    // overriding code
  }
}
```

Figure 8.8C

```
public class Test
{
  public static void main( String[] args )
  {
    Shape shapeObj = new Shape();
    Rectangle rectObj = new RectangleObject();
    shapeObj.calcArea();
    rectObj.calcArea();
  }
}
```

Revisiting the Circle and Cylinder Class with Polymorphism

We worked with the Circle and Cylinder classes to demonstrate inheritance just a bit earlier in the chapter. Now, we will be using the existing code from that and working in concepts of polymorphism. The changes we will be making to the Circle and Cylinder class are relatively basic. We will be demonstrating method overloading by adding a few more constructors with different parameters. Add one more constructor to the Circle class. A constructor without parameters already exists and this new constructor should have 1 `double` parameter and the `radius` instance variable should be set to the value of the parameter. The method header should be as follows: `public Circle( double r )`.

As for the Cylinder class, we will be adding ne constructor as well. This constructor will contain two `double` parameters, representing the radius and height. Then, the `radius` and `height` private instance variables should be set to the value of the parameters. Keep in the that the Cylinder subclass cannot access the private `radius` variable and the `super` keyword will need to be used. The method header should be as follows: public `Cylinder( double r, double h )`. Once you are done, match your code with the following code.

Figure 8.9A | Circle.java

```
1  public class Circle
2  {
3    private double radius;
4
5    public Circle()
6    {
7      radius = 1.0;
8    }
9
10   public Circle( double r )
```

```
11      {
12         radius = r;
13      }
14
15      public double getRadius()
16      {
17         return radius;
18      }
19
20      public void setRadius( double r )
21      {
22         radius = r;
23      }
24
25      public double findArea()
26      {
27         return radius * radius * Math.PI;
28      }
29   }
```

Figure 8.9B | Cylinder.java

```
1    public class Cylinder extends Circle
2    {
3       private double height;
4
5       public Cylinder()
6       {
7          super();
8          height = 1.0;
9       }
10
11      public Cylinder( double r, double h )
12      {
13         super(r);
14         height = h;
15      }
16
17      public double getHeight()
18      {
19         return height;
20      }
```

```
21
22    public void setHeight( double h )
23    {
24      height = h;
25    }
26
27    public double findVolume()
28    {
29      return findArea() * height;
30    }
31  }
```

The code above should be easy to understand as we have looked at examples of method overriding and overloading already. If you have any troubles with this, reread this section on polymorphism.

8.5 Abstract Classes and Methods:

Abstract Classes

Abstract classes are classes that cannot be instantiated to objects. Most of the classes we have worked with so far have been developed so that they can eventually become objects. However, abstract classes are not meant to be objects. You may be wondering what the purpose of the abstract classes is. The purpose for abstract classes is to serve as superclasses and provide a base for subclasses. The subclasses of an abstract class are called concrete classes as they fill in all of the missing pieces within abstract classes. You can think of an abstract class as an outline that all of its subclasses must follow and is not meant to become an object itself.

Abstract Methods

Abstract methods are just like abstract classes in that they don't do what you're typically accustomed to expecting. Abstract methods are the methods within an abstract class and they only have a header. This means that abstract methods do not have any method body or implementation. All they have is a simple method signature. The purpose of abstract methods is to provide an outline for the concrete subclasses. The subclasses are required to give an implementation for all of the abstract methods so it's a way of ensuring that the subclasses include some specific functions.

For example, let's say we have a Shape class. Usually within a shape, you want to find the area of it but the method of finding the area is unique depending on what type of shape you are working with. The various types of shapes would be the subclasses and the Shape class would be the abstract superclass. Within the Shape class, we know that we want to make all of the subclasses have a function to calculate area so we will have an abstract area() method to ensure that the subclasses do so as well. Again, remember, we will not have any implementation for the abstract method, and this makes sense because we aren't sure how to implement calculating area until we know the specific shape. Note that abstract methods are only available in abstract classes. But, that does not mean that an abstract class cannot have an ordinary method with an implementation.

abstract **keyword**

We utilize the abstract keyword to indicate which classes and methods are abstract. To implement this, all we have to do is add the abstract keyword to the class or method declaration right after the public keyword. Take a look at this example below to see how easily we can use abstract classes and methods.

Figure 8.10A | Shape.java

```
1   public abstract class Shape
2   {
3     private String name;
4
5     public Shape( String shapeName )
6     {
7       name = shapeName;
8     }
9
10    public String getName()
11    {
12      return name;
13    }
14
15    public void setName( String n )
16    {
17      name = n;
18    }
19
20    public abstract int area( int l, int w );
21  }
```

Figure 8.10B | Circle.java

```
1   public class Circle extends Shape
2   {
3     private int radius;
4
5     public Circle( int circleRadius, String shapeName )
6     {
7       super(shapeName);
8       radius = circleRadius;
9     }
10
11    public int area( int l, int w)
12    {
13      return l * w;
14    }
15  }
```

In this example, the Shape class is the abstract class and we indicate that by making its class declaration `public abstract class Shape`. All we need to do is throw in that `abstract` keyword and we're all set. The same applies for abstract methods. The Shape class has one abstract method, the `area()` method. Our method declaration for it looks like `public abstract int area( int l, int w );`. Notice how we have a semicolon at the end instead of braces for the method body since abstract methods don't have bodies. Everything else within the abstract class, such as a private instance variables or constructors, can be typically expected within an ordinary class as well.

The Circle class is the concrete class because it is the subclass of the Shape class. This time we don't need to use the `abstract` keyword. One of the requirements of this concrete class is to provide method implementations for all abstract methods in the superclass. Therefore, the `area()` method must have a method body, which you can see on Lines 11-14 in Figure 8.10B. The remainder of the subclass is, again, standard.

Creating Employees

It's your turn to take a shot at demonstrating your understanding of abstract classes by creating employees. Create an abstract class Employee and a concrete subclass Dev. The abstract class Employee should have 3 private instance variables: name (`String`), address (`String`), and number (`int`). It should also have the abstract method `computePay()` that doesn't take in any parameters and returns a `double`. Don't forget to use the `abstract` keyword to indicate the use of an abstract class or abstract method.

The Dev subclass should have 1 private instance variable weeklySalary (`int`) and it will be set to a value of 2000. Because the superclass (Employee) of the Dev class contains an abstract method (computePay()), the Dev class must provide an implementation for this method. The Dev class should return the weeklySalary multiplied by 52. Don't worry about constructors for the sake of this practice exercise. Once you are done, match your code with the following code.

Figure 8.11A | Employee.java

```
1  public abstract class Employee
2  {
3    private String name;
4    private String address;
5    private int number;
6
7    public abstract double computePay();
8  }
```

Figure 8.11B | Dev.java

```
1  public class Dev extends Employee
2  {
3    private int weeklySalary = 2000;
4
5    public double computePay()
6    {
7      return weeklySalary * 52;
8    }
9  }
```

Just like the Shape and Circle example we just looked at, the Employee superclass is the abstract class, as indicated by the abstract keyword. We have a few instance variables and the abstract method computerPay() that has no implementation. The subclass Dev extends the Employee class and provides the required method body for the computePay() method. Everything is pretty evident from the examples we've looked at and you can now see how the abstract classes and their concrete classes operate.

8.6 Creating and Using Interfaces:

Understanding Interfaces

Our next topic is an interface and the interesting thing about it is that it is very similar to an abstract class. An interface is a group of related empty-bodied methods. The term "empty-bodied method" maybe remind you of an abstract method and interfaces are actually *only* made of public abstract methods. The purpose of an interface is to establish a general structure without all of the details. It's almost like an abstract class in that it's a skeletal outline. Just like a concrete class gives bodies to the abstract methods of an abstract class, the implementing class (the subclass of an interface) implements the methods of an interface. You may be finding a lot of similarities between interfaces and abstract classes but they're actually different as well something we will discuss a bit later in this chapter.

Interface Declaration and Use

When we declare an interface, we use the `interface` keyword in place of the `class` keyword. Since all methods of an interface must be public and abstract, the method headers do not contain the `public` and `abstract` keywords. Just like with abstract methods, we have no method bodies and just the headers. With inheritance, the subclass uses the `extends` keyword. Interfaces replaces the `extends` keyword with the `implements` keyword. Take a look at this example to see how an interface and its implementing class can be used.

Figure 8.12A | Animal.java

```
1  public interface Animal
2  {
3    void eat();
4    void run();
5  }
```

Figure 8.12B | Dog.java

```
1  public class Dog implements Animal
2  {
3    public void eat()
4    {
5      System.out.println( "Dog eats" );
6    }
7
8    public void run()
9    {
10     System.out.println( "Dog runs" );
11   }
12 }
```

Using interfaces is as simple as replacing a few keywords. We saw the `class` keyword get replaced by the `interface` keyword and the `extends` keyword by the `implements` keyword. With a few minor changes, we were successfully able to use interfaces. Pay close attention to how small the interface code is and that's how it's meant to be. The method headers are shorter than usual and an interface is a simple outline for the implementing classes to follow, just as an abstract class is for its concrete subclasses.

Creating an Animal Interface

As you can probably tell from the title, we will be creating an Animal interface. This interface should have 4 methods: eat(), run(), turn(), and hide(). All of these methods have a void return type. Remember that because this is an interface, there should not be any implementations for any of the methods and only the method headers should be present. Once you are done, match your code with the following code.

Figure 8.13 | Animal.java

```
1   public interface Animal
2   {
3       void eat();
4       void run();
5       void turn();
6       void hide();
7   }
```

This entire interface is only 7 lines and this just a way of making sure you can create an interface. It's easy to develop as you long as you the interface keyword and have the method headers that only include the return type, method name, and parameters.

8.7 Abstract Class vs. Interface:

As you may have realized, abstract classes and interfaces are similar enough that both can be used interchangeably in certain situations. However, looking at the nuances of their use cases, it becomes clear which one is appropriate in a situation.

1. An abstract class can have instance variables, while an interface cannot.
2. Both an abstract class and an interface cannot be instantiated into an object.
3. All of the methods in an interface have to be abstract methods while an abstract class can have some methods implemented as well.
4. Classes use the extends keyword to connect with abstract classes and the implements keyword for interfaces.

The primary difference between the two is that interfaces are used to set rigid rules for other classes in regards to functions that they must have. Interfaces only serve that purpose. However, with an abstract class, there is a potential for instance variables and implemented methods which gives a lot of added flexibility so that the subclasses can have a foundation as well. Both are very useful and which one you use really does depend on the context.

8.8 Chapter Summary:

Chapter 8 was probably one of the the most important chapters of the entire textbook because it goes over inheritance and polymorphism. Be sure to remember the relationships and functions of the superclass and subclass through inheritance. In addition, know what polymorphism is and how it relates to method overloading and overriding. Understand what abstract classes and interfaces are and when they are used.

Multiple Choice Questions

1) Which of the following keywords is used to implement inheritance between two classes?

(A) `implements`

(B) `extends`

(C) `final`

(D) `const`

For Questions 2 - 4, refer to the following code.

```
public class A
{
  int n = 100;

  public A(){}
  public void display()
  {
    System.out.println("Displaying the contents of Class A");
    System.out.println("n: " + n);
  }
}
```

```
public class B extends A
{
  int n = 10;

  public B(){}
  public void display()
  {
    System.out.println("Displaying the contents of Class B");
    System.out.println("n: " + n);
  }
}
```

2) Which of the following code segments should be added to the method body for the `display()`

method in Class B to execute the `display()` method from Class A as well?

(A) `System.out.println("Displaying the contents of Class A");`
     `System.out.println("n: " + n);`

(B) `System.out.println("Displaying the contents of Class B");`
     `System.out.println("n: " + n);`

(C) `super.display();`

(D) None of the above

3) What will be displayed upon execution of this code segment?

```
B b = new B();
b.display();
```

(A) Displaying the contents of Class A
    n: 100
    Displaying the contents of Class B
    n: 10

(B) Displaying the contents of Class B
    n: 10
    Displaying the contents of Class A
    n: 100

(C) Displaying the contents of Class B
    n: 10

(D) Compile time error

4) Refer to the following code. What will be displayed upon execution of the display() method in Class C?

```
public class C extends B
{
  public C(){}
  public void display()
  {
    super.display();
    System.out.println("Displaying the contents of Class C");
  }
}
```

(A) Displaying the contents of Class A
    n: 100
    Displaying the contents of Class B
    n: 10

(B) Displaying the contents of Class B
    n: 10
    Displaying the contents of Class C

(C) Displaying the contents of Class B
    n: 10

(D) None of the above

For Questions 5 - 9, refer to the following code.

```java
public class FirstClass
{
  int x = 0;

  public FirstClass(int x)
  {
    this.x = x;
  }
  private void increment()
  {
    x++;
  }
  public final void add(int y) {
    x += y;
  }
  public void display()
  {
    System.out.print(x);
  }
}


public class SecClass extends FirstClass
{
  public SecClass(int x)
  {
    super(x);
  }
  public void display()
  {
    add(2);
    super.display();
  }
}
```

5) Which methods are inherited by the SecClass from the FirstClass?

(A) FirstClass(int x), add(int y), display()

(B) FirstClass(int x)

(C) add(int y), display()

(D) FirstClass(int x), display()

6) What will be displayed upon execution of this code segment?

```
SecClass sc = new SecClass(3);
sc.display();
```

(A) 1

(B) 5

(C) 3

(D) 2

7) Is the method `increment()` in the `FirstClass` is inherited by the `SecClass`?

(A) Yes, all non-constructor `public` methods are inherited

(B) Yes, it has a `void` return type

(C) No, it's a `private` method

(D) No, only constructor methods are inherited

8) What will be displayed upon execution of this code segment?

```
FirstClass fc = new FirstClass(3);
fc.display();
fc = new SecClass(3);
fc.display();
```

(A) 33

(B) 32

(C) 35

(D) 31

9) In order to inherit the following method, what are any changes, if any, that need to be made?

```
private void increment() { x++; }
```

(A) `private final void increment() { x++; }`

(B) `private static void increment() { x++; }`

(C) `public void increment() { x++; }`

(D) No changes needed

10) Which of the following keywords is used to access the methods of the superclass?

(A) `private`

(B) `super`

(C) `public`

(D) `static`

11) Which of the following statements correctly demonstrates inheritance?

(A) `public class A extends B{}`

(B) `public class B implements A{}`

(C) `public class A super B{}`

(D) `public class A{class B{}}`

For Question 12, consider the following statement.

```
public class BMW extends Car
{
  // code
}
```

12) What will result upon execution of this code segment?

```
Car C = new Car();
Car C1 = new BMW();
```

(A) Compile time error

(B) Run time error

(C) No error

(D) Exception

For Questions 13 - 15, consider the following code.

```
public class Calculations
{
  int result;

  public Calculations(int x, int y)
  {
    System.out.println("Calculations");
  }
  public void add(int x, int y)
  {
    result = x + y;
    System.out.println("Addition Result: "+ result);
  }
  public void sub(int x, int y)
  {
    result = x - y;
    System.out.println("Difference Result: " + result);
  }
  public void mult(int x, int y)
  {
    result = x * y;
    System.out.println("Product Result: " + result);
  }
}
```

13) What will be displayed upon execution of the `addSub()` method?

```
public class MyCalc extends Calculations
{
  public void addSub()
  {
    super.add(10, 20);
    super.sub(20, 10);
  }
  // more code
}
```

(A) `Addition Result: 30 Difference Result: 10`

(B) Compile time error

(C) `Addition Result: 200 Difference Result: 10`

(D) None of the above

14) Which of the following code segments will allow use of the superclass constructor?

```
public class MyCalc extends Calculations
{
  public MyCalc(int x, int y)
  {
    // add code here
  }
}
```

(A) `super(x, y);`

(B) `Calculations cal = new Calculations(x, y);`

(C) `MyCalc m = new MyCalc();`

(D) A and B

15) What will be displayed upon execution of this code segment?

```
MyCalc m = new MyCalc(3, 2);
```

(A) Compile time error

(B) `Calculations`

(C) `Addition Result: 5 Difference Result: 1`

(D) None of the above

16) Which of the following keywords is used to access the interface?

(A) `implements`

(B) `extends`

(C) `final`

(D) `access`

17) Which of the following relationships represents polymorphism?

(A) HAS-A

(B) HAS-HAS

(C) IS-A

(D) None of the above

18) Which of the following is a type of polymorphism?

(A) Method overriding

(B) Method overloading

(C) A and B

(D) None of the above

19) Consider following code.

```
public interface Display
{
  void contents();
}


public class A
{
  // code
}
```

If the above Class A wants to access the interface Display, what needs to be added to its class declaration?

(A) public class A implements Display

(B) public class A extends Display

(C) public class A implements contents

(D) Display.contents();

For Questions 20 - 21, consider the following code.

```
public abstract class Person
{
  public abstract void printDetails();
}



public class Student extends Person
{
  public void printDetails()
  {
    System.out.print("Student");
  }
}



public class Employee extends Person
{
  public void printDetails()
  {
    System.out.print("Employee");
  }
}
```

20) What will be displayed upon execution of this code segment?

```
Person P1 = new Student();
P1.printDetails();
```

(A) `Person`

(B) `Student`

(C) `Employee`

(D) `Student Employee`

21) Presume that the code for the Employee class is replaced by the following.

```
public class Employee extends Student
{
  public void printDetails()
  {
    super.printDetails();
    System.out.print("Employee");
  }
}
```

What will be displayed upon execution of this code segment?

```
Employee P1 = new Employee();
P1.printDetails();
```

(A) Person

(B) Student

(C) Employee

(D) StudentEmployee

22) Consider the following code.

```
public void add(int x)
{
  x = x + 1;

}
public void add(int x, int y)
{
  x = x + y;
}
```

The above code is an example of which of the following?

(A) Method overriding

(B) Method overloading

(C) Inheritance

(D) Encapsulation

For Questions 23 - 25, consider the following code.

```
public class A
{
  public A()
  { // empty constructor }

  public void printNumber(int num)
  {
    System.out.println("A: " + num + " ");
  }
  public void printNumber(int num1, int num2)
  {
    System.out.println("Numbers: " + num1 + ", " + num2 + " ");
  }
  public double printNumber(double num)
  {
    System.out.println("Decimals: " + num + " ");
    return num;
  }
}
```

23) What will be displayed upon execution of this code segment?

```
A a = new A();
a.printNumber(10);
a.printNumber(10, 20);
```

(A) `10 20`

(B) `A: 10 Numbers: 10, 20`

(C) `10 10, 20`

(D) Compile time error

24) What will be displayed upon execution of this code segment?

```
A a = new A();
a.printNumber(10.5);
```

(A) 10.5

(B) A: 10 Numbers: 10, 20

(C) 10

(D) None of the above

25) What will be displayed upon execution of this code segment?

```
A a = new A();
double b = a.printNumber(10.5);
System.out.print("b: " + b + " ");
a.printNumber(5);
a.printNumber(5, 6);
```

(A) b: 10.5 A: 5 numbers: 5, 6

(B) decimals: 10.5 b: 10.5 a: 5 numbers: 5, 6

(C) 10

(D) None of the above

26) Which of the following statements is true about the inheritance?

I. A superclass inherits the properties of the subclass.

II. A subclass inherits the properties of the superclass.

III. A superclass can have multiple subclasses.

(A) I only

(B) I and II

(C) II and III

(D) II only

27) Which of the following statements is true about abstract classes?

I. An abstract class can be initialized.

II. An abstract class must have abstract methods.

III. An abstract class can have abstract methods.

(A) I only

(B) I and II

(C) II and III

(D) III only

28) Which of the following statements is true about interfaces?

I. An interface may not contain instance variables.

II. A class can implement more than one interface.

III. An interface can be extended.

(A) I only

(B) I and II

(C) I, II and III

(D) III only

29) What will be displayed upon execution of this code segment?

```
String str1 = "Tommy";
String str2 = "Tommy";
int result = str1.compareTo(str2);
System.out.println(result);
```

(A) 0

(B) 10

(C) -1

(D) 2

Answers and Explanations

Answer Key

1. B
2. C
3. C
4. B
5. C
6. B
7. A
8. C
9. C
10. B
11. A
12. C
13. A
14. D
15. B
16. A
17. C
18. C
19. A
20. B
21. D
22. B
23. B
24. D
25. B
26. C
27. D
28. B
29. A

Explanations

1) **(B)** The `extends` keyword is used to implement inheritance.

2) **(C)** The `super` keyword allows you to call a method from the superclass.

3) **(C)** Only the `display()` method of Class B is executed.

4) **(B)** The `super` keyword leads to the execution of the Class B `display()` method first and then of the Class C one.

5) **(C)** All non-constructor, public methods are inherited.

6) **(B)** The value is increased by 2 and outputted.

7) **(A)** All non-constructor, public methods are inherited.

8) **(C)** The first class does not change the value of 3 and prints it out. The second class increases it by 2 and then prints it out.

9) **(C)** The method needs to be `public` to be inherited.

10) **(B)** The `super` keyword allows for superclass method access.

11) **(A)** A class declaration with the `extends` keyword demonstrates inheritance.

12) **(C)** Both are valid declarations.

13) **(A)** The `super` keyword calls the methods from the superclass and yields the output seen in Choice A.

14) **(D)** A and B access the superclass constructor, albeit in different ways.

15) **(B)** The superclass constructor is executed.

16) **(A)** The `implements` keyword allows a class to access an interface.

17) **(C)** Polymorphism is represented by an IS-A relationship.

18) **(C)** Method overloading and overriding are two examples of polymorphism.

19) **(A)** The `implements` keyword allows a class to access an interface.

20) **(B)** The `printDetails()` method of the `Student` class is executed.

21) **(D)** The superclass method is executed and then the subclass method is

22) **(B)** Method overloading is when 2 methods have the same method signature except for the parameters.

23) **(B)** This is another example of method overloading. The method called depends on the number of and types of the parameters.

24) **(D)** `Decimals: 10.5` is outputted. None of the answers have that choice.

25) **(B)** The method called depends on the number of and types of the parameters, which determines the output.

26) **(C)** A subclass inherits from a superclass. A superclass can have multiple subclasses but a subclass can only have one superclass.

27) **(D)** An abstract class cannot be initialized and it does not have to contain only abstract methods.

28) **(B)** Choice C correctly iterates through the array and determines the max value.

29) **(A)** The compareTo( ) method returns 0 when the 2 Strings are equal to each other.

Chapter 9 Recursion, Algorithms, and Labs

9.1 Chapter Overview:

Congratulations! You have successfully made it to the final chapter of content covered on the AP Computer Science exam. In this chapter, we will be learning some higher level concepts that are essential to improving as a programmer. We will also be going over the labs that are now a part of the AP Computer Science curriculum to see what important concepts you can derive from them. In this chapter, logic and iterations will be used frequently.

9.2 Recursive Methods:

Understanding Recursive Methods

A recursive method is a method that calls itself. Take a second to process that. A recursive method is kind of like a loop and is often referred to as "a method within a method." The best way to understand how a recursive method functions is to see an example.

Figure 9.1 | RecursionTest1.java

```
1   public class RecursionTest1
2   {
3     public static void test( int n )
4     {
5       if ( n > 0 )
6       {
7         System.out.println(n);
8         test( n - 1 ); // recursion
9       }
10    }
11
12    public static void main( String[] args )
13    {
14      test(3);
15    }
16  }
```

Output

```
> run RecursionTest1
3
2
1
```

The `test()` method is a recursive method. It is considered a recursive method because of Line 8. In Line 8, the `test()` method calls `test()`, or essentially calls itself. To understand what recursion does, let's look at the output that comes about from calling `test(3)` in the main method. As you can see, a total of 3 integers are printed even though the `test()` method only print one integer out. This means that the `test()` method was executed 3 times due to recursion.

On the first time, the `test()` method is run, n is equal to 3 and, since 3 is greater than 0, 3 is printed out and `test(2);` is called. On the second iteration, 2 is printed out and `test(1);` is called because 2 is greater than 0. At this point, you may have realized that this method will keep calling itself until n becomes less than or equal to 0. n is slowly getting smaller with every method call. The `test()` method continues getting called until `test(0);` is run and nothing happens and the method terminates. This entire process of calling the same method over and over again (bears some resemblance to the for loop) is what recursion is all about. This was a very simple example of it. Soon, you will see how recursion can be used to accomplish complex functions and objectives.

Recursive Method Properties

There are a few properties of recursive methods that you should know to look out for. On the AP Computer Science exam, you do not have to write out your own methods so recursion does not show up on the free response portion. However, on the multiple choice section, you are often asked to evaluate recursive methods and determine what their output will be or how many times a method will be executed. Knowing the properties of a recursive method is useful because it allows for more efficient evaluation of recursion.

The first, and most important component of a recursive method is its base case. The base case is the condition that is checked for upon every execution of the method to determine when the method should terminate. Just like a for loop, with a recursive method, you should ideally be getting closer and closer to the base case so that the recursive method does not continue infinitely. Every case that is not at the base case is known as a non-base case. Another way that recursion is like a loop is that it is used to simplify code and you use it logically to make your life as a programmer simpler. Although recursion is useful, it is particularly inefficient for large sets. This means something like `test(100)` would not be ideal as it would be a slow route compared to other options. However, recursion is perfect for situations where you have a small set of numbers.

Practical Uses for Recursion

As we start building more complicated programs, you will notice that recursion will apply to more situations. The first example is the Fibonacci series which goes as follows: 0, 1, 1, 2, 3, 5... The nth number of this series is sum of the 2 numbers before it. As you can tell, you need to reuse the same method to get the nth number and recursion enables you to do that. Furthermore, you can use recursion to implement factorials. An example of a factorial is 5! = 5 x 4 x 3 x 2 x 1. Last but not least, you can print out patterns like the one below.

```
******
*****
****
***
**
*
```

Notice how for all of these examples, you are using the same method (recursion) with different numbers (repeated method calls).

Recursion vs. Iteration

Recursion and iteration are awfully similar but they have their differences as well. Both involve repetition and can, technically speaking, run for an infinite amount of time. With iteration, you are repeating a code block through a statement like a for loop, but, with recursion, repeated method calls enable that same functionality. In addition, both have a base case, or a termination test to prevent them from repeating the same function infinitely. Between the two, iteration is preferred over recursion because it uses less memory. Only use recursion when iteration can't do the job, or you are specifically asked to use recursion.

Printing Asterisk Patterns

One example where we can use recursion is to print a pattern of asterisks as mentioned in an earlier subsection. Below, you can see a recursive method, commented to indicate its parts, that does just that.

Figure 9.2 | PrintingPatterns.java

```java
public class PrintingPatterns
{
  public static void printPattern( int n )
  {
    if ( n > 0 ) // base case
    {
      for ( int i = 1; i <= n; i++ )
      {
        System.out.print("*");   // print out n *s on a line
      }
      System.out.println(); // next row starts on new line
      printPattern( n - 1 ); // n-1 = non-base case
    }
  }

  public static void main( String[] args )
  {
    printPattern(5);
  }
}
```

Output

```
> run PrintingPatterns
*****
****
***
**
*
```

The printPattern() method, every time it is called, prints out an asterisk (*) n amount of times through a for loop. The recursive part comes in when we recall the method to print out the next row of asterisks with one less asterisk through printPattern(n - 1);. Clearly, the output reflects what we wanted through the printPattern(5); method call.

Calculating Factorials

The factorial of a number is defined is the product of natural numbers from one to that particular number.

Mathematically, n! = 1 * 2 * 3 * .... * (n-1) * n

For example, the factorial of 4 is 4! = 1 * 2 * 3 * 4 = 24

The objective of this program is to model factorials so that we can calculate the factorial of any number using recursion. Create a Java program that calculates and outputs the factorial of any number using recursion. For example, if our program were to calculate the factorial of 10, 3628800 would be outputted. Once you are done, refer to the code below to compare your work.

Figure 9.3 | Factorial.java

```
1   public class Factorial
2   {
3     public static void main( String[] args )
4     {
5       System.out.println( "3! = " + calcFactorial(3) );
6     }
7
8     public static int calcFactorial( int n )
9     {
10      if ( n == 0 )
11      {
12        return 1;
13      }
14      else
15      {
16        return n * calcFactorial( n - 1 );
17      }
18    }
19  }
```

Output

```
> run Factorial
3! = 6
```

The calcFactorial() method is a recursive method. It multiplies n by one less than n until n is equal to 0, at which point, the method terminates. That's why calcFactorial(3) yields 3 x 2 x 1 and, eventually 6.

Printing the Fibonacci Series

The Fibonacci Sequence is the series of numbers: 0, 1, 1, 2, 3, 5, 8, 13, 21, 34... The next number is found by adding up the two numbers before it.

The objective of this program is to model the Fibonacci series. Create a Java program that calculates and outputs a Fibonacci series consisting of 10 numbers using recursion. For example, if I wanted to calculate a Fibonacci series of 10 numbers, 0 1 1 2 3 5 8 13 21 34 should be outputted. Make sure that the program is extendable so that you can find the series for *n* numbers. Instead of using recursion, use iteration with for loops. Once you have completed, compare your code to the code below.

Figure 9.4 | Fibonacci.java

```
1  public class Fibonacci
2  {
3    public static void main( String[] args )
4    {
5      int numPrinted = 10;
6      int[] series = new int[numPrinted];
7
8      // Create first 2 series elements
9      series[0] = 0;
10     series[1] = 1;
11
12     // Create series
13     for ( int i = 2; i < numPrinted; i++ )
14     {
15       series[i] = series[i-1] + series[i-2];
16     }
17
18     // Print series
19     System.out.println( "Fibonacci Series of " + numPrinted + " numbers!" );
20     for ( int i = 0; i < numPrinted; i++ )
21     {
22       System.out.print( series[i] + " " );
23     }
24   }
25 }
```

Output

```
> run Fibonacci
Fibonacci Series of 10 numbers!
0 1 1 2 3 5 8 13 21 34 >
```

Using an array to store the series makes your life a lot easier. Using for loops, we are able to determine each value in the Fibonacci series by adding the last two elements of the array and printing out the entire series. In this case, we use iteration, but recursion could have done the job as well. The two are interchangeable in most cases, but iteration is the more efficient option so that's why we opted for it.

9.3 Sorting Algorithms:

Understanding Sorting Algorithms

An *algorithm* is a process or set of rules to be used in calculations or other problem-solving operations. Whenever you want to complete a task that involves multiple steps, you follow an algorithm, or the list of all the steps. Logically, a sorting algorithm is a process to order a set of numbers in ascending ordered. Below, you can see two lines of numbers. The first before the algorithm is implemented and the second is after.

```
3   5   9   1   8
```

```
1   3   5   8   9
```

As expected, the line of numbers after the algorithm has been arranged in increasing order. There are many different methods, or algorithms, of ordering numbers. Do you start by looking in the middle of a list? In the front? In the back? We will be exploring multiple types of sorting algorithms to compare efficiency and implementation.

Selection Sort

Selection sort is also known as the "search and swap" algorithm. It's finds the smallest element in the array a[n] and makes it exchange positions with the element at a[0]. Then, it finds the smallest element within the subarray of a[1] to a[n-1] and so on and so forth. It continues this process until there are only 2 elements, a[n-2] and a[n-1], left. The smaller of the 2 elements is stored as a[n-2] and the larger as a[n-1] and the list is successfully sorted. The process of searching for the smallest element is repeated n - 1 times.

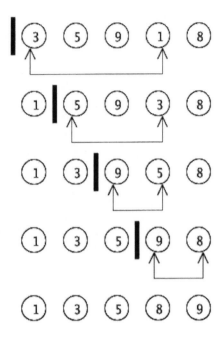

Figure 9.5

As you can see in the figure above, the algorithm looks for the smallest number in the list to the right of the vertical line and the list continues to grow shorter as the smallest numbers are placed at the front.

Insertion Sort

Insertion sort is a sorting algorithm that goes element by element and inserts it into a sorted list. It splits a list into sorted and unsorted lists and then moves each element in the unsorted list one-by-one to its appropriate place in the sorted list. The initial sorted list consists solely of a[0] and the unsorted list of a[1] to a[n-1]. The figure below will make the process of insertion sort much clearer.

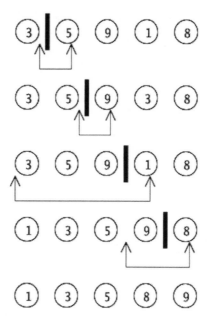

Figure 9.6

The sorted list is to the left of the vertical line and the unsorted list to the right. Each time, the algorithm takes the first element from the unsorted list and puts it in a sorted place within the sorted list. Like selection sort, the process of placing the first element of the unsorted list into the sorted list is repeated n - 1 times. The worst case for this algorithm is if the original list is in descending order because that will require the maximum amount of moving and comparing elements. On the other hand, the best situation is if the original list is already sorted so none of the elements will be moved and there will be a minimal number of comparisons. Both insertion and selection sort are inefficient for big lists.

Mergesort

Mergesort is an algorithm that takes a recursive approach to sorting. The first step in mergesort is to recursively split a list until it made of n sublists, each containing an individual element as you can see in left half of Figure 9.7. Then, we recursively merge sublists (right half of Figure 9.7) until the we get one list, which ends up being sorted. When two lists are merged, they merge so that they form a combination of the 2 lists sorted.

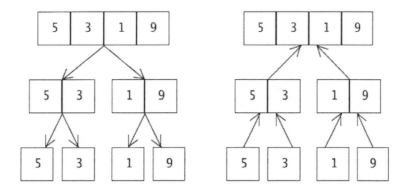

Figure 9.7

There is no worst or best case for mergesort because the array is split and merged based on the number of elements, not the ordering of the elements. The primary disadvantage of this method is that it creates a temporary array which takes up space and can become a concern with large lists.

9.4 Searching Algorithms:

Understanding Searching Algorithms

A searching algorithm is an algorithm that can be used to find the location of a specific number within a list of numbers. The number, or value, that the algorithm tries to locate is often referred to as the "key". A searching algorithm typically reports the first occurrence of the key and returns the index of the its location. If the value cannot be found within the list, -1 is returned.

Linear Search

Linear search, also known as sequential search, is a very simple searching algorithm. It starts at the first element and keep going until it locates the key or there aren't anymore elements to check. This searching algorithm will work regardless of whether the list is sorted. However, if there are two occurrences of the key in the list, the index of the first occurrence is the one that will be returned. The ideal situation for a linear search is that the key is the first element because it requires only one comparison. The worst case is that the key is in the last spot in the list or is not a part of a list at all. When you have an unsorted list, your options are relatively limited and your best choice is to go with a standard linear search.

Binary Search

Unlike linear search, binary search is a search algorithm designed for lists that are already sorted. It uses a "divide-and-conquer" approach. Binary search goes to the middle element of the list and compares it to the key. If the middle element is greater than the key, the algorithm focuses on the smaller half of the list and goes to the middle of that halve. The algorithm search the larger half of the list if the key is smaller than the middle element.

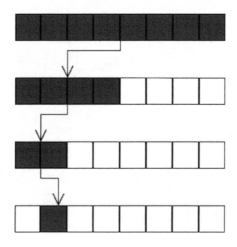

Figure 9.8

The best case for binary search is if the key is equal to the middle element and the worst case is if the key is at the end of a sublist or is not in the list.

Code for Searching Algorithms

Figure 9.9 | SearchTest.java

```java
1   public class SearchTest
2   {
3     public static void main(String[] args)
4     {
5       int[] intArray = {5, 6, 8, 2, 3};
6       System.out.println(linearSearch(intArray, 2));
7
8       int[] intArray2 = {2, 6, 78, 234, 456, 767};
9       System.out.println(binarySearch(intArray2, 767 ));
10    }
11
12    public static int linearSearch(int[] array, int key)
13    {
14      int size = array.length;
15
16      for (int i = 0; i < size; i++)
```

```
17      {
18        if (array[i] == key)
19        {
20          return i;
21        }
22      }
23      return -1; // couldn't find key
24    }
25
26    public static int binarySearch(int[] array, int key)
27    {
28      int low = 0;
29      int high = array.length - 1;
30
31      while (low <= high) // more elements to search
32      {
33        int middle = low + (high - low) / 2;
34
35        if (key < array[middle])
36        {
37          high = middle - 1;
38        }
39        else if (key > array[middle])
40        {
41          low = middle + 1;
42        }
43        else
44        {
45          return middle;
46        }
47      }
48      return -1;
49    }
50 }
```

Output

```
> run SearchTest
3
5
```

The code above has two methods, one for linear search and one for binary search. You do not need to know the code for these algorithms for AP Computer Science test but knowing it will increase your understanding of search algorithms.

The method body for the `linearSearch()` method is straightforward. There is a for loop that iterates through the list of numbers and returns the index once the key is found in the list. If the for loop iterates and doesn't return anything (meaning the key was not found in the list), -1 is returned.

For binary search, we use a while loop and keep alternating the bounds for the sublists we are finding the middle of. Like linear search, if the loop completes and nothing is returned, -1 gets returned. The most important part of the logic behind this while loop is that we keep comparing the key with the middle of whatever sublist we look at and then adjusting our sublists based on that until we are able to zero in on the key, if it exists.

9.5 AP Computer Science A Labs:

Although the labs are newly added to the AP Computer Science curriculum, there will be no questions directly regarding the labs on the AP test. Instead, the questions will focus on the concepts emphasized and demonstrated in these labs. The subsections below outline the important concepts of each lab and you can refer to past text for reference if you have forgotten the concept. You can access the student guides for the labs on the *CollegeBoard* website.

The Elevens Lab

- *Math.random()* for shuffling
- Abstract classes
- Writing a subclass
- Polymorphism
- Inheritance
- Arrays

The Magpie Lab

- Conditionals (if-else statement when searching)
- *Math.random()* for random selection
- String methods for manipulating Strings
- ArrayLists and arrays
- while loops

The Picture Lab

- Two-dimensional arrays
- Manipulating two-dimensional arrays
- Using the for-each loop with arrays

9.6 Chapter Summary

And that's it! That covers all of the content for AP Computer Science A! We learned about two very important concepts, recursion and searching/sorting algorithms. Know how to evaluate recursive code. Understand the logic behind each type of algorithm and know which one should be used when. Look over the labs online and review concepts you don't understanding by tracing back to past chapters. It's been a very long ride and your hard work will definitely be rewarded!

Multiple Choice Questions

1) A function which calls itself is known as a

(A) Final method

(B) Static method

(C) Recursive method

(D) Constant method

2) Which of the following statement are true?

I. Recursive function is the function which calls itself.

II. Recursion can be efficiently applied to huge data.

III. Recursion usage to large amount of data can cause memory issue.

(A) I only

(B) II only

(C) I and II

(D) I and III

3) Refer to the following code.

```
public void func(int n)
{
  while(n > 1)
  {
    System.out.println("n: " + n);
    n = n - 1;
  }
}
```

Which of following code is correct recursive replacement for the code above? You can assume n will be greater than or equal to 1.

```
(A) public void func(int n)
    {
      func(n - 1);
    }
```

```
(B) public int func(int n)
    {
      if (n == 1)
      {
        return n;
      }
      System.out.println("n: " + n);
      func(n - 1);
    }
```

```
(C) public void func(int n)
    {
      System.out.println("n: " + n);
    }
```

(D) None of the above

4) Consider the following code.

```
public int prod(int p)
{
  if (p == 1)
  {
    return 1;
  }
  else
  {
    return  p * prod(p - 1);
  }
}
```

What will be displayed upon execution of this code segment?

```
int p = prod(5);
System.out.println(p);
```

(A) 10

(B) 100

(C) 120

(D) None of the above

For Questions 5 - 6, refer to the following method.

```java
public void func(int n)
{
  if (n == 0)
  {
    System.out.print(" ");
  }
  else
  {
    System.out.print(n + " ");
    func(n - 1);
  }
}
```

5) What will be the output if we pass the integer 3 to the method?

(A) 3 2 1

(B) 3 2

(C) 3 2 1 0

(D) None of the above

Assume we replace the else block of the method with the code below.

```java
else
{
  System.out.println(n);
  func(--n);
  return;
}
```

6) What will be the output if we pass the integer 3 to the updated method?

(A) 3 2 1

(B) 3 2

(C) 3 2 1 0

(D) None of the above

7) Which of the following statement is true?

I. Recursion can be used in two-dimensional array problems.

II. Divide and conquer algorithms can use recursion.

III. The worst case for linear search occurs when the item is the last element in the array.

(A) I only

(B) II only

(C) I and III

(D) I, II, and II

8) Consider the following code segment.

```
public int bin(int n, int k)
{
  if (k == 0 || n == k)
  {
    return 1;
  }
  else
  {
    return bin(n - 1, k - 1) + bin(n - 1, k);
  }
}
```

What will be returned by the above code if we pass n = 8 and k = 3?

(A) 56

(B) 24

(C) 15

(D) 36

9) Consider the following code segment.

```
public void bin(int n, int k)
{
  if (k == 0 || n == k)
  {
    return 1;
  }
  else
  {
    return bin(n - 1, k - 1) + bin(n - 1, k);
  }
}
```

What will be returned by the above code if we pass n = 10 and k = 5?

(A) 56

(B) 182

(C) 252

(D) 256

10) If the user enters a positive integer, the `printEvent()` method should print out all the even numbers between 1 and that positive integer using recursion.

```
public void printEven(int num)
{
  if (num == 1)
  {
     return;
  }
  else
  {
    // Code goes here
  }
}
```

Which of the following code segments is appropriate for the else block?

```
(A) if (num % 2 == 0)
    {
       System.out.println(num);
    }
    printEven(num - 1);
```

```
(B) while (num >1)
    {
       if(num % 2 == 0)
       {
         System.out.println(num);
       }
       num = num - 1;
    }
```

```
(C) for (int i = 0; i < num; i++)
    {
       if (num % 2 == 0)
       {
          System.out.println(num);
       }
       num = num-1;
    }
```

(D) None of the above

11) Which of the following sorting algorithms uses recursion?

I. Insertion Sort

II. Mergesort

III. Selection Sort

(A) I only

(B) II only

(C) I and III

(D) II and III

12) Consider the following method.

```
public int pro(int x)
{
  if(x == 1)
  {
    return x;
  }
  else
  {
    return x * pro(x-2);
  }
}
```

What will be returned by pro(5)?

(A) 15

(B) 120

(C) 1

(D) None of the above

13) Which of the following techniques is used by selection sort?

(A) Insert

(B) Delete

(C) Random

(D) Swap

14) Sequential search is also known as

(A) Binary search

(B) Linear search

(C) Random search

(D) Circular search

For Questions 15 - 16, consider the following code segment representing linear search.

```
public int search(int[] a, int key)
{
  int size = a.length;
  for (int i = 0;i < size; i++)
  {
    if (a[i] == key)
    {
      return i;
    }
  }
  return -1;
}
```

15) If an integer array has the following elements 12, 81, 19, 45, and 89 and has been passed to the search method with a key of 81, what does the above method return?

(A) 1

(B) 2

(C) 3

(D) -1

16) If an integer array has the following elements 10, 20, 45, 60, and 70 and has been passed to the search method with a key of 11, what does the above method return?

(A) 1

(B) 2

(C) -1

(D) 0

For Questions 17 - 18, consider the following class.

```
public class Merge
{
  int[] a;
  int[] temp;
  int length;

  public void sort(int Arr[])
  {
    this.a = Arr;
    this.length = Arr.length;
    this.temp = new int[length];
    doMerge(0, length - 1);
  }
  private void doMerge(int low, int high)
  {
    if (low < high)
    {
      int mid = lowerIndex + (higherIndex - lowerIndex) / 2;
      doMergeSort(low, mid);
      doMergeSort(mid+ 1, high);
      mergeBoth(low, mid, high);
    }
  }
  private void mergeBoth(int low, int mid, int high)
  {
    for (int i = low; i <= high; i++)
    {
      temp[i] = a[i];
    }
    int i = low;
    int j = mid+ 1;
    int k = low;
    while (i <= mid && j <= high)
    {
      if (temp[i] <= temp[j])
      {
        a[k] = temp[i];
        i++;
      }
      else
      {
```

```
        a[k] = temp[j];
        j++;
      }
      k++;
    }
    while (i <= mid)
    {
      a[k] = temp[i];
      k++;
      i++;
    }
  }
  public static void main(String [] args)
  {
    // code goes here
  }
}
```

17) If we want to print the sorted version of the following array: [14 3 19 2 11 89 77], which of the following code segments needs to be placed in the main method?

```
(A) int[] input = {14, 3, 19, 2, 11, 89, 77};
    Merge m = new Merge();
    m.sort(input);
    for (int i : input)
    {
      System.out.print(i + " ");
    }
```

```
(B) Merge m = new Merge();
    m.doMerge(input);
```

```
(C) for (int i : input)
    {
      System.out.print(i + " ");
    }
```

(D) None of the above

18) If [33 11 55 44 77 66 10] is given as the input, from which number do the comparisons start?

(A) 55

(B) 44

(C) 77

(D) 11

19) Sorting algorithms for a particular data is chosen based on which factor(s) of the following

(A) Input data size

(B) Run-time efficiency

(C) Space utilization

(D) all of the above

20) Which of the following statements are true based on the following condition?

i = 0, a[i] < a[k] where a[k] is the last element

I. a[i] is the smallest element in the array

II. a[k] is the highest element in the array

III. k+1 is the size of the array.

(A) I only

(B) II only

(C) III only

(D) II and III

For Questions 21 - 22, consider the following sorting method.

```
public static int[] sort(int[] arr)
{
  int temp;
  for (int i = 0; i < arr.length - 1; i++)
  {
    for (int j = 1; j < arr.length - i; j++)
    {
      if (arr[j - 1] > arr[j])
      {
        temp = arr[j - 1];
        arr[j - 1] = arr[j];
        arr[j] = temp;
      }
    }
  }
  return arr;
}
```

21) If we pass an array to the method above, in what form will the method return it?

(A) In descending order

(B) In ascending order

(C) Unsorted

(D) Run time error

22) If [10 9 2 15 11] is passed to the method, what will the array be after the second iteration of the outer loop?

(A) [9 10 2 15 11]

(B) [9 2 10 11 15]

(C) [2 9 10 11 15]

(D) [10 9 11 15 2]

23) Which of the following statements are true?

I. Mergesort uses divide and conquer technique.

II. Insertion sort can be applied efficiently to large amount of data.

III. A list must be sorted in order to use binary search on it.

(A) I only

(B) II only

(C) I and III

(D) II and III

24) On an average case how many comparisons are required for selection sort?

(A) n!

(B) n - 1

(C) n / 2

(D) nlogn

Answers and Explanations

Answer Key

1. C
2. D
3. B
4. C
5. A
6. A
7. D
8. A
9. C
10. A
11. B
12. A
13. D
14. B
15. A
16. C
17. A
18. B
19. D
20. C
21. B
22. C
23. C
24. C

Explanations

1) (C) A recursive method is a method that calls itself within its body.

2) (D) Recursion does not work well with large amount of data. It is inefficient and can cause a memory issue.

3) (B) Choice B is the only choice that demonstrates recursion. It successfully models the while loop. It would not work if we could not assume that n was greater than or equal to 1.

4) (C) The calculation becomes the factorial of 5 which equals 5 x 4 x 3 x 2 x 1 = 120.

5) (A) This recursive method is like a for loop and gets called from 3 to 0 and prints out 3 2 1.

6) **(A)** The new else block has the same functionality as the first one. If the `--  --n` was `n--  --` we would have an infinite loop.

7) **(D)** All of the statements are true. Recursion can be applied in many cases and two worst cases for linear search are if the key is the last element or if the key is not in the list.

8) **(A)** This can take a while to evaluate but it's recursion and you have to keep making method calls until you get to `k = 0` or `n = k`.

9) **(C)** Same methodology as the previous question.

10) **(A)** Choices B and C aren't recursive. Choice A implements recursion and correctly checks whether `num` is even.

11) **(B)** Mergesort is the only sorting algorithm we have gone over that uses recursion.

12) **(A)** Evaluate the recursive method. x iterates down, going from 5 to 3 to 1.

13) **(D)** Selection sort swaps the start of the list with the smallest element in the list.

14) **(B)** Sequential search and linear search are interchangeable terms.

15) **(A)** The code represents linear search. 81 is the element at index 1.

16) **(C)** The code represents linear search. The key is not in the array so -1 is returned.

17) **(A)** The code represents mergesort. Choice A is the only choice that uses the `sort()` method, the right method to correctly arrange the array.

18) **(B)** The code represents mergesort. It first compares the middle element, as seen in the `doMerge` method.

19) **(D)** Input data size, run-time efficiency, and space utilization all influence sorting algorithm choice.

20) **(C)** I and II are not guaranteed as it isn't said the the array is sorted. `k + 1` must be the size if `a[k]` is the last element.

21) **(B)** The code models selection sort and orders the code in ascending order.

22) **(C)** Insertion sort does not work well with a large amount of data as it becomes a very slow process.

23) **(C)** The first condition becomes `false` and the second condition `true` so Line 2 is printed out and the if-else statement stops evaluating as soon as one block is executed.

24) **(C)** Selection sort required `n / 2` comparisons because the average array will be half sorted and half unsorted.

Practice Test 1

Multiple Choice Portion

COMPUTER SCIENCE A

SECTION I

Time - 1 hour and 15 minutes

Number of questions - 40

Percent of total grade - 50

Directions: Determine the answer for each of the following questions or incomplete statements, using the available space for any necessary scratch work. Then decide which is the best of the choices given and fill in the corresponding oval on the answer sheet. No credit will be given for anything written in the examination booklet. Do not spend too much time on any one problem.

Notes:

- Assume that the classes listed in Quick Reference found in the Appendix have been imported where appropriate.
- Assume that declarations of variables and methods appear within the context of an enclosing class.
- Assume that method calls are not prefixed with an object or class name and are not shown within a complete class definition appear within the context of an enclosing class.
- Unless otherwise noted in the question, assume that parameters in method calls are not `null`.

1) Consider the following code segment.

```
int a = 0;
int i = 4;

while (a < 4)
{
  a = a + 4;
  System.out.println(a + " ");
}
```

What is the output of above code segment?

(A) Nothing, the loop terminates at start

(B) 4 5

(C) 4

(D) 0 4

(E) 4 4

2) Consider the incomplete method below. The method square() is intended to return the square of number passed to it.

```
public int square(int x)
{
  // missing code
}
```

Which of the code segments shown below can be used to replace // missing code so that square() will work as intended?

(A) return x * x;

(B) return x ^ 2;

(C) return x * 2;

(D) All of the above

(E) None of the above

3) Consider the following code segment.

```
String l = "zeshan";

for (int i = l.length() - 1; i >= 0; i--)
{
   System.out.print(l.charAt[i]);
}
```

What is the output of above code segment?

(A) shanze

(B) nshzea

(C) hzeasn

(D) nahsez

(E) None of the above

4) Consider the incomplete method below. The method index() is intended to return the index of number passed to it in the array. If the number is not found, the method returns -1.

```
public int index(int x)
{
   int[] array={1,2,3,5};

   // missing code
}
```

Which of the code segments shown below can be used to replace // missing code so that index() will work as intended?

```
(A) for (int i = 0; i < 4; i++)
    {
      if (x == array[i])
      {
        return i;
      }
    }
    return -1;
```

```
(B) for (int i = 0; i < 4; i++)
    {
      if (x == array[i])
      {
        return i;
      }
      else
      {
        return i;
      }
    }
    return -1;
```

```
(C) for (int i = 0; i < 4; i++)
    {
      if (x == array[i])
      {
        return i;
      }
    }
```

```
(D) for (int i = 0; i < 4; i++)
    {
      if (x == array[i])
      {
        return i;
      }
      else
      {
        return i;
      }
    }
```

(E) None of the above

5) Consider the following method.

```
public void checkMarks(int x)
{
  if (x <= 40)
  {
    System.out.println("You have failed ");
  }
  else if (x >= 60)
  {
    System.out.println("You have passed ");
  }
  else
  {
    System.out.println("We are sorry ");
  }
}
```

What is printed as a result of the call `checkMarks(50)`?

(A) `We are sorry`

(B) `You have passed`

(C) `You have failed`

(D) `You have failed We are sorry`

(E) None of these

6) The Java compiler _____.

(A) Translates Java source code to byte code

(B) Creates classes

(C) Creates executable files

(D) Produces the Java interpreter

(E) All of above

7) Consider the following code segment.

```
String str = new String("Zeshan");
System.out.println(str.length());
```

What is the output of the above code?

(A) 0

(B) 7

(C) 6

(D) 5

(E) None of the above

8) Consider the following code segment.

```
int s = 0;
int j = 0;
int f = 3;
int temp = (j * 4) + (f * f);
System.out.println(temp);
```

What is the output of above code segment?

(A) 9

(B) 0

(C) 3

(D) 6

(E) None of the above

9) Consider the following code segment.

```
System.out.printf("%s\n%s\n%s\n", "*", "***", "*****");
```

What is the output of above code segment?

(A) * *** *****

(B) *
    ***
    ****

(C) *
    ***
    *****

(D) *****
    ****
    *

(E) *
    ****
    *****

10) Every class declaration must begin with which of the following keywords?

(A) `public`

(B) `static`

(C) `protected`

(D) `private`

(E) None of above

11) Consider the following method grade().

```
public void grade(int studentGrade)
{
  if (studentGrade >= 90)
  {
    System.out.println("A");
  }
  else if (studentGrade >= 80)
  {
    System.out.println("B");
  }
  else if (studentGrade >= 70)
  {
    System.out.println("C");
  }
  else if (studentGrade >= 60)
  {
    System.out.println("D");
  }
  else
  {
    System.out.println("F");
  }
}
```

What is printed as a result of the call grade(59)?

(A) A

(B) F

(C) D

(D) B

(E) None of the above

12) Assume that variables x and y are of type `double`.

```
!(x < y) && !(x > y)
```

The expression above is equivalent to which of the following?

(A) `true`

(B) `false`

(C) `x == y`

(D) `x != y`

(E) `!(x < y) && (x > y)`

13) Consider the following code segment.

```
int x = 24;
int y = 30;
while (y != 30)
{
   int z = x % y;
   x = y;
   y = z;
}

System.out.println(x);
```

What is the output of above code segment?

(A) 0

(B) 6

(C) 12

(D) 24

(E) 30

14) Consider the following code segment.

```
public class MyClass
{
  public MyClass()
  {
    // code
  }

  // more code
}
```

To instantiate MyClass, which of the following statements should you use?

(A) MyClass mc = new MyClass();

(B) MyClass mc = MyClass();

(C) MyClass mc = new MyClass;

(D) MyClass mc = MyClass;

(E) None of the above

15) Consider the following code segment.

```
submarine.drive(depth);
```

Which of the following statements must be true?

(A) submarine is a class and drive is a method

(B) drive is a class and submarine is a method

(C) submarine is a variable

(D) drive is a variable

(E) None of the above

For Questions 16 - 18, refer to the following code.

```
public class Person
{
  private String name;
  private int age;

  public person(String name, int age)
  {
    this.name = name;
    this.age = age;
  }
  public int getName()
  {
    return name;
  }
  public int getAge()
  {
    return age;
  }
  public void setName(String name)
  {
    this.name = Name;
  }
}
```

16) Which of the following code segments correctly accesses the name attribute?

```
I.    Person p = new Person("zeshan", 14);
      String name = p.getName();
```

```
II.   Person p = new Person("zeshan", 14);
      String name;
      name = p.getName();
```

```
III.  Person p = new Person(zeshan, 14);
      String name = p.getName();
```

(A) I only

(B) II only

(C) I and II

(D) I, II and III

(E) III only

17) Which of the following code segments correctly sets "zeshan" to be the name of the AccessPerson object?

I. `AccessPerson.setName(zeshan);`

II. `AccessPerson.setName("zeshan");`

III. `Person AccessPerson = new Person(ali, 14);`
     `AccessPerson.setName("zeshan");`

(A) I only

(B) I and III only

(C) I, II and III

(D) III only

(E) II only

18) Which of the following code segments does not compile?

```
I.    Person p = new Person(zeshan, 14);
      String name = p.getName();
```

```
II.   Person p = new Person(zeshan, 14);
      name = p.getName();
```

```
III.  Person p = new Person("zeshan", 14);
      String name = p.getName();
```

(A) I, II and III

(B) I only

(C) II only

(D) III only

(E) I and II

19) Consider the following code segment.

```
int x = 5;
int y = 2;
System.out.println(x / y - (double) (x / y));
```

What will be printed after running this code?

(A) 0

(B) 1

(C) 0.5

(D) 5.5

(E) None of the above

20) Consider the following code segment.

```
if (x > 2)
{
    x = x * 2;
}
else if (x > 4)
{
    x = 0;
}
```

Which of the following code segments is equivalent to the code above?

```
I.    x + 4;
```

```
II.   if (x > 2)
      {
          x = x * 2;
      }
```

```
III.  if (x > 4)
      {
          x = 0;
      }
```

(A) I only

(B) II only

(C) III only

(D) I, II and III

(E) None of the above

For Questions 21 - 22, refer to the following code segment.

```
Object o = "abc";
boolean b = o.equals("a,b,c");

Object o2 = b;
String t = (String) o;

System.out.println(o2);
System.out.println(o == t);
```

21) What will be the result of the execution of the following statement?

```
System.out.println(o2);
```

I. true

II. false

III. Compile time error

(A) II only

(B) I only

(C) III only

(D) I and II

(E) None

22) What will be the result of the execution of the following statement?

```
System.out.println(o == t);
```

I. true

II. false

III. Compile time error

(A) I only

(B) II only

(C) III only

(D) I and III

(E) None

23) Consider the following code segment.

```
1   Integer i = new Integer(0);
2   if (!(i.equals(0)))
3   {
4       System.out.println(i + " does not equal to " + 0);
5   }
6   else
7   {
8       System.out.println("Done");
9   }
```

Which of the following is true?

I. The code will not compile

II. Done will be printed out

III. There is an error on Line 1

(A) I only

(B) I and III only

(C) II only

(D) I and II only

(E) III only

24) Consider the following code segment.

```
double a = Math.random();
double b;
```

Which of the following statements can be used to assign b a random value in between 0.5 and 5.5?

(A) b = a + 0.5;

(B) b = a + 0.5 * 5.0;

(C) b = a * 5.0;

(D) b = a * 5.0 + 0.5;

(E) b = a * 5.5;

25) Consider the following class declarations.

```
public class ClassOne
{
  private int x;

  public ClassOne()
  {
    x = 0;
  }

  public ClassOne(int y)
  {
    x = y;
  }
}
```

```
public class ClassTwo
{
  public ClassTwo()
  {
    super(0);
  }
}
```

Which of the following statements will not successfully compile?

(A) `ClassOne c1 = new ClassOne();`

(B) `ClassOne c2 = new ClassOne(5);`

(C) `ClassOne c3 = new ClassTwo();`

(D) `ClassTwo c4 = new ClassTwo();`

(E) `ClassTWo c5 = new ClassTwo(5);`

26) Consider the following code segment.

```
for (int k = 0; k < 20; k = k + 2)
{
   if (k % 3 == 1)
   {
      System.out.print(k + " ");
   }
}
```

What will be displayed upon execution of the code?

(A) 4 10 16

(B) 4 5 6 7 2 4 5

(C) 3

(D) 5 64 22 33

(E) None of the above

27) Consider the following code segment.

```
int a = 6;
int b = 4;
int c = 3;
a -= b + c;
b += a - c;
c -= a + b;
System.out.println(a + " " + b + " " + c);
```

What will be displayed upon execution of the code?

(A) -1 2 4

(B) -2 4 -1

(C) 4 2 1

(D) -1 0 4

(E) 4 3 6

For Questions 28 - 29, refer to following code.

```
public int f(int y)
{
  return y + 2;
}



public int g(int y)
{
  return y * 2;
}
```

28) What will be printed when we execute the following code segment?

```
int y = 1;
y += f(g(6)) - g(f(6));
System.out.println(y);
```

(A) 0

(B) -1

(C) -2

(D) 3

(E) 4

29) What will be printed when we execute the following code segment?

```
int y = 1;
y += f(g(2)) - g(f(4));
System.out.println(y);
```

(A) -4

(B) -6

(C) -8

(D) -2

(E) 1

For Questions 30 - 31, refers to the following code.

```
int y = 1;
int x = 123;
while (x > 0)
{
   y *= 10;
   y += x % 10;
   x /= 10;
}
```

30) What will be printed when we execute the following code segment?

```
System.out.println(y);
```

(A) 1000

(B) 1320

(C) 1321

(D) 1329

(E) None of the above

31) What will be printed when we execute the following code segment?

```
System.out.println(x);
```

(A) 0

(B) 1

(C) 2

(D) 3

(E) 4

For Questions 32 - 34, refer to the following code.

```
public static void divider(int[] a, int[] q, int[] r)
{
  q[0] = a[0] / 5;
  r[0] = a[0] % 5;
}
```

32) What will be printed when we execute the following code segment?

```
int[] x = {21, 22, 23};
int[] y = new int[3];
int[] z = {21, 22, 23};

divider(x, y, z);
System.out.println(x[0]);
```

(A) 41

(B) 31

(C) 21

(D) 0

(E) 33

33) What will be printed when we execute the following code segment?

```
int[] x = {21, 22, 23};
int[] y = new int[3];
int[] z = {21, 22, 23};

divider(x, y, z);
System.out.println(y[1]);
```

(A) 0

(B) 1

(C) 2

(D) 3

(E) 4

34) What will be printed when we execute the following code segment?

```
int[] x = {21, 22, 23};
int[] y = new int[3];
int[] z = {21, 22, 23};

divider(x, y, z);
System.out.println(z[2]);
```

(A) 21

(B) 22

(C) 23

(D) 24

(E) 25

35) Consider the following code segment.

```
int x = 2005;

for (int j = 0; j < 50; j++)
{
   x = (x + 3) / 2;
}
```

What will the value of x be after the code has been executed?

(A) 0

(B) 1

(C) 2

(D) 3

(E) 65

36) Consider the following code segment.

```
int x = 0;

if (<condition 1>)
{
   x++;
}
if (<condition 2>)
{
   x++;
}
if (<condition 3>)
{
   x++;
}
```

Assume that none of the conditions can influence the value of x. What are the possible final values of x after the code segment is executed?

(A) 0 only

(B) 1 only

(C) 0 or 1

(D) 1, 2, or 3

(E) 0, 1, 2, or 3

37) Consider the following code segment.

```
int odd = 1;

if(odd)
{
  System.out.println("odd");
}
else
{
  System.out.println("even");
}
```

Which of the following statements is always true?

I. "Odd" will be printed

II. "Even" will be printed

III. A compile time error will occur

(A) I only

(B) II only

(C) III only

(D) I and II

(E) II and III

38) Consider the following code segment.

```
1  int x = 0;
2  while (1)
3  {
4    System.out.print("x plus one is " + (x + 1));
5  }
```

Which of the following statements is true?

I. Syntax error in Line 1

II. Syntax error in Line 2

III. An infinite loop will occur

(A) I only

(B) II only

(C) I and II

(D) I and III

(E) III only

39) Which of the following statements legally declares, constructs, and initializes an array?

(A) `int[] myList = {"1", "2", "3"};`

(B) `int[] myList = {5, 8, 2};`

(C) `int[] myList = {5, 8, "2"};`

(D) `int[] myList = {"5", 8, 2};`

(E) `int[] myList = {5, 8, 2}`

40) Consider the following code segment.

```
double d = Math.round(2.5 + Math.random());
System.out.println(d);
```

What will be the output of the above code?

(A) `2.0`

(B) `3.0`

(C) `4.0`

(D) `5.0`

(E) `4.5`

Free Response Portion

COMPUTER SCIENCE A

SECTION II

Time - 1 hour and 45 minutes

Number of questions - 4

Percent of total grade - 50

Directions: SHOW ALL YOUR WORK. REMEMBER THAT PROGRAM SEGMENTS ARE TO BE WRITTEN IN JAVA.

Notes:

- Assume that the classes listed in Quick Reference found in the Appendix have been imported where appropriate.
- Unless otherwise noted in the question, assume that parameters in method calls are not null and the methods are called only when their preconditions are satisfied.
- In writing solutions for each question, you may use any of the accessible methods that are listed in classes defined in that question. Writing significant amounts of code that can be replaced by a call to one of these methods may not receive full credit.

1) This question involves reasoning about one-dimensional and two-dimensional arrays of integers. You will write 3 static methods, all of which are in a single enclosing class, named `CalculateArray` (not shown). The first method returns the sum of first and last element of a one-dimensional array. The second method returns the total amount of prime numbers in a one-dimensional array. The third method returns the sum of diagonal elements of a specified two-dimensional array.

(a) Write a static method "'sumFi" that calculates and returns the sum of the first and last elements of the one-dimensional array received by the method.

```
public static int sumFi(int[] arr)
```

(b) Write a static method `primeCount` that determines and returns the number of the prime numbers in the one-dimensional array received by the method.

```
public static int primeCount(int[] arr)
```

(c) Write a static method `diagonalSum` that calculates and returns the sum of diagonal elements of the specified two-dimensional array (below).

```
3    4    5
7   66    6
4    2   21
```

```
public static int diagonalSum()
{
   int[][] arr = {{3, 4, 5}, {7, 66, 6}, {4, 2, 21}};
```

2) This question involves reasoning about `boolean` methods. You will write two static methods, all of which are in a single enclosing class, named `EqualityCheck` (not shown). The first method returns `true` if three `int` values received by the method are equal to each other; the second method returns `true` if none of the three `int` values received by the method are equal.

(a) Write a static method `allEquals` that returns `true` if the three `int` values the method receives are equal. All 3 values should be equal to each other. If they are not equal, the method should return `false`.

```
public static boolean allEquals(int a, int b, int c)
```

(b) Write a static method noneEquals that returns true if none of the three int values received by the method are equal. This means that all 3 values received should be unique for true to be returned. If two or more values are equal to each other, the method should return false.

```
public static boolean noneEquals(int a, int b, int c)
```

3) An online bank system takes care of many functions, most notably the user account withdrawal, deposit, and pin verification. The information is updated or validated with the Account class given below.

```
public class Account
{
  int availableBalance;
  int pin;

  public Account(int balance, int pin)
  {
    this.pin = pin;
    availableBalance = balance;
  }

  public boolean validatePin(int pin)
  {
    // implementation needed
  }

  public void withdraw(int amount)
  {
    // implementation needed
  }

  public void deposit(int amount)
  {
    // implementation needed
  }
}
```

(a) Write the implementation of the `validatePin` method takes a pin and check whether it is equal to the stored pin or not. If it is equal, `true` is returned and `false` otherwise.

```
public boolean validatePin(int pin)
```

(b) Write the implementation for the deposit method that takes the value given to it and increases the balance of the account accordingly.

```
public void deposit(int amount)
```

(c) Write the implementation for the `withdraw` method that takes the value given to it and decreases the balance of the account accordingly.

```
public void withdraw(int amount)
```

4) This question involves reasoning about Strings. You have to implement two related methods that appear in the same class (not shown). The first method takes a single String parameter and returns the palindrome of it, or the reverse of it. The second method takes the reverse string and returns the String in its correct form.

(a) Write a method `palindrome`, which takes a String and returns the reverse of it. If the String is empty, the method returns `String is empty`.

Value Given	Value Returned
"moksh"	"hskom"
""	String is empty

```
public static String palindrome(String s)
```

(b) Write a method `initialString`, which takes a reverse String and returns the correct version of it. If the String is empty, the method returns `String is empty`.

Value Given	Value Returned
"hskom"	"moksh"
String is empty	""""

```
public static String initialString(String s)
```

Answers and Explanations

Answer Key (Section I)

1. C
2. A
3. D
4. E
5. A
6. E
7. C
8. A
9. C
10. A
11. B
12. B
13. D
14. A
15. A
16. C
17. E
18. E
19. E
20. B
21. A
22. A
23. C
24. D
25. E
26. A
27. D
28. B
29. B
30. C
31. A
32. C
33. A
34. C
35. D

36. **E**

37. **C**

38. **B**

39. **B**

40. **B**

Explanations

Section I

1) **(C)** The while loop terminates only after the while loop is implemented once since the condition is no longer satisfied when a = 4.

2) **(A)** The value of x ^ 2 can only be represented as x * x or as Math.pow(x, 2). All other implementations are incorrect.

3) **(D)** The function is reversing any string that is placed as a parameter, in this case, the String "zeshan". The function is printing the last character first, the second to last character second, etc., thereby reversing the string.

4) **(E)** None of these implementations of code set the else code to return -1. All of them return i or there is no implementation of the else method.

5) **(A)** The value 50 doesn't satisfy the if condition or the if else condition.

6) **(E)** The Java compiler's main functions relate to converting the user given code into code that can be read by the machine.

7) **(C)** The length of the string str is 6.

8) **(A)** If the order of operations is followed: temp = (0) + (9) = 9.

9) **(C)** This output has the various Strings on separate lines and each line has the correct number of Strings.

10) **(A)** We make classes public so that they can interact with other classes.

11) **(B)** The value of 59 only satisfies the condition of else.

12) **(B)** Since the boolean expression is true && false which produces false since the && operator requires both statements to be true for the expression to come out true.

13) **(D)** The condition of the while loop isn't satisfied, therefore the code in the while loop will not be executed.

14) **(A)** The constructor has no parameters and the object is declared correctly.

15) **(A)** The basic syntax is class.methodName(parameters).

16) **(C)** Only I and II pass Strings as the first argument when the constructor method is called.

17) **(E)** Only II uses a String when it is needed.

18) **(E)** In I, zeshan isn't in quotation marks and in II, the data type of the variable name isn't declared.

19) **(E)** The output is 0.0 based on the (in order) parenthesis, `double` cast, division and subtraction.

20) **(B)** If the first condition is `true`, the second one has to be `true` as well. Since this is an if-else statement, the second else if block will never get executed because the first one will become `true` first.

21) **(A)** o doesn't equal "a,b,c".

22) **(A)** o equals `t`.

23) **(C)** The code is implemented correctly and accurately.

24) **(D)** `Math.random()` produces values between 0 and 1 and when multiplied by 5 the values produced range from 0 and 5. When we add 0.5, the values range from 0.5 to 5.

25) **(E)** `ClassTwo` doesn't have a constructor that has one parameter.

26) **(A)** The values of `k` that will be tested are 2, 4, 6, 8, 10, 12, 14, 16, 18, and 20. The only values of `k` such that `k % 3 = 1` are 4, 10, and 16.

27) **(D)** The value ends up being `a = 6 - (4 + 3) = -1`. `b` ends up being `b = 4 + (-1 - 3) = 0`. `c` ends up being `c = 3 - (-1) = 4`.

28) **(B)** When the values of `f(g(6))` and `g(f(6))` are solved out the value of y becomes 1 - 2 = -1.

29) **(B)** The values of `f(g(2))` and `g(f(4))` are solved out the value of y becomes 6 - 12 = -6.

30) **(C)** The various values of y are 10, 13, 130, 132, 1320, and 1321. (Remember, the decimal truncates!)

31) **(A)** The while loop ends only when the value of `x` isn't greater than 0 and 0 is the only value that isn't greater than 0.

32) **(C)** The value of `x[0]` doesn't change.

33) **(A)** The value of `y[1]` is 0 because the `y[1]` was never set to any other value.

34) **(C)** The value of `z[2]` doesn't change.

35) **(D)** the value of x changes until x = 3. [(3 + 3) / 2 =3]

36) **(E)** If all the conditions were satisfied the value of x would be 3, and if some were satisfied the value of x could be 1 or 2. If none of the conditions were satisfied the value of x is 0.

37) **(C)** The expression `odd` isn't a `boolean` expression.

38) **(B)** The expression `1` isn't a `boolean` expression.

39) **(B)** Only Choice B follows the basic syntax for declaring and initializing an array.

40) **(B)** The value at maximum is less than 1 and only when the expression `(2.5 + Math.random())` equals 3.5 the value will be equal to 4.0.

Section II

1)

(a)

```
public static int sumFi(int[] arr)
{
  return arr[0] + arr[arr.length - 1];
}
```

Access the first and last elements of the array and add them together.

(b)

```
public static int primeCount(int[] arr)
{
  int primeNumbersSum = 0;

  for (int n = 0; n < arr.length; n++)
  {
    boolean prime = true;

    for (int j = 2; j < arr[n].length; j++)
    {
      if (arr[n] % j == 0 )
      {
        prime = false;
        break;
      }
    }

    if (prime && arr[n] != 1)
    {
      primeNumbersSum++;
    }
  }

  return primeNumbersSum;
}
```

Iterate through all of the elements of the array and use another for loop and modulus to find the prime numbers. Keep count of the number of prime numbers.

(c)

```java
public static int diagonalSum()
{
  int[][] arr = {{3, 4, 5}, {7, 66, 6}, {4, 2, 21}};

  int diagSum = 0;

  for (int i = 0; i < arr.length; i++)
  {
    for (int j = 0; j < arr[i].length; j++)
    {
      if (i == j)
      {
        diagSum += arr[i][j];
      }
    }
  }

  return diagSum;
}
```

Use 2 for loops to iterate through the array and check for when the indices of the row and column are equal to know that you have encountered a diagonal element.

2)

(a)

```
public static boolean allEquals(int a, int b, int c)
{
  if (a == b && b == c)
  {
    return true;
  }
  else
  {
    return false;
  }
}
```

Use an if statement to see if all of the elements are equal to each other and return a value accordingly.

(b)

```
public static boolean noneEquals(int a, int b, int c)
{
  if (a != b && b!= c && a != c)
  {
    return true;
  }
  else
  {
    return false;
  }
}
```

Use an if statement to see if all of the elements are NOT equal to each other and return a value accordingly.

3)

(a)

```
public boolean validatePin(int pin)
{
  if (pin == this.pin)
  {
    return true;
  }
  else
  {
    return false;
  }
}
```

Use an if statement to compare the pins and return a value accordingly.

(b)

```
public void deposit(int amount)
{
  availableBalance += amount;
}
```

Increase the balance accordingly.

(c)

```
public void withdraw(int amount)
{
  availableBalance -= amount;
}
```

Decrease the balance accordingly.

4)

(a)

```
public static String palindrome(String s)
{
  if (s == "")
  {
    return "String is empty";
  }

  String reversed = "";

  for (int i = s.length() - 1; i >= 0; i--)
  {
    reversed = reversed + s.substring(i, i + 1);
    System.out.println(reversed);
  }

  System.out.println(reversed);
}
```

Use a for loop to iterate through each letter of the String from right to left and append each letter to the returned String.

(b)

```
public static String initialString(String s)
{
  if (s == "")
  {
    return "String is empty";
  }

  String initial = "";

  for (int i = s.length() - 1; i >= 0; i--)
  {
    initial = initial + s.substring(i, i + 1);
    System.out.println(initial);
  }

  System.out.println(initial);
}
```

Same code as last part.

Practice Test 2

Multiple Choice Portion

COMPUTER SCIENCE A

SECTION I

Time - 1 hour and 15 minutes

Number of questions - 40

Percent of total grade - 50

Directions: Determine the answer for each of the following questions or incomplete statements, using the available space for any necessary scratch work. Then decide which is the best of the choices given and fill in the corresponding oval on the answer sheet. No credit will be given for anything written in the examination booklet. Do not spend too much time on any one problem.

Notes:

- Assume that the classes listed in Quick Reference found in the Appendix have been imported where appropriate.
- Assume that declarations of variables and methods appear within the context of an enclosing class.
- Assume that method calls are not prefixed with an object or class name and are not shown within a complete class definition appear within the context of an enclosing class.
- Unless otherwise noted in the question, assume that parameters in method calls are not null.

1) Consider the following code segment.

```
while (0 > 4)
{
  System.out.println("You are hacked");
}
```

What is the output of the above code segment?

I. Compile time error

II. You are hacked

III. Loop prints infinitely

(A) I only

(B) II only

(C) III only

(D) II and III

(E) None

2) Consider the following code segment.

```
1  int i = 0;
2  while (i < 4)
3  {
4    System.out.println("Infinite loop");
5  }
```

How many times is Line 4 executed?

(A) 4

(B) Infinite times

(C) 0

(D) 5

(E) 3

For Questions 3 - 4, refer to the following code.

```
public static int sum(int[] a)
{
    int result = 0;
    String newName = "name";

    for (int i = 0; i < a.length; i++)
    {
        result = result + a[i];
    }
    newName = name + "1";
    return result;
}
```

3) Consider the following code segment.

```
int[] array= {1, 2, 3, 4, 5, 7};
sum(array);
```

What is the value of `result` when the `sum(array)` call is made?

(A) 22

(B) 33

(C) 44

(D) 55

(E) 66

4) Consider the following code segment.

```
int[] array= {1, 2, 3, 4, 5, 7};
sum(array);
```

What is the value of newName when the sum(array) call is made?

(A) name1

(B) name

(C) 12345

(D) 54321

(E) 12111

5) Consider the incomplete method. The method `checkLength()` is intended to return the length of the String passed to it.

```
public int checkLength(String s)
{
  // missing code
}
```

Which of the code segments shown below can be used to replace `// missing code` so that `checkLength()` will work as intended?

```
(A) int length = s.length;
    return length;
```

```
(B) int length = s.length();
    return length;
```

```
(C) length = s.length();
    return length;
```

```
(D) int length = length();
    return length;
```

(E) None of the above

6) Consider the incomplete method. The method indexElement() is intended to return the element at specified index passed. The possible indices are 0, 1, 2, and 3.

```
public int index(int x)
{
  int[] array = {1, 2, 3, 5};

  // missing code
}
```

Which of the code segments shown below can be used to replace // missing code so that index() will work as intended?

```
(A) int element = array[x];
```

```
(B) int element = array[x];
    return element;
```

```
(C) element = array[x];
    return element;
```

```
(D) int element = array;
    return element;
```

(E) None of the above

7) Consider the following code segment.

```
int values[] = {1, 2, 3, 4, 5, 6, 7, 8};

for (int i = 0; i < x; i++)
{
  System.out.println(values[i]);
}
```

What value of x will allow all elements in the values[] array to be printed out?

(A) 6

(B) 7

(C) 8

(D) 9

(E) 3

For Questions 8 - 9, refer to the following information.

```
1   public class Test
2   {
3     public static void main(String[] args)
4     {
5       int total = 0;
6       int[] i = new int[3];
7
8       for (int j = 1; j <= i.length; j++)
9       {
10        total += (i[j] = j);
11        System.out.println(total);
12      }
13    }
14  }
```

8) What is the output of the above program?

(A) 5

(B) 6

(C) 7

(D) All of the above

(E) None of the above; the system will throw an `ArrayIndexOutOfBoundsException`

9) What will be the output if we remove Line 3 of the `Test` class?

(A) Compile time error

(B) 5

(C) 6

(D) 7

(E) 9

10) Consider the following code with interface Calculate implemented by the Display class.

```
public interface Calculate
{
  int var = 0;
  void cal(int item);
}



public class Display implements Calculate
{
  int x;
  public void cal(int item)
  {
    if (item < 2)
    {
      x = var;
    }
    else
    {
      x = item * item;
    }
  }
}



public class Interfaces
{
  public static void main(String args[])
  {
    Display[] arr = new Display[3];

    for (int i = 0; i < 3; i++)
    {
      arr[i] = new display();
    }
    arr[0].cal(0);
    arr[1].cal(1);
    arr[2].cal(2);
    System.out.print(arr[0].x + " " + arr[1].x + " " + arr[2].x);
  }
}
```

What will the output be if the main method of `Interfaces` is executed?

(A) 0 1 2

(B) 0 2 4

(C) 0 4 2

(D) 0 0 4

(E) Compile time error

11) Consider the following code segment with parent class A and child class B.

```
public class A
{
  int i;
}



public class B extends A
{
  int j;
  public void display()
  {
    super.i = j + 1;
    System.out.println(j + " " + i);
  }
}



public class Inheritance
{
  public static void main(String args[])
  {
    B obj = new B();
    obj.i = 1;
    obj.j = 2;
    obj.display();
  }
}
```

What will the output be if the main method of Inheritance is executed?

(A) 2 2

(B) 3 3

(C) 2 3

(D) 3 2

(E) 4 2

12) What will be displayed upon execution of this code segment?

```
int[] myarr = new int[10];
for (int i = 0 ; i < myarr.length; i++)
{
  myarr[i] = i + 1;
}
for (int i = 0; i < myarr.length; i++)
{
  System.out.print(myarr[i]);
}
```

(A) 0 1 2 3 4 5 6 7 8 9

(B) 12345678910

(C) 1 2 3 4 5 6 7 8 9 10

(D) myarr 1 2 3 4 5 6 7 8 9 10

(E) None of the above

13) Consider the following code segment.

```
public class Output
{
  public static void main(String args[])
  {
    String c = "Hello I love java";
    boolean var;
    var = c.startsWith("hello");
    System.out.println(var);
  }
}
```

What is the output of the above code?

(A) true

(B) false

(C) 0

(D) 1

(E) 3

14) Consider the following code segment.

```
String s1 = new String("AbraCadabra");
String s3;
s3 = s1.substring(1, 5);
System.out.println(s3);
```

What is the output of the above code?

(A) braC

(B) baCILLO

(C) AbraC

(D) raCI

(E) braCI

15) What will be displayed upon execution of this code segment?

```
int [] a = {1, 2, 3, 4, 5, 6, 7, 8, 9, 10};
for (int i = 0; i < a.length; i++)
{
  if (a[i] % 2 == 0)
  {
    System.out.print(a[i] + " ");
  }
}
```

(A) 1 3 4 5 6 7

(B) 2 4 6 8 10

(C) 1 2 3 4 5

(D) 2 4 5 6 7

(E) None of the above

16) Consider the following code segment.

```
int j;
for (int i = 0; i < 14; i++)
{
  if (i < 10)
  {
    j = 2 + i;
  }
  System.out.println("j: " + j + " i: " + i);
}
```

What error is expected during the compilation?

I. Local variable j may not have been initialized

II. Syntax error

III. No error

(A) II only

(B) I and II only

(C) III only

(D) I only

(E) I, II, and III

17) Consider the following code segment.

```
public boolean boolCheck(int x)
{
  if (x == 0)
  {
    return true;
  }
  else
  {
    return false;
  }
}
```

For what values of x does the method boolCheck() return true?

(A) 1

(B) 2

(C) 3

(D) 0

(E) 4

18) Consider the following code segment.

```
int m = 20;
int n = 2;
int temp;

for (int count = 1; count <= 20; count++)
{
  temp = m;
  m = n + count;
  n = temp - count;
}
```

What are the values of m and n after executing the code?

(A) m: 20 n: -8

(B) m: 9 n: -9

(C) m: 30 n: -8

(D) m: 29 n: -6

(E) m: 4 n: -5

19) Consider the following code segment.

```
String s = "JAVA";
System.out.println(s.substring(1, 5).substring(1, 4).substring(0, 3));
```

What is the output of above code segment?

(A) Compile time error

(B) JA

(C) VA

(D) JAV

(E) JAVA

20) Consider the following code segment.

```
public int bin (int n, int k)
{
  if (k == 0 || n == k)
  {
    return 1;
  }
  else
  {
    return bin(n - 1, k - 1) + bin(n - 1, k);
  }
}
```

What will be the output for the above code if we pass n = 8 and k = 3?

(A) 56

(B) 24

(C) 15

(D) 36

(E) None of the above

21) Consider the following method.

```
1  public void printer(int i)
2  {
3    while (i < 10)
4    {
5      System.out.println("Printing......");
6      i++;
7    }
8  }
```

What should the value of i be in the printer() method so that Line 5 is executed 10 times?

(A) 5

(B) 0

(C) 10

(D) 15

(E) 7

22) Consider the following code segment.

```
1  int count = 0;
2  while (count++ < 10)
3  {
4    System.out.println("Line " + count);
5  }
```

How many times is Line 4 executed?

(A) 5

(B) 6

(C) 7

(D) 9

(E) 10

For Questions 23 - 24, refer to the following code.

```java
public class Employee
{
  private String EmpId;
  private String Name;
  private double Salary;

  public Employee(String EmpId, String Name, double Salary)
  {
    this.EmpId = EmpId;
    this.Name = Name;
    this.Salary = Salary;
  }
  // Setter and Getter methods
}
```

```java
Employee[] emp = new Employee[50];
```

23) Which of the following code segments can be used to print the maximum salary?

```java
(A) for (int i = 0; i < emp.length; i++)
    {
      int max = 0;
      if (emp.getSalary() > max)
      {
        max = emp.getSalary();
      }
    }
    System.out.println(max);
```

```
(B) int max = Employee[0];
    for (Employee e : emp)
    {
      if (e.getSalary() > max)
      {
        max = e.getSalary();
      }
    }
    System.out.println(max);
```

```
(C) if(emp[i].getSalary > emp[i + 1].getSalary())
    {
      max = emp[i].getSalary();
    }
    System.out.println(max);
```

```
(D) for (int i = 0; i > emp.length; i--)
    {
      int max = 0;
      if (emp.getSalary() < max)
      {
        max = emp.getSalary();
      }
    }
    System.out.println(max);
```

(E) None of the above

24) Which of the following code segments represents the total salary of all the employees?

```
(A) double total_sal = 0.0;
    for (Employee e : Emp)
    {
      total_sal = e.getSalary();
    }
```

```
(B) double total_sal = 0.0;
    for (Employee e : Emp)
    {
      total_sal = e[i].getSalary();
    }
```

```
(C) double total_sal = 0.0;
    for (Employee e : Emp)
    {
      total_sal += e.getSalary();
    }
```

```
(D) double total_sal = 0.0;
    for (Employee e : Emp)
    {
      total_sal += Emp.getSalary();
    }
```

(E) None of the above

25) Consider the following code segment.

```
1  for (int i = 0; i < 5; i++)
2  {
3    for (int j = 0; j < 5; j++)
4    {
5      System.out.print("*");
6    }
7  }
```

How many times is Line 5 executed?

(A) 10

(B) 15

(C) 20

(D) 25

(E) 30

26) Consider the following output.

```
1   1
2   22
3   333
4   4444
5   55555
```

Which of the following code segments produces the desired output?

```
I.    for (int i = 1; i <= 5; i++)
      {
        for (int j = i; j > 0; j--)
        {
          System.out.print(i);
        }
        System.out.println();
      }
```

```
II.   for (int i = 0; i < 5; i++)
      {
        for (int j = 0; j < i; j++)
        {
          System.out.print(i);
        }
        System.out.println();
      }
```

```
III.  for (int i = 1; i <= 5; i++)
      {
        for (int j = i; j > 0; j--)
        {
          System.out.print(i);
        }
      }
```

(A) I only

(B) II only

(C) III only

(D) I and II

(E) I, II and III

27) Consider the following code segment.

```
for (int k = 0; k < 20; k += 2)
{
  if (k % 3 == 1)
  {
    System.out.print(k + " ");
  }
}
```

What is the output of above code segment?

(A) 16 4 10

(B) 4 10 16

(C) 10 4 16

(D) 4 10 4

(E) 4 4 4

28) Consider the following code segment.

```
for (int j = 1; j <= 1; j++)
{
  for (int k = 1; k <= 1; k = k * 2)
  {
    System.out.println(j + " " + k);
  }
}
```

What is the output of above code segment?

(A) 1 1

(B) 2 2

(C) 3 3

(D) 4 4

(E) 0 0

29) Consider the code segment.

```
public class Boo
{
  public Boo(String s) { /* implementation not shown */ }
  public Boo() { /* implementation not shown */ }
}



public class Bar extends Boo
{
  public Bar() { /* implementation not shown */ }
  public Bar(String s)
  {
    super(s);
  }

  public void zoo()
  {
    // missing code
  }
}
```

Which of the following code segments can be used to instantiate a object?

(A) `Boo f = new Bar();`

(B) `Bar f = new Boo(String s);`

(C) `Bar f = new Boo;`

(D) `Bar f = Boo(String s);`

(E) None of the above

30) Consider the following code.

```
public void add(int x)
{
  x = x + 1;

}
public void add(int x, int y)
{
  x = x + y;
}
```

The above code is an example of which of the following?

(A) Method overriding

(B) Method overloading

(C) Inheritance

(D) Encapsulation

(E) Implementation

31) Consider the following code segment.

```java
int arr[][] = new int[3][];
arr[0] = new int[1];
arr[1] = new int[2];
arr[2] = new int[3];
int sum = 0;

for (int i = 0; i < 3; ++i)
{
  for (int j = 0; j < i + 1; ++j)
  {
    arr[i][j] = j + 1;
  }
}

for (int i = 0; i < 3; ++i)
{
  for (int j = 0; j < i + 1; ++j)
  {
    sum += arr[i][j];
  }
}
System.out.print(sum);
```

What is the output of above code?

(A) 11

(B) 10

(C) 13

(D) 14

(E) 0

32) Consider the following code segment.

```
int arr[] = new int[] {0, 1, 2, 3, 4, 5, 6, 7, 8, 9};
int n = 6;
n = arr[arr[n] / 2];
System.out.println(arr[n] / 2);
```

What is the output of above code segment?

(A) 3

(B) 2

(C) 5

(D) 1

(E) 0

33) Consider the following code segment.

```
char array_variable [] = new char[10];
for (int i = 0; i < 10; ++i)
{
  array_variable[i] = 'i';
  System.out.print(array_variable[i] + "");
}
```

What is the output of the above code segment?

(A) 111111111

(B) iiiiiiiiii

(C) iiii

(D) iiiiii

(E) iiii

34) Consider the following code segment.

```
int g = 3;
System.out.print(++g * 8);
```

What is the output of above code segment?

(A) 32

(B) 34

(C) 28

(D) 33

(E) 35

35) Consider the following code segment.

```
boolean var1 = true;
boolean var2 = false;
if (var1)
{
   System.out.println(var1);
}
else
{
   System.out.println(var2);
}
```

What is the output of above code segment?

(A) 0

(B) 1

(C) true

(D) false

(E) None of the above

36) Consider the following code segment.

```
boolean var1 = true;
boolean var2 = false;
System.out.println((var2 & var2));
```

What is the output of above code segment?

(A) `true`

(B) `false`

(C) Syntax error

(D) Compile time error

(E) None of the above

37) Consider the following code segment.

```
String var1 = 65.5;
String var2 =  97.8;
System.out.println((int) var1 + " " + (int) var2);
```

What is the output of above code segment?

(A) 65 97

(B) 97 65

(C) 67 65

(D) 87 9

(E) 90 65

38) Which of the following would compile without error?

(A) `int a = Math.abs(-5);`

(B) `int a = Math.abs(5.5);`

(C) `int a = Math.abs(5F);`

(D) A and B

(E) None of the above

39) Which of the following are valid calls to Math.max?

I. `Math.max(1, 4)`

II. `Math.max(1, 4.8)`

III. `Math.max(1.1, 4)`

(A) I only

(B) II only

(C) III only

(D) I, II and III

(E) II and III

40) Which is the valid declaration to of a boolean?

I. `boolean b1 = 0;`

II. `boolean b2 = "true";`

III. `boolean b3 = true;`

(A) I only

(B) II only

(C) III only

(D) I, II and III

(E) None of these

Free Response Portion

COMPUTER SCIENCE A

SECTION II

Time - 1 hour and 45 minutes

Number of questions - 4

Percent of total grade - 50

Directions: SHOW ALL YOUR WORK. REMEMBER THAT PROGRAM SEGMENTS ARE TO BE WRITTEN IN JAVA.

Notes:

- Assume that the classes listed in Quick Reference found in the Appendix have been imported where appropriate.
- Unless otherwise noted in the question, assume that parameters in method calls are not null and the methods are called only when their preconditions are satisfied.
- In writing solutions for each question, you may use any of the accessible methods that are listed in classes defined in that question. Writing significant amounts of code that can be replaced by a call to one of these methods may not receive full credit.

1) This question involves reasoning about one-dimensional and two-dimensional arrays of integers. You will write three static methods, all of which are in a single enclosing class, named `ArrayAction` (not shown). The first method returns the sum of number of columns and number of rows in a two-dimensional array. The second method returns the sum of largest and smallest number in a one-dimensional array. The third method returns the sum of the even numbers in a one-dimensional array.

(a) Write a static method `rowColSum` that returns the sum of total number of rows and total number of columns in the two-dimensional array passed to the method.

```
public static int rowColSum(int[][] array)
```

(b) Write a static method `rangeSum` that returns the sum of the largest and smallest number in the one-dimensional array passed to the method.

```
public static int rangeSum(int[] a)
```

(c) Write a static method evenSum that returns the sum of all the even numbers in the one-dimensional array passed to the method.

```
public static int evenSum(int[] a)
```

2) You have to manage sets with the IntSet class, shown below. You have to write three methods to maintain, modify, and check the set.

```
public class IntSet
{
  int[] set;

  public IntSet(int size)
  {
    set = int[size];
  }

  // more code, not shown

  public void append(int x)
  {
    // implementation goes here
  }

  public void remove(int x)
  {
    // implementation goes here
  }

  public boolean isIn(int x)
  {
    // implementation goes here
  }
}
```

(a) Write a method that replaces the last value at the end of the set. However, if the value being added is already in the set, then the value is not added and Value already exists is printed out.

```
public void append(int x)
```

(b) Write a method that finds the value passed to it in the set and changes it to 0. However, if the value being deleted is not in the text, Value does not exist is printed out.

```
public void remove(int x)
```

(c) Write a method to determine whether a particular value passed to the method exists in the set. If it does, true is returned. If not, false is returned.

```
public boolean isIn(int x)
```

3) This question involves reasoning about the rational class methods. You will write three methods, all of which are in a single enclosing class, named Rational (shown below). The first method returns the greatest common divisor between the numbers passed to the method; the second method writes its numbers in p/q form; the third method returns the sum of the denominator and numerator.

```
public class Rational
{
  int numerator;
  int denominator;

  public Rational(int n, int d)
  {
    numerator = n;
    denominator = d;
  }

  // more methods to be implemented
}
```

(a) Write a method that take two `int` arguments and returns the greatest common divisor among the two.

```
public int gcd(int n, int d)
```

(b) Write a method `rationalForm` that prints the numerator and denominator in p/q form. If the denominator is zero, the method simply prints `Math error`.

```
public void rationalForm(int n, int d)
```

(c) Write a method `pqSum` that returns the sum of the numerator and the denominator.

```
public int pqSum(int n, int d)
```

4) Consider two classes: superclass `Point` and subclass `ColorPoint`. The two classes work together and need to have their constructors and inheritance relationship implemented. The code below demonstrates the starting point for each class.

```
public class Point
{
   int x;
   int y;

   // constructor needs to be implemented
}



public class ColorPoint extends Point
{
   String color;

   // constructor needs to be implemented
}
```

(a) Write a constructor for the Point class. The constructor should have two parameters and assign each of the parameters to an instance variable in the constructor body.

```
public Point(int a, int b)
```

(b) Write a constructor for the ColorPoint class. The constructor should have three parameters and assign each of the parameters to an instance variable in the constructor body. Use the super keyword in your implementation.

```
public ColorPoint(int a, int b, String c)
```

(c) Write a `toString` method for the `ColorPoint` class. Do NOT use the predefined method. The method should print out the color.

```
public void toString()
```

Answers and Explanations

Answer Key (Section I)

1. E
2. B
3. A
4. A
5. B
6. B
7. C
8. E
9. A
10. E
11. C
12. B
13. B
14. A
15. B
16. C
17. D
18. C
19. A
20. A
21. B
22. E
23. E
24. C
25. D
26. A
27. B
28. A
29. A
30. B
31. B
32. D
33. B
34. A
35. C

36. **B**

37. **A**

38. **A**

39. **A**

40. **C**

Explanations

Section I

1) **(E)** The condition is `false` so nothing is printed at all.

2) **(B)** The condition remains `true` forever because the value of `i` is not modified in the while loop body.

3) **(A)** The method finds the sum of the array, which is `1 + 2 + 3 + 4 + 5 + 7` which equals 22.

4) **(A)** `newName` is exactly as it is defined in the method: `name + "1"` which equals `name1`.

5) **(B)** Choice B correctly initializes `length` and returns the value of `length`.

6) **(B)** Choice B correctly initializes `element` and returns the value of `element`.

7) **(C)** There are 8 elements in the array so `i` should be 0, 1, 2, 3, 4, 5, 6, and 7 at some point to sum up every element.

8) **(E)** There is no element `j[3]`.

9) **(A)** We can execute any code without defining the main method.

10) **(E)** The initialization of the `Displays` object is incorrect.

11) **(C)** The value of `j` remains the same and the value of `i` is `j + 1`. Therefore, `j = 2` and `i = 3`.

12) **(B)** The values of the elements of `myarr` go from 1 to 10 thanks to the for loops. The elements are printed out with no spaces in between them.

13) **(B)** The `startsWith` method is case sensitive and returns `false`.

14) **(A)** The substring is from index 1 to 4.

15) **(B)** The for loop and if statement check for the even elements in the array.

16) **(C)** No error. Everything is implemented correctly.

17) **(D)** `true` is only returned when `x` is equal to 0.

18) **(C)** Iterate through the for loop to see how the values of `m` and `n` continue to change until you reach `count = 2`, at which point the for loops stops iterating and you get the final values for `m` and `n`.

19) **(A)** Some of the indices used with the `substring` method are too large and do not exist in the `String` we are working with.

20) **(A)** Evaluate using recursion.

21) **(B)** With 0, i will start at 0 and go up to 9, which leads to 10 iterations.

22) **(E)** Going from 0 to 10 leads to 10 successful iteration of the body of the while loop.

23) **(E)** All the code segments have some type of error. Some don't initialize max correctly and others have incorrect logic.

24) **(C)** This implementation correctly finds the individual employee salary values and adds them to the total salary.

25) **(D)** The outer loop and inner loop each iterate 5 times. 5 x 5 = 25.

26) **(A)** Only I uses the for loops to get all 5 rows and spaces the elements out correctly as well.

27) **(B)** The for loop prints out all even numbers in between 0 and 18 that give a remainder of 1 when divided by 3.

28) **(A)** Each for loop only iterates once.

29) **(A)** superclass f = new subclass(); Only Choice A follows that rule.

30) **(B)** Method overloading is having two methods with the same method signature except for the parameters.

31) **(B)** The for loops for processing the get a final sum of 10.

32) **(D)** Upon evaluation, we are printing out 3 / 2 which is equal to 1 based on integer division.

33) **(B)** The for loop is set to iterate 10 times so i is printed 10 times as well.

34) **(A)** g is incremented before the multiplication so 4 * 8 = 32.

35) **(C)** The value of var1 is true so the if condition is satisfied.

36) **(B)** (false & false) = false.

37) **(A)** The (int) cast truncates decimals.

38) **(A)** Only Choice A passes an int argument.

39) **(A)** The Math.max method requires that both arguments be of the same type.

40) **(C)** Only III gives the boolean variable a true or false value.

Section II

1)

(a)

```
public static int rowColSum(int[][] array)
{
  return array.length + array[0].length;
}
```

Access the number of rows and number of columns using the lengthvariable.

(b)

```
public static int rangeSum(int[] a)
{
  int max = Integer.MIN_VALUE;
  int min = Integer.MAX_VALUE;
  int sum;

  for (num : a)
  {
    if (num > max)
    {
      max = num;
    }
    else if (num < min)
    {
      min = num;
    }
  }

  sum = max + min;
  return sum;
}
```

Set max to the lowest possible value and min to the highest possible value. Continue to update their values as you come across larger and smaller elements.

(c)

```java
public static int evenSum(int[][] a)
{
  int sum = 0;

  for (num : a)
  {
    if (num % 2 == 0)
    {
      sum += num;
    }
  }

  return sum;
}
```

Use the enhanced for statement to iterate through the array and the % operator to determine whether an element is even.

2)

(a)

```
public void append(int x)
{
  boolean isInSet = false;

  for (num : set)
  {
    if (num == x)
    {
      isInSet = true;
    }
  }

  if (!isInSet)
  {
    set[set.length - 1] = x;
  }
  else
  {
    System.out.println("Value already exists");
  }
}
```

Create a boolean variable to track whether the value is in the set and use a for each loop and and if statement to decide whether to replace the last element or not.

(b)

```
public void remove(int x)
{
  boolean isInSet = false;

  for (num : set)
  {
    if (num == x)
    {
      isInSet = true;
      num = 0;
    }
  }

  if (!isInSet)
  {
    System.out.println("Value does not exist");
  }
}
```

Check if the value is in the set just like the last part. If it is, replace it with 0 and then use a boolean variable to determine what you should do.

(c)

```
public boolean isIn(int x)
{
  for (n : set)
  {
    if (n == x)
    {
      return true;
    }
  }

  return false;
}
```

Use an enhanced for statement to iterate through the elements of the array and see if any of them matches the value you are looking for.

3)

(a)

```
public int gcd(int n, int d)
{
  boolean isDBigger = (d > n);
  int gcd = 1;

  if (isDBigger)
  {
    for (int i = 1; i <= n; i++)
    {
      if (d % i == 0 && n % i == 0)
      {
        gcd = i;
      }
    }
  }
  else
  {
    for (int j = 1; j <= d; j++)
    {
      if (d % j == 0 && n % j == 0)
      {
        gcd = j;
      }
    }
  }
}
```

Find out which of the parameters is bigger to decide what value you will iterate up to. Find common divisors based on the number being visible by both parameters.

(b)

```
public void rationalForm(int n, int d)
{
  if (d == 0)
  {
    System.out.println("Math error");
  }
  else
  {
    System.out.println(n + " / " + d);
  }
}
```

Use an if statement to find out if the denominator is 0 and then print accordingly.

(c)

```
public int pqSum(int n, int d)
{
  return n + d;
}
```

Add the two parameters to find the sum.

4)

(a)

```
public Point(int a, int b)
{
   x = a;
   y = b;
}
```

Simply assign the instance variables the parameter values.

(b)

```
public ColorPoint(int a, int b, String c)
{
   super(a, b);
   color = c;
}
```

Use the super keyword to call the constructor from the superclass for the first two parameters and assign the third to the instance variable.

(c)

```
public void toString()
{
   System.out.println(color);
}
```

Print out the color after overriding the method.

Practice Test 3

Multiple Choice Portion

COMPUTER SCIENCE A

SECTION I

Time - 1 hour and 15 minutes

Number of questions - 40

Percent of total grade - 50

Directions: Determine the answer for each of the following questions or incomplete statements, using the available space for any necessary scratch work. Then decide which is the best of the choices given and fill in the corresponding oval on the answer sheet. No credit will be given for anything written in the examination booklet. Do not spend too much time on any one problem.

Notes:

- Assume that the classes listed in Quick Reference found in the Appendix have been imported where appropriate.
- Assume that declarations of variables and methods appear within the context of an enclosing class.
- Assume that method calls are not prefixed with an object or class name and are not shown within a complete class definition appear within the context of an enclosing class.
- Unless otherwise noted in the question, assume that parameters in method calls are not null.

1) Consider the following code segment.

```
1  String s = "Hello World";
2  int i = s.indexOf('o');
3  int j = s.lastIndexOf('l');
4  System.out.print(i + " " + j);
```

What will be displayed upon execution of this code segment?

(A) 4 8

(B) 5 9

(C) 4 9

(D) 5 8

(E) None of the above

2) Consider the following code segment.

```
String[] names = new String[10];
System.out.println(names);
```

What will be displayed upon execution of this code segment?

(A) Null

(B) Memory location of the array

(C) 0 0 0 0 0 0 0 0 0 0

(D) Run time error

(E) None of the above

For Questions 3 - 5, refer to following student class

```
public class Employee
{
  private String name;
  private double salary;
  private boolean isManager;
  public Employee(String name, double salary, boolean isMang)
  {
    // missing code
  }

  /* Setter and getter methods implementation not shown */


  public void displayable()
  {
    // missing code
  }

  public Employee salincrement(Employee E)
  {
    // missing code
  }
}
```

3) Which of the following code segments is a valid way of instantiating an Employee object?

```
I.    Employee E = new Employee();
```

```
II.   String n = "Tom";
      double s = 20000;
      boolean is_m = true;
      Employee E = new Employee(n, s, is_m);
```

```
III. Employee E = new Employee(String name,boolean ismanager,double salary);
```

(A) I only

(B) II only

(C) I and II

(D) I and III

(E) III only

4) Consider the following implementation of the constructor of the Employee class.

```
public Employee(String name, double salary, boolean isMang)
{
  this.name = name;
  this.salary = salary;
  this.isManager = isMang;
}
```

Which of the following code segments is an appropriate implementation of the displayable() method if its purpose is to print out the details to Employee?

(A) System.out.print(name + " " + salary + " " + isManager + " ");

(B) System.out.print(Employee.name + " ");
    System.out.print(Employee.salary + " ");
    System.out.print(Employee.isManager + " ");

(C) System.out.println(E.getName() + " " + E.getSalary());

(D) System.out.println(Employee.getName() + " " + Employee.getSalary());

(E) None of the above

5) Consider the following implementation for the salincrement() method.

```
public Employee salincrement(Employee E)
{
  if (E.isManager == true)
  {
    double sal =  E.getSalary() * 2;
    E.setSalary(sal);
    return E;
  }
  else
  {
    return E;
  }
}
```

If the code below is executed, what will the output be?

```
public static void main(String[] args)
{
  Employee E = new Employee("Tom", 200000, true);
  E.displayable();
  Employee E_DUP = E.salincrement(E);
  E_DUP.displayable();
}
```

(A) Tom 200000.0 true

(B) Tom 200000.0 true Tom 400000.0 true

(C) Tom 200000 true Tom 400000 true

(D) Compile time error

(E) None of the above

6) Consider the following code segment.

```
public void printmethod(int n)
{
  if (n < 0)
  {
    System.out.println("- ");
  }
  else
  {
    System.out.print(n + " ");
    printmethod(n - 3);
  }
}
```

What will be the output for printmethod(5)?

(A) 5 3

(B) Infinite loop

(C) 5 2 -

(D) 5 3 1

7) Consider the following classes.

```java
public class A
{
   int x = 10;
   int y = 20;

   public void display_A()
   {
      System.out.println(x + " " + y);
   }
}
```

```java
public class B
{
   int x = 20;
   int y = 10;

   public void display_B()
   {
      System.out.println(x + " " + y);
   }
}
```

```java
public class C extends A, B
{
   int x = 30;
   int y = 40;
   A a = new A();
   a.display_A();
}
```

What will be the output for the above code?

(A) Run time error

(B) 10 20

(C) Compile time error

(D) 30 40

(E) None of the above

8) Which of the following code segments populates a two-dimensional with 0 as each element?

```
int[][] matr = new int [3][4];
```

(A)
```
for (int r = 0; r < 3; r++)
{
    for (int c = 0; c < 4; c++)
    {
        matr[r][c] = 0;
    }
}
```

(B)
```
for (int r = 0, c = 0; r < 3, c < 4; r++)
{
    matr[r][c]=0;
}
```

(C)
```
for ( int r = 0, c = 0; r < 3, c < 4; r++, c--)
{
    matr[r][c] = 0;
}
```

(D) B and C

(E) None of the above

9) Refer to the following code segment.

```
ArrayList<String> cars = new ArrayList<String>();
```

Which of the following code segments add a value to the ArrayList?

(A) cars.add("BMW");

(B) cars.remove("BMW");

(C) cars.insert("BMW");

(D) A and C

(E) None of the above

10) Consider the following code segment.

```
public static void main(String [] args)
{
   int a;
   int b;
   int c;
   a = 100;
   b= ++a;
   c = b++ + ++a;
   System.out.println(a + " " + b + " " + c);
}
```

What will be the output for the above code?

(A) 100 101 201

(B) 101 101 202

(C) 102 102 203

(D) 101 102 202

(E) None of the above

11) Consider the following code segment.

```
public static void main(String[] args)
{
  int[] a = {1, 2, 3, 4, 5, 6, 7, 8, 9, 10};
  for (int i = 0; i < a.length; i++)
  {
    System.out.print(a[i] + " ");
    System.out.print(a[i] + " ");
  }
}
```

(A) 1 2 3 4 5 6 7 8 9 10

(B) 1 1 2 2 3 3 4 4 5 5 6 6 7 7 8 8 9 9 10 10

(C) 1 2 3 4 5 6 7 8 9

(D) 1 1 2 2 3 3 4 4 5 5 6 6 7 7 8 8 9 9

(E) None of the above

12) Which of the while loops is equivalent to the for loop below?

```
for (int x = 5; x <= 50; x += 5)
{
        System.out.print(" " + x);
}
```

```
(A) int x = 5;
    while (x <= 50)
    {
      System.out.print(" " + x);
      x += 5;
    }
```

```
(B) while (x <= 50)
    {
      int x = 5;
      System.out.print(" " + x);
      x += 5;
    }
```

```
(C) while (int x = 5; x <= 50)
    {
      System.out.print(" " + x);
      x += 5;
    }
```

```
(D) int x = 5;
    while (x <= 50; x += 5)
    {
      System.out.print(" " + x);
    }
```

For Questions 13 - 15, refer to the following classes.

```java
public class Author
{
  private String name;
  private int noofpub;

  public Author(String name, int noofpub)
  {
    // missing code
  }
  public String getName()
  {
    // missing code
  }
  public int getNoofpub()
  {
    // missing code
  }
}


public class Book
{
  private String title;
  private double price;
  private Author author;

  public Book(String title, double price)
  {
    /* Implementation */
  }
  public String getTitle()
  {
    /* Implementation */
  }
  public double getPrice()
  {
    /* Implementation */
  }

  /* Other methods (not shown) */
}
```

13) Consider the following implementation of the Book constructor.

```
public Book(String title, double price)
{
  this.title = title;
  this.price = price;
  this.author = new Author("Steven", 2);
}
```

What is the relationship between the Book and the Author classes?

(A) Inheritance

(B) Composition

(C) Aggregation

(D) Polymorphism

(E) None of the above

14) Consider the following implementation of the Book constructor.

```
public Book(String title, double price)
{
  this.title = title;
  this.price = price;
  this.author = new Author("Steven", 2);
}
```

Which of the following code segments is a valid way of creating an Author object?

I. Author A = new Author("Tom", 3);

II. Book B = new Author("Tom", 3);

III. Book B = new Book("xyz", 35.0);

(A) I only

(B) II only

(C) I and II

(D) I and III

(E) III only

15) Consider the following declaration.

```
private Book[] books;
```

Which of the following code segments prints the details of each book in the books array?

```
(A) System.out.println(title);
    System.out.println(price);
```

```
(B) for (Book b : books)
    {
      System.out.println(b.getTitle());
      System.out.println(b.getPrice());
    }
```

```
(C) System.out.println(b.getTitle());
    System.out.println(b.getTitle());
```

```
(D) for (Book b : books)
    {
      System.out.println(title);
      System.out.println(price);
    }
```

(E) None of the above

16) Which of the following code segments randoms picks values?

(A) `Math.min()`

(B) `Math.pickrandom()`

(C) `Math.random()`

(D) `Math.pow()`

(E) B and C

17) Which of the following statements is true about abstract classes?

I. An abstract class can be initialized.

II. An abstract class must have abstract methods.

III. An abstract class can have abstract methods.

(A) I only

(B) I and II

(C) II and III

(D) III only

(E) II only

18) In an exam, there are 50 questions, each worth 1 point. One point is awarded for every correct answer and one point deducted for every mistake or omission. The exam has been graded and the result is saved as a `boolean` array called `question[]`. Which of the following code segments correctly calculates and outputs the total score?

```
(A) int sum_c = 0;
    int sum_f = 0;
    for (int i = 0; i < question.length; i++)
    {
      if (question[i] == true)
      {
        sum_c = sum_c + 1;
      }
    }
    sum_f = 50 - sum_c;
    int total = sum_c - sum_f;
    System.out.println(total);
```

```
(B) for (int i = 0; i < question.length; i++)
    {
      if (question[i] == true)
      {
        sum_c = sum_c + 1;
      }
    }
```

```
(C) int sum_c = 0;
    int sum_f = 0;
    for (i = 0; i < question.length; i++)
    {
      if (question[i] = true)
      {
        sum_c = sum_c + 1;
      }
    }
    sum_f = 50 - sum_c;
    int total = sum_c - sum_f;
    System.out.println(total);
```

```
(D) int sum_c = 0;
    int sum_f = 0;
    for (i = 0; i < question.length; i++)
    {
      if (question[i] == false)
      {
        sum_c = sum_c + 1;
      }
    }
    sum_f = 50 - sum_c;
    int total = sum_c - sum_f;
    System.out.println(total);
```

(E) None of the above

For Questions 19 - 20, consider following code segment:

```
ArrayList<Integer> mem = new ArrayList();
int length = 10;
for (int i = 0; i < length; i++)
{
   mem.add(i * 20);
}
```

19) Which of the following code segments can be used to print out the elements at index 5 and 9?

(A) `System.out.println(mem.get(5));`
     `System.out.println(mem.get(9));`

(B) `System.out.println(mem[5]);`
     `System.out.println(mem[6]);`

(C) `System.out.println(mem.get(5) && mem.get(9));`

(D) Both A and C

(E) None of the above

20) Which of the following code segments can be used to print out the sum of all of the elements in the ArrayList?

```
(A) int sum = 0;
    for (int i = 0; i > length; i++)
    {
      sum += mem.get(i);
    }
    System.out.println("Sum is: " + sum);
```

```
(B) int sum = 0;
    for (int i = 0; i < length; i++)
    {
      sum += mem.get(i);
    }
    System.out.println("Sum is: " + sum);
```

```
(C) for (int i = 0; i < length; i++)
    {
      int sum = 0;
      sum += mem.get(i);
    }
    System.out.println("Sum is: " + sum);
```

(D) A and B

(E) None of the above

21) Consider the following method.

```
public void strcom(String str1, String str2, String str3)
{
  System.out.print(str1.equals(str2) + " ");
  System.out.print(str1.equals(str3) + " ");
  System.out.print(str2.equalsIgnoreCase(str3));
}
```

What will be the output if strcom("java.com","Java.com","JAVA.COM")?

(A) `false false true`

(B) `true false true`

(C) `false true true`

(D) `false false false`

(E) Compile time error

22) Consider the following code.

```
public class Round extends Shape
public class Rectangle extends Shape

public class Oval extends Round
public class Square extends Rectangle
```

Assuming each class has a default constructor, which of the following declarations are valid, based on the code above?

```
I.    Shape S = new Round();
      Round R = new Oval();
```

```
II.   Shape S = new Oval();
      Shape S1 = new Square();
      Square S2 = new Square();
```

```
III.  Square S = new Rectangle();
```

(A) I only

(B) II only

(C) I and II

(D) I, II, and III

(E) III only

23) If a, b, c are integers, which of the following will be true based on this expression?

```
(a < b && b < c && c > a) = true
```

(A) b is greater than a

(B) c is the greatest

(C) a is the greatest

(D) A and B

(E) Not enough information

24) Which of the following relationships represents polymorphism?

(A) HAS-A

(B) HAS-HAS

(C) IS-A

(D) MANY-TYPES

(E) None of the above

25) Consider the following code segment.

```
ArrayList<String> al = new ArrayList<String>();
al.add("abc");
al.add("xyz);
al.add(("opm");
for (String s : al)
{
   System.out.println(s + " ");
}
```

What will be the output for the above?

(A) abc xyz opm

(B) abcxyzopm

(C) abc-xyz-opm

(D) Compile time error

(E) None of the above

26) Which of the following statement is true about inheritance?

(A) Inheritance is shown by using `implements` keyword.

(B) One class can inherit two classes.

(C) The `super` keyword can be used to inherit the superclass constructor.

(D) Inheritance is not commonly used in Java programming.

(E) All of the above are false.

27) Consider the following code segment.

```
int num = (int) (Math.random() * 5) + 3;
System.out.println("num = " + num);
```

What will the output be?

(A) Integer between 3 and 8

(B) Integer between 0 to 8

(C) Integer between 0 to 50

(D) Integer between 1 and 8

(E) None of the above

28) Consider the following code segment.

```
String Str = "Super keyword";
System.out.println( Str.substring(3,8));
```

What will the output be?

(A) erke

(B) keywo

(C) per k

(D) er ke

(E) er key

For Questions 29 - 30, consider the following sorting method.

```
public static int[] sort(int[] arr)
{
  int temp;
  for (int i = 0; i < arr.length - 1; i++)
  {
    for (int j = 1; j < arr.length - i; j++)
    {
      if (arr[j - 1] > arr[j])
      {
        temp = arr[j - 1];
        arr[j - 1] = arr[j];
        arr[j] = temp;
      }
    }
  }
  return arr;
}
```

29) If we pass an array to the method above, in what form will the method return it?

(A) In descending order

(B) In ascending order

(C) Unsorted

(D) Run time error

(E) Random order

30) If [10 9 2 15 11] is passed to the method, what will the array be after the second iteration of the outer loop?

(A) [9 10 2 15 11]

(B) [9 2 10 11 15]

(C) [2 9 10 11 15]

(D) [10 9 11 15 2]

(E) [9 2 10 15 11]

31) Consider the following code segment.

```
int n = 100;
for (int i = 0; i < 10; i++)
{
    n = n + n++;
}
System.out.println(n);
```

What will be the output?

(A) 102401

(B) 10240

(C) 102400

(D) 1024

(E) None of the above

32) Consider the following method.

```
public int findele(int[] a, int key)
{
    for (int i = 0; i < a.length; i++)
    {
        if (key == a[i])
        {
            System.out.println("Element found");
        }
    }
}
```

What will be the output if the following array is passed and the key is 30.

```
int[] a = {12, 15, 67, 30, 80, 67};
```

(A) Compile time Error

(B) Run time Error

(C) No output

(D) Element found

(E) None of the above

33) Refer to the following classes.

```java
public class A
{
  int i = 100;
}
```

```java
public class B extends A
{
  int i = 101;
}
```

What will be the output if the following code is executed?

```java
public static void main(String[] args)
{
  A a = new B();
  B b = new B();
  System.out.println(a.i + " " + b.i);
}
```

(A) 100 100

(B) 101 100

(C) 100 101

(D) 101 101

(E) None of the above

34) Consider the following method.

```
public static void sort(int[] arr)
{
  int n = arr.length;
  for (int j = 1; j < n; j++)
  {
    int k = arr[j];
    int i = j - 1;
    while ((i > -1) && (arr[i] > k))
    {
      arr[i+1] = arr[i];
      i--;
    }
    arr[i+1] = k;
  }
}
```

The following array is passed to the sort method.

```
int[] arr = {10, 3, 4, 2, 1, 14, 12, 11};
sort(arr);
```

What will be the sequence of elements at the completion of the 3rd iteration of the for loop?

(A) 2, 3, 10, 4, 1, 14, 12, 11

(B) 2, 3, 4, 10, 1, 14, 12, 11

(C) 2, 10, 3, 4, 1, 14, 12, 11

(D) 2, 3, 4, 10, 1, 11, 12, 14

(E) None of the above

For Questions 35 - 36, refer to the following class.

```java
public class Student
{
  private String id;
  private double gpa;
  private int marks;

  public Student(String id, double gpa, int marks)
  {
    this.id = id;
    this.gpa = gpa;
    this.marks = marks;
  }

  // getter and setter methods (not shown)
  // other methods (not shown)
}
```

35) Consider the following code segment.

```
Student[] studs = new Student[10];

public void highestgpa()
{
  /* Implementation goes here */
}
```

Which of the following implementations is a valid method of calculating the highest GPA among students in the studs array?

```
(A) double max = 0.0;

    for (Student s : studs)
    {
      if (s.getGpa() > max)
      {
        max= s.getGpa();
      }
    }
    System.out.println("Highest gpa: " + max);
```

```
(B) if (s.getGpa() > max)
    {
      max = s.getGpa();
    }
```

```
(C) for (Student s : studs)
    {
      double max = 0.0;

      if (s.getGpa() > max)
      {
        max = s.getGpa();
      }
    }
    System.out.println("Highest gpa: " + max);
```

```
(D) for (Student s : studs)
    {

      double max = 0.0;

      while (s.getGpa() > max)
      {
        max = s.getGpa();
      }
    }
    System.out.println("Highest gpa: " + max);
```

(E) None of the above

36) Consider the following code segment.

```
public void averagemarks()
{
  /* Implementation goes here */
}
```

Which of the following implementations is a valid method of calculating the average marks among students in the studs array?

```
(A) double avg = 0.0;
    double sum = 0.0;

    for (Student s : studs)
    {
      sum = s.getMarks();
    }
    System.out.println(avg);
```

```
(B) double avg = 0.0;
    double sum = 0.0;

    for (Student s : studs)
    {
      sum += s.getMarks();
    }
    avg = sum / studs.length;
    System.out.println(avg);
```

```
(C) for (Student s : studs)
    {
      sum += s.getMarks();
    }
```

```
(D) double avg = 0.0;
    double sum = 0.0;

    for (Student s : studs)
    {
      sum += s.getMarks();
    }
    avg = sum / studs.length();
    System.out.println(avg);
```

(E) None of the above

37) Refer to the following class.

```
public class X
{
  public methodA(int x)
  {
    System.out.println("x : " + x);
  }

  public methodA(int x, int y)
  {
    System.out.println("x : " + x + " " + y);
  }
}
```

Which of the following concepts does the method represent?

(A) Method overriding

(B) Method overloading

(C) Inheritance

(D) Polymorphism

(E) B and D

38) Consider the following method.

```
public void number(int num)
{
  int num1 = 0;

  while (num != 0)
  {
    num1 = num1 * 10;
    num1 = num1 + num % 10;
    num = num / 10;
  }

  System.out.println(num1);
}
```

What will be the output if number(125) ?

(A) 8

(B) 521

(C) 125

(D) 10

(E) None of the above

39) Refer to the following classes.

```java
public class X
{
  public void methoda(int a)
  {
    System.out.println("Integer" + " ");
  }
  public void methoda(double d)
  {
    System.out.println("Double" + " ");
  }
}
```

```java
public class Y extends X
{
  public void methoda(double d)
  {
    System.out.println("Double in class Y" + " ");
  }
}
```

What will be the output if the following code is executed?

```java
public static void main(String[] args)
{
  Y y = new Y();
  y.methoda(100);
  y.methoda(100.0);
}
```

(A) 100 100.0

(B) Integer Double

(C) Integer Double in class Y

(D) Double Double in class Y

(E) Double in class Y Integer

40) Which of the following statements are true?

I. Mergesort uses the divide and conquer technique.

II. Insertion sort can be applied efficiently to large amount of data.

III. A list must be sorted in order to use binary search on it.

(A) I only

(B) II only

(C) I and III

(D) II and III

(E) III only

Free Response Portion

COMPUTER SCIENCE A

SECTION II

Time - 1 hour and 45 minutes

Number of questions - 4

Percent of total grade - 50

Directions: SHOW ALL YOUR WORK. REMEMBER THAT PROGRAM SEGMENTS ARE TO BE WRITTEN IN JAVA.

Notes:

- Assume that the classes listed in Quick Reference found in the Appendix have been imported where appropriate.
- Unless otherwise noted in the question, assume that parameters in method calls are not null and the methods are called only when their preconditions are satisfied.
- In writing solutions for each question, you may use any of the accessible methods that are listed in classes defined in that question. Writing significant amounts of code that can be replaced by a call to one of these methods may not receive full credit.

1) This question involves reasoning about one-dimensional and two-dimensional arrays of integers. You will write two static methods, all of which are in a single enclosing class, named Arrays (not shown). The first method returns the index of number passed to it in the array. The second method returns the middle element in a one-dimensional array.

(a) Write a method indexSearch which returns the index of the number passed to it if it exists in the array passed to it. It returns the index of the first occurrence of the numbers it's looking for. If the number cannot be found, -1 is returned.

```
public static int indexSearch(int[] arr, int x)
```

(b) Write a method middleNum that returns the middle element of an array as long as the array has an odd-numbered length. If not, the method returns -1.

```
public static int middleNum(int[] arr)
```

2) You will write three static methods, all of which are in single enclosing class, named createLogin (not shown). The first method checks information about the username. The second method checks the length of the password. The third method calculates and returns the age of the user.

(a) Write a method username that returns true if the name passed to it does not contain "a", "e", "i", "o", "u" and its length is less than 8. Otherwise, it returns false.

```
public boolean username(String name)
```

(b) Write a method checkPass that returns true if the password length is greater than 6 and false otherwise.

```
public boolean checkPass(String password)
```

(c) Write a method ageCal that returns the current age of the user based on the year of birth given. You may assume the current year to be 2016.

```
public int ageCal(int yearOfBirth)
```

3) This question involves reasoning about the implementation of the interfaces. You will write 2 different interfaces for different purposes. The first Interface will contain the method `isPrime`. The second interface will contain the method `canSquareRoot`.

(a) Write an interface with method `isPrime` that will eventually check whether a number passed to it is prime. It will return a `boolean` value.

(b) Write an interface with the method `canSquareRoot` that will eventually return a `boolean` value representing whether we can find the square root of a number passed to it.

4) You have to implement two static methods that will appear in the same class (not shown). The first method takes a single number parameter and returns its factorial. The second method counts the number of even numbers in between the number given and 1.

(a) Write a static method `factorial` that returns the factorial of a given number.

```
public static int factorial(int f)
```

(b) Write a static method evenCounter that returns the total even numbers in between 1 and the number passed to the method.

```
public static int evenCounter(int endingNumber)
```

Answers and Explanations

Answer Key (Section I)

1. C
2. B
3. C
4. A
5. B
6. C
7. B
8. A
9. A
10. *C**
11. B
12. A
13. B
14. D
15. B
16. C
17. D
18. A
19. A
20. B
21. A
22. E
23. B
24. C
25. A
26. C
27. A
28. D
29. B
30. C
31. C
32. D
33. C
34. B
35. A

36. **B**
37. **B**
38. **B**
39. **C**
40. **C**

Explanations

Section I

1) **(C)** The index of the first "o" is 4 and the index of the last "l" is 9.

2) **(B)** Whenever, you print an array like such, you will print the memory location of the array.

3) **(C)** When you are instantiating an object, you must use actual values instead of the implementation used in III.

4) **(A)** Simply print out each of the instance variables in the class.

5) **(B)** Whenever the computer prints a `double`, it adds one decimal point even if it's a whole number.

6) **(C)** The value of 5 minus 3 is 2. And 2 minus 3 is less than 0 so a dash was printed.

7) **(B)** Since there is no constructor for `Class A` and the variables are initialized in the class, you will get the values stated in the class.

8) **(A)** Only Choice A correctly uses nested for loops to access all elements in the array.

9) **(A)** The `add` method is the correct way of adding to an `ArrayList`.

10) **(C)** Since one increment operator was before the number, it is completed before the addition begins.

11) **(B)** This for loop contains two statements in the loop, both of which must be completed before the loop's condition variable increments.

12) **(A)** Choice A is the only choice that accounts for the initial condition, termination condition, and the increment shown in the for loop.

13) **(B)** Composition is used to model objects that contain other objects.

14) **(D)** Only I and III follow the syntax of an object instantiation.

15) **(B)** This implementation of the code correctly uses the getter methods which gets the price and name of the book from each object.

16) **(C)** The `Math.random()` function picks a random value.

17) **(D)** An abstract class cannot be initialized and it does not have to contain only abstract methods.

18) **(A)** Only Choice A comprehensively and correctly meets all of the requirements for the code segment.

19) **(A)** Use the get() method to access elements of an ArrayList.

20) **(B)** An ordinary for loop and the get() method allow you to calculate the sum.

21) **(A)** The method equals is case-sensitive.

22) **(E)** Only a square can be a rectangle. A rectangle cannot be a square.

23) **(B)** From the code statement, one can see that a < b < c.

24) **(C)** Polymorphism is represented by an IS-A relationship.

25) **(A)** The code for printing the values is correctly implemented.

26) **(C)** The super keyword can be used to inherit the superclass constructor.

27) **(A)** The random value is between 3 and 8 because the function is multiplied by 5 and then 3 added to it.

28) **(D)** The String is cut short to go from index 3 to 7.

29) **(B)** The code models selection sort and orders the code in ascending order.

30) **(C)** Insertion sort does not work well with a large amount of data as it becomes a very slow process.

31) **(C)** If you loop through the calculations several times, you will get 102400.

32) **(D)** The number 30 was an element in the array.

33) **(C)** The value of the variables for each class remains the same.

34) **(B)** Iterate through the loop 3 times and identify the sorting method to see how the array is modified at each step.

35) **(A)** The initialization of the variable max is done correctly and in the correct location.

36) **(B)** Length isn't a method for arrays. It's a property.

37) **(B)** Method overloading is the same name except a different number of parameters.

38) **(B)** Evaluate the while loop until the termination condition is met.

39) **(C)** This can be seen in the step by step implementation of the code. The Class y extends x so all the methods of x can be used in Class y.

40) **(C)** The first condition becomes false and the second condition true so Line 2 is printed out and the if-else statement stops evaluating as soon as one block is executed.

Section II

1)

(a)

```
public static int indexSearch(int[] arr, int x)
{
  for (int i = 0; i < arr.length; i++)
  {
    if (arr[i] == x)
    {
      return i;
    }
  }
  return -1;
}
```

Iterate element by element until one of them matches the key. This is an implementation of linear search.

(b)

```
public static int middleNum(int[] arr)
{
  if (arr.length % 2 != 0)
  {
    int index = (arr.length / 2);
  }
  else
  {
    return -1;
  }
}
```

Check if the length is odd and then divide the length by 2 to get the middle element. Account for integer division.

2)

(a)

```
public boolean username(String name)
{
  if (name.length < 8)
  {
    if (name.indexOf("a") == -1 && name.indexOf("e") == -1 && name.indexOf("i") \
== -1 && name.indexOf("o") == -1 && name.indexOf("u") == -1)
    {
      return true;
    }
  }
  else
  {
    return false;
  }
}
```

First check the length. Then, check if the the indexOf method returns -1 for any of the vowels to see if they are in the String.

(b)

```
public boolean checkPass(String password)
{
  if (password.length > 6)
  {
    return true;
  }
  else
  {
    return false;
  }
}
```

Check to see if the length is greater than 6 and return a value accordingly.

(c)

```
public int ageCal(int yearOfBirth)
{
  int currentYear = 2016;
  int age = currentYear - yearOfBirth;
  return age;
}
```

Subtract the birth year from 2016 and return the value.

3)

(a)

```
public interface AnyName
{
  public boolean isPrime(int num);
}
```

An interface should not have methods with implementations. Just have the method signature of the proposed method.

(b)

```
public interface AnyName
{
  public boolean canSquareRoot(int num);
}
```

An interface should not have methods with implementations. Just have the method signature of the proposed method.

4)

(a)

```
public static int factorial(int f)
{
  if (f == 0)
  {
    return 1;
  }
  else
  {
    return n * factorial(n - 1);
  }
}
```

Use recursion to find the factorial. Other methods can be employed as well. Refer to Chapter 9 for an explanation of recursion.

(b)

```
public static int evenCount(int endingNumber)
{
  int numOfInts = 0;

  for (int i = 1; i <= endingNmber; i++)
  {
    if (i % 2 == 0)
    {
      numOfInts++;
    }
  }

  return numOfInts;
}
```

Iterate through all of the numbers between 1 and the endingNumber ' and increment the return value if a value is divisible by 2.

Thank you for reading.

Made in the USA
Middletown, DE
22 March 2016